OLIMPIO FANTUZ/4CORNERS ©

IRELAND

TOP SIGHTS, AUTHENTIC EXPERIENCES

THIS EDITION WRITTEN AND RESEARCHED BY

oes

Lonely Planet's
Ultimate Ireland Itinerary

This is Lonely Planet's ultimate Ireland itinerary, which ensures you'll see the best of everything the country has to offer.

For other recommended paths to travel, check out our itineraries section (p18). For inspiration on themed travel, see If You Like... (p24).

From left: Temple Bar (p61), Dublin; Ring of Kerry (p206); Carrick-a-Rede Rope Bridge (p171), County Antrim

POM POM/SHUTTERSTOCK ©; CARL BRUEMMER/DESIGN PICS/GETTY IMAGES ©; WADE EARLE/GETTY IMAGES ©

Week 1

Dublin to Cork

1 **Dublin** (p34) deserves at least three days. The first two are for exploring the city itself. The third is for a day trip south to Powerscourt and Glendalough in **County Wicklow** (p94).

🚌 1¾ hours; or
🚗 1½ hours

2 Head southwest for a day spent discovering the medieval delights of **Kilkenny** (p246).

🚌 3 hours; or
🚗 2 hours

3 A car allows you to visit the impressive Rock of Cashel before staying overnight in **Cork** (p182), Ireland's gourmet capital. Spend next morning in the city followed by an afternoon at Blarney Castle.

🚌 2 hours; or
🚗 1¾ hours

Culdaff

Portstewart

ANTRIM COAST p158

Bushmills

Cushendun

Buncrana

Derry/Londonderry

Larne

LAND

Kells

**NORTHERN
IRELAND**

Antrim

Bangor

Omagh

Lough
Neagh

★ BELFAST p226

Portadown

Downpatrick

Monaghan

Newry

Cavan

IRELAND

Dundalk
Bay

COUNTIES MEATH & LOUTH p82

Kells

Drogheda

Mullingar

Howth

Athlone

★ DUBLIN p34

Newbridge

COUNTY WICKLOW p94

rr

Roscrea

Wicklow

Carlow

KILKENNY CITY p246

Cashel

Enniscorthy

New Ross

ARY

Clonmel

Wexford

Waterford

Rosslare
Harbour

Dungarvan

ghal

SCOTLAND

Isle of
Man

IRISH SEA

Bangor

Cardigan
Bay

WALES

Middleton

ATLANTIC OCEAN

Welcome to Ireland

Don't think the Ireland of postcards is just a two-dimensional fiction: it very much exists. You'll find it along the peninsulas of the southwest, in the brooding loneliness of Connemara and the dramatic wildness of the Aran Islands.

Ireland has modernised dramatically, but some things endure. Brave the raging Atlantic on a crossing to Skellig Michael or spend a summer's evening in the yard of a thatched-cottage pub and you'll experience an Ireland that has changed little in generations.

History presents itself everywhere: from the breath-taking monuments of prehistoric Ireland at Brú na Bóinne, to the fabulous ruins of a rich monastic past at Glendalough and Clonmacnoise. Ireland's more recent history is visible in the Titanic Quarter in Belfast and the forbidding Kilmainham Gaol in Dublin.

Throughout your travels you will be overwhelmed by the cultural choices on offer – see a play by one of the theatrical greats in Dublin, experience a traditional music 'session' in a west-Ireland pub or attend a rock gig in a Limerick saloon. The Irish summer is awash with festivals celebrating everything from flowers in bloom to high literature.

The Ireland of postcards very much exists...

ATLANTIC OCEAN

Dungloe

IR

Glencolumbcille

Donegal

Donegal Bay

Pollatomish

Ballycastle

Sligo

Boyle

Newport

Castlebar

Knock

Westport

COUNTY GALWAY p110

Lough Mask

Cong

Clifden

Lough Corrib

Cashel

Ballinasloe

Galway

Ballyvaughan

Lough Derg

ARAN ISLANDS p130

Gort

E

Doolin

Nenagh

COUNTY CLARE p140

Ennis

Kilkee

Limerick

Kilrush

Tipperary

COUNTY TIPPER p260

Tralee

Mallow

Dingle

Killarney

COUNTY KERRY p202

COUNTY CORK p182

Yo

Kenmare

Cork

Bantry

Skibbereen

0 | 100 km
0 | 50 miles

N

Week 2

Cork to Galway

❶ From Cork head west to **Kerry** (p202) and base yourself in Killarney for three days while exploring Killarney National Park and making day trips around the scenic Ring of Kerry and Dingle peninsulas. Pray that good weather allows a boat trip to unforgettable Skellig Michael.

🚌 4 hours; or
🚗 3 hours

❷ Travel north to **Galway** (p110), where four days will allow you to enjoy the city's lively pubs, and make day trips to County Clare, Connemara and the Aran Islands (drivers can take in Clare on the way from Killarney to Galway).

🚌 5 to 6 hours; or
🚗 4½ hours

Staying Longer

Galway to Belfast

❶ It's a long haul from Galway via Dublin to **Belfast** (p226), capital of Northern Ireland. Allow at least one day to take in the city sights, and another to make a day trip north along the **Antrim Coast** (p158) to the Giant's Causeway.

🚌 2¼ hours; or
🚗 2 hours

❷ Finish your grand tour of Ireland back in **Dublin** (p34), and if time allows make a day trip to the prehistoric splendour of Brú na Boinne.

Contents

In Focus

Survival Guide

Plan Your Trip
Ireland's Top 12

Dublin

Ireland's capital (p34) and largest city by some stretch is the main gateway into the country, and it has enough distractions to keep visitors engaged for at least a few days. From world-class museums and entertainment, superb dining and top-grade hotels, Dublin has all the baubles of a major international metropolis. But the real clinchers are Dubliners themselves, who are friendlier, more easygoing and welcoming than the burghers of virtually any other European capital. And it's the home of Guinness.

From left: Temple Bar (p61); harpist on the streets of Dublin

NORADOA/SHUTTERSTOCK ©

HAOLIANG/GETTY IMAGES ©

Connemara Peninsula

A filigreed coast of tiny coves and beaches is the beautiful border of the Connemara Peninsula (p114) and the wild waters of the Atlantic. Wandering characterful roads bring you from one village to another, each with trad pubs and restaurants serving seafood chowder cooked from recipes that are family secrets. Inland, the scenic drama is even greater. In desolate valleys, green hills, wildflowers and wild streams reflecting the blue sky provide elemental beauty.
Top: Kylemore Abbey (p129), County Galway; Bottom: seafood chowder

Glendalough & County Wicklow

St Kevin knew a thing or two about magical locations when he chose a remote cave on a glacial lake nestled at the base of a forested valley as his monastic retreat. He inadvertently founded a settlement (p100) that would later prove to be one of Ireland's most dynamic universities and, in our time, one of the country's most beautiful ruined sites.

5

Galway City

One word to describe Galway City (p120)? Craic! Ireland's liveliest city literally hums through the night at music-filled pubs where you can hear three old guys playing spoons and fiddles, or a hot, young band. Join the locals as they bounce from place to place, never knowing what fun lies ahead but certain of the possibility. Add in local bounty such as the famous oysters and nearby adventure in the Connemara Peninsula and the Aran Islands and the fun never ends.

4

Dingle

Dingle (p221) is the name of both the picturesque peninsula jutting into the Atlantic from County Kerry, strewn with ancient ruins, and its delightful main town, the peninsula's beating heart. Fishing boats unload fish and shellfish that couldn't be any fresher if you caught it yourself, many pubs are untouched since their earlier incarnations as old-fashioned shops, artists sell their creations (including beautiful jewellery with Irish designs) at intriguing boutiques, and toe-tapping trad sessions take place around roaring pub fires.

GEORGE KARBUS PHOTOGRAPHY/GETTY IMAGES ©

RISH PUNCH/DESIGN PICS/GETTY IMAGES ©

Brú na Bóinne

Looking at once ancient and yet eerily futuristic, Newgrange's immense, round, white-stone walls topped by a grass dome is one of the most extraordinary sights you'll ever see. Part of the vast Neolithic necropolis Brú na Bóinne (p86; the Boyne Palace), it contains Ireland's finest Stone Age passage tomb, predating the Egyptian pyramids by some six centuries. Most extraordinary of all is the tomb's alignment with the sun at the time of the winter solstice.
Right: Knowth burial mound (p88)

Cliffs of Moher

Bathed in the golden glow of the late-afternoon sun, the iconic Cliffs of Moher (p144) are but one of the splendours of County Clare. From a boat bobbing below, the towering stone faces have a jaw-dropping dramatic beauty that's enlivened by scores of sea birds, including cute little puffins. Down south in Loop Head, pillars of rock towering above the sea house abandoned stone cottages whose very existence is inexplicable.

Antrim Coast

County Antrim's Causeway Coast (p166) is an especially dramatic backdrop for *Game of Thrones* filming locations. Put on your walking boots by the swaying Carrick-a-Rede rope bridge, then follow the rugged coastline for 16½ spectacular kilometres, passing Ballintoy Harbour (aka the Iron Islands' Lordsports Harbour) and the geological wonder of the Giant's Causeway's outsized basalt columns (p162), as well as cliffs and islands, sandy beaches and ruined castles, before finishing with a dram at the Old Bushmills Distillery.

Right: Carrick-a-Rede Rope Bridge (p171)

9

Cork City

The Republic's second city (p190) is second only in terms of size – in every other respect it will bear no competition. A tidy, compact city centre is home to an enticing collection of art galleries, museums and – most especially – places to eat. From cheap cafes to top-end gourmet restaurants, Cork City excels (p186), although it's hardly a surprise given the county's exceptional foodie reputation. At the heart of it is the simply wonderful English Market, a covered produce market that is an attraction unto itself.

From left: English Market (p186); buildings along the River Lee

Belfast

Northern Ireland's capital city (p226) is buzzing with confidence, having reinvented itself as a tourist hot-spot packed with Victorian architecture, world-class museums and lively pubs. Attractions range from Titanic Belfast, a celebration of the world's most famous ocean liner (built and launched here in 1911), to the black taxi tours of West Belfast's political murals, a reminder of the strife that scarred the city in the last decades of the 20th century.

Top: Belfast city lights; Above left: Titanic quarter (p230); Above right: Belfast locals enjoying a drink

10

Ring of Kerry

Driving around the Ring of Kerry (p206) is an unforgettable experience in itself, but you don't need to limit yourself to the main route. Along this 179km loop around the Iveragh Peninsula there are countless opportunities for detours. Near Killorglin, it's a short hop up to the beautiful, little-known Cromane Peninsula. Between Portmagee and Waterville, you can explore the Skellig Ring. The peninsula's interior offers mesmerising mountain views. And that's just for starters.

Kilkenny City

From its regal castle to its soaring medieval cathedral, Kilkenny (p246) exudes a permanence and culture that have made it an unmissable stop on journeys to the south and west. Its namesake county boasts scores of artisans and craftspeople and you can browse their wares at Kilkenny's classy shops and boutiques. Chefs eschew Dublin in order to be close to the source of Kilkenny's wonderful produce and you can enjoy the local brewery's concoctions at scores of delightful pubs.

Plan Your Trip
Five-Day Itinerary

DAVID SOANES PHOTOGRAPHY/GETTY IMAGES ©

Dublin to Meath

Short on time? Dublin has enough to entertain you for at least three days, leaving you two to devote to day trips from the capital. Even on a quick trip here you'll see some of the country's top highlights.

❶ Dublin (p34)

Start with the city's big hitters – Trinity College, the Book of Kells and the Guinness Storehouse. Then take in a collection or two: the Chester Beatty Library is worth an hour at least, as is the National Museum – Archaeology & History.

On day two, amble through St Stephen's Green before checking out the National Gallery. In the afternoon, head west and visit the Irish Museum of Modern Art and/or the fabulous Kilmainham Gaol. On day three, explore the north side of the city – a walk down O'Connell St will lead you to the Dublin City Gallery – The Hugh Lane. In the evening, take in a performance at either the Abbey Theatre or the Gate.

➡ Dublin to County Wicklow
🚗 1 hour; along M11, then right on R755; or
🚌 4 hours; organised bus tour from Dublin Tourism, includes Powerscourt Estate.

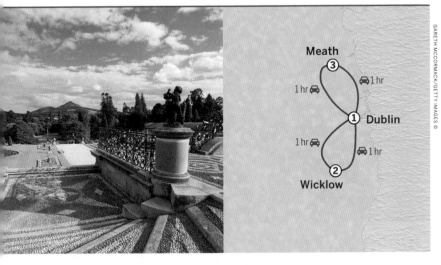

GARETH MCCORMACK/GETTY IMAGES ©

❷ County Wicklow (p94)

Immediately south of Dublin is the wild countryside of County Wicklow. If you only have one day, we recommend a guided tour during which you'll visit the county's showpiece attractions and be back in time for dinner. First up is the aristocratic mansion house and manicured gardens of Powerscourt, just a short drive outside the city boundary.

On day four, continue southwest through the granite scenery of the Wicklow Mountains to explore the the monastic ruins at Glendalough, one of the most scenic parts of the country, before returning to Dublin.

◯ Dublin to County Meath
🚗 1 hour; along M1, left on N51; or
🚌 4 hours; organised bus tour with Dublin Tourism.

❸ County Meath (p82)

On day five, head north into County Meath and back into prehistory by visiting the stunning Neolithic passage grave complex of Brú na Bóinne, which predates both Stonehenge and the pyramids of Egypt. From here, whether driving or on an organised tour, you can also visit Tara, where the high kings of Ireland resided in Celtic times. Also nearby is the site of Battle of the Boyne, where in 1690 Catholic and Protestant forces clashed under the leadership of King James II and King William III respectively, setting the course of Irish history for the next 300 years.

From left: Entrance to St Stephen's Green (p50), Dublin;
gardens and forecourt at Powerscourt Estate (p98)

Plan Your Trip
10-Day Itinerary

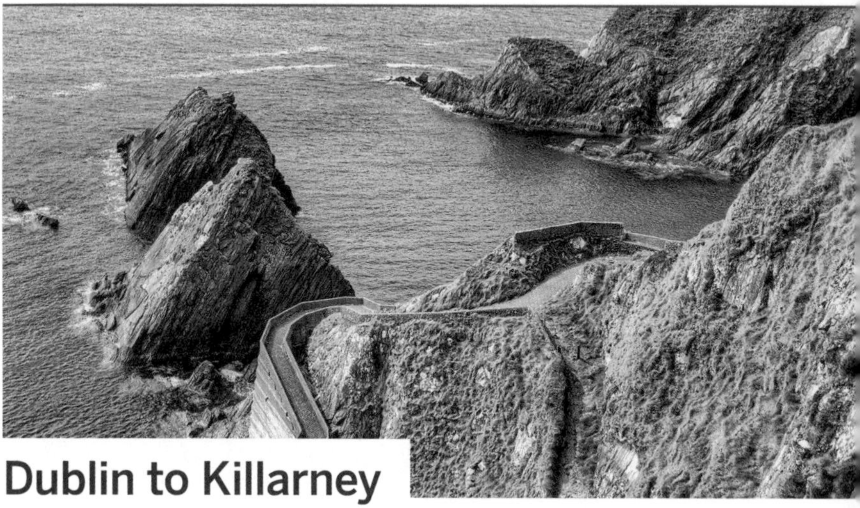

Dublin to Killarney

If you've only got 10 days and you must see the best of the country, you won't have time to linger too long anywhere, but if you manage it correctly, you'll leave with the top highlights in your memory – and on your memory card.

❶ Dublin (p34)

A one-day whistle-stop tour of the capital should include visits to Trinity College and the Book of Kells, the National Museum – Archaeology and the Guinness Storehouse. Make sure you also sample a pint of Guinness in one of the city's collection of superb pubs.

⊙ Dublin to Galway

🚗 3 hours via M6; or

🚌 3½ hours from Dublin's Busáras to Galway Bus Station; or

🚌 3 hours from Dublin's Heuston Station to Galway's Ceannt Station.

❷ Galway (p110)

Plan on three nights based in Galway city, and spend the first full day soaking in the city's aesthetic delights: a visit to the museum, a stroll along the river, and a meal followed by a drink (or four) and a live *céilidh* (session of traditional music and dancing) in a traditional old pub like Tig Cóilí.

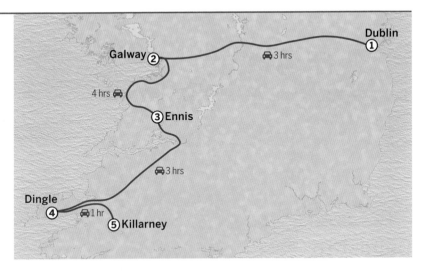

On the second day, take a drive to Clifden in Connemara, heading out via the coast, lunching in Clifden, and returning via Oughterard on lovely Lough Corrib.

○ **Galway to Ennis**
🚗 4 hours to Ennis via Cliffs of Moher

❸ Ennis (p148)

Drive south from Galway via Kinvara and the coastal road around the bare limestone scarps of the Burren to visit the Cliffs of Moher, before staying overnight in the town of Ennis, where you can take in a trad music session in one of its many pubs.

○ **Ennis to Dingle**
🚗 3 hours via M18, N21 and N86

❹ Dingle (p221)

Moving south again, cross into County Kerry and make for Dingle, on its eponymous peninsula. Explore the town on the after-

noon you arrive, and stay for two nights. The following morning take a harbour cruise to see Fungi the dolphin, and in the afternoon motor around Slea Head Drive with its stunning prehistoric monuments – not to mention the views!

○ **Dingle to Killarney**
🚗 One hour via N86

❺ Killarney (p214)

Allow for two nights based in Killarney. When you arrive from Dingle mid-morning, spend the rest of the day exploring Killarney National Park, making sure to take in Muckross House and a boat trip on Lough Leane. The following day, drive (or take a coach tour) around the scenic splendours of the famous Ring of Kerry (180km).

Above left: Dingle Peninsula (p221)

Plan Your Trip
Two-Week Itinerary

Belfast to Galway

This tourist trail takes in many of Ireland's most famous attractions and passes through spectacular countryside. It's almost 1500km in length, so you could dash around it in under a week, but what would be the point of rushing? You won't be disappointed on this route.

❶ Belfast (p226) & County Antrim (p158)

For the first two nights you're based in Northern Ireland's lively capital. Spend one day exploring the city's superb sights – Titanic Belfast and the political murals of West Belfast are must-sees – and one day on a driving tour around the Antrim coast to the Giant's Causeway, and back to Belfast (240km round trip).

➲ **Belfast & County Antrim to Dublin**
🚗 2 hours via the A1 and M1.; or
🚆 2¼ hours; Belfast Central to Dublin Connolly.

❷ Dublin (p34)

A one-day whistle-stop tour of the capital should include visits to Trinity College and the Book of Kells, the National Museum – Archaeology and the Guinness Storehouse. Make sure you also sample a pint of Guinness in one of the city's collection of superb pubs.

➲ **Dublin to Kilkenny**
🚗 1½ hours via M7 and M9; or
🚆 1¾ hours; Dublin Heuston to Kilkenny MacDonagh station.

HONEY CLOVERZ/SHUTTERSTOCK ©

❸ Kilkenny (p246)

Head southwest to Kilkenny to explore its medieval heritage – castle, cathedral, and city walls, plus art and crafts shops, riverside walks, and a plethora of pubs.

➲ **Kilkenny to Cork**
🚗 2½ hours via R693 and M8

❹ Cork (p182)

It's an hour's drive west from Kilkenny to the Rock of Cashel, giving you time to visit this spectacular site before continuing south to Cork via Blarney Castle. Spend two nights in Cork, giving you time to take in the English Market, stroll the city streets, and make a side trip to Midleton or Cobh.

➲ **Cork to Kinsale**
🚗 40 minutes via the R600; or
🚌 50 minutes from Cork bus station to Pier Rd stop.

❺ Kinsale (p197)

Indulge yourself with a day of shopping, eating and lounging around in the lovely yachting harbour of Kinsale. Spend a night here so you can enjoy a restaurant meal of some of Ireland's finest seafood.

➲ **Kinsale to Killarney**
🚗 1½ hours via L3201 and N22.

❻ Killarney (p214)

Allow for two nights based in Killarney, exploring nearby Killarney National Park, and driving (or taking a coach tour) around the Ring of Kerry (180km).

➲ **Killarney to Galway**
🚗 5 hours via Cliffs of Moher; or
🚌 4 hours; Killarney bus station direct to Galway bus station.

❼ Galway (p110)

Drive north to Galway via the Cliffs of Moher, and spend three nights there; see the Dublin to Killarney itinerary (p20) for what to do.

From left: Killarney National Park (p210);
Cork City (p190)

Plan Your Trip
If You Like...

Traditional Pubs

Séhán Ua Neáchtain One of Ireland's best-known traditional pubs, located in Galway. (p124)

John Mulligan's The most famous of Dublin's traditional pubs and a star of film and TV – where it usually plays itself. (p75)

Tynan's Bridge House A typical country pub, except it's in the middle of Kilkenny city. (p258)

Crown Liquor Saloon The most famous of Belfast's Victorian pubs. (p242)

King's Head An ancient pub in the heart of Galway city, with parts dating to the 14th century. (p117)

Scenic Drives

Ring of Kerry Probably Ireland's most famous – and popular – scenic route. (p206)

Connemara Coast An off-the-beaten-track meander along a gorgeous coastline. (p114)

Slea Head Drive Historic sites abound on this tour of County Kerry's most southwestern point. (p224)

Antrim Coast Northern Ireland's best scenic route culminates with the Giant's Causeway. (p158)

Festivals

Kilkenny Arts Festival Medieval Kilkenny shows its artistic side. (p255)

Cat Laughs Comedy Festival Comics from around the world descend on Kilkenny every year. (p255)

Willie Clancy Irish Music Festival You can hear some of the best traditional music in the world at this annual do on the Clare coast. (p150)

Galway Arts Festival The city goes arts- and fun-crazy for two weeks. (p122)

Galway International Oyster Festival Locally produced oysters washed down with Guinness to a lively musical soundtrack. (p122)

ZKBLD/SHUTTERSTOCK ©

Good Food

Dublin The republic's capital is the best place in Ireland for range of cuisines. (p72)

Belfast From pub grub to gourmet feasts, Belfast's foodie rep is growing. (p239)

Cork City The gourmet capital of Ireland, Cork is famous for its championing of local produce. (p186)

Kinsale Home to some of Ireland's best seafood restaurants, as well as a fine farmers market. (p197)

Ballymaloe House The hotel, restaurant and cookery school where Darina Allen kicked off Ireland's entire foodie scene in the 1970s. (p196)

Irish Music

An Droichead Excellent music sessions at a Belfast arts centre dedicated to Irish culture. (p239)

Miltown Malbay Every pub in this County Clare town features outstanding Irish trad sessions. (p152)

Tig Cóilí Galway's best trad sessions are held in a pub whose name means 'house of music'. (p116)

Whelan's Dublin's top live-music venue. (p70)

Courtney's A timeless Killarney pub that hosts regular trad sessions. (p217)

Ancient Monuments

Brú na Bóinne Europe's most impressive Neolithic burial site. (p86)

Clonmacnoise Ireland's finest monastic site. (p118)

Skellig Michael Monastic settlement clinging to a rock since the 6th century. (p208)

Dún Aengus Stunning Stone Age fort perched perilously on Inishmór's cliffs. (p134)

Glendalough Ruins of a once-powerful monastic city in stunning surroundings. (p100)

From left: Oyster plate; Connemara landscape (p125)

Plan Your Trip
Month by Month

SLOW IMAGES/GETTY IMAGES ©

February

Bad weather makes February the perfect month for indoor activities. Some museums launch new exhibits, and it's a good time to visit the major towns and cities.

☆ Six Nations Rugby

Ireland, winners of the 2015 championship, play their three home matches at the Aviva Stadium in the Dublin suburb of Ballsbridge. The season runs from February to April.

⚜ Jameson Dublin International Film Festival

Most of Dublin's cinemas participate in the country's biggest film festival (www.jdiff.com), a two-week showcase for new Irish and international films that features local flicks, art-house films from across the globe and advance releases of mainstream movies.

March

Spring is in the air, and the whole country is getting ready for arguably the world's most famous parade. Dublin's is the biggest, but every town in Ireland holds one.

⚜ St Patrick's Day

Ireland erupts into one giant celebration on 17 March (www.stpatricksday.ie), but Dublin throws a five-day party around the parade (attended by 600,000), with gigs and festivities that leave the city with a giant hangover.

April

The weather is getting better, the flowers are beginning to bloom and the festival season begins anew. Seasonal attractions start to open up around the middle of the month or at Easter.

☆ Circuit of Ireland International Rally

Northern Ireland's most prestigious rally race – known locally as the 'Circuit' (www.circuitofireland.net) – sees over 130 competitors throttle and turn through some 550km of Northern Ireland and parts of the Republic over two days at Easter.

☆ Irish Grand National

Ireland loves horse racing, and the race that's loved the most is the Grand National (www.

fairyhouse.ie), the showcase of the national hunt season that takes place at Fairyhouse in County Meath on Easter Monday.

☆ World Irish Dancing Championships

There's far more to Irish dancing than Riverdance. Every April, some 4500 competitors from all over the world gather to test their steps and skills against the very best. The location varies from year to year; see www.irishdancingorg.com.

May

The May Bank Holiday (on the first Monday) sees the first of the busy summer weekends as the Irish take to the roads to enjoy the budding good weather.

☆ North West 200

Ireland's most famous road race (www. northwest200.org) is also the country's biggest outdoor sporting event; 150,000-plus people line the triangular route to cheer on some of the biggest names in motorcycle racing. Held in mid-May.

✵ Fleadh Nua

The third week of May sees the cream of the traditional music crop come to Ennis, County Clare, for one of the country's most important festivals (www.fleadhnua.com).

June

The bank holiday at the beginning of the month sees the country spoilt for choice as to what to do. Weekend traffic gets busier as the weather gets better.

☆ Irish Derby

Wallets are packed and fancy hats donned for the best flat-race festival in the country (www.curragh.ie), run during the first week of the month.

✵ Bloomsday

Edwardian dress and breakfast of 'the inner organs of beast and fowl' are but two of the elements of the Dublin festival celebrating

From left: St Patrick's Day parade, Dublin; World Irish Dancing Championships

16 June, the day on which Joyce's *Ulysses* takes place; the real highlight is retracing Leopold Bloom's steps.

July

There isn't a weekend in the month that a major festival doesn't take place, while visitors to Galway will find that the city is in full swing for the entire month.

☆ Longitude

A mini-Glastonbury in Dublin's Marlay Park, Longitude (www.longitude.ie) packs them in over three days in mid-July for a feast of EDM, nu-folk, rock and pop. In 2015 Hozier and Chemical Brothers were the big headliners.

August

Schools are closed, the sun is shining (or not!) and Ireland is in holiday mood. Seaside towns and tourist centres are at their busiest as the country looks to make the most of its time off.

☆ Galway Race Week

The biggest horse-racing festival (www.galwayraces.com) west of the Shannon is not just about the horses, it's also a celebration of Irish culture, sporting gambles and elaborate hats.

☆ Fleadh Cheoil na hÉireann

The mother of all Irish music festivals (www.comhaltas.ie), usually held at the end of the month, attracts in excess of 250,000 music lovers and revellers to whichever town is playing host – there's some great music amid the drinking.

☆ Rose of Tralee

The Irish beauty pageant sees wannabe Roses plucked from Irish communities throughout the world competing for the ultimate prize. For everyone else, it's a big party.

September

Summer may be over but September weather can be surprisingly good, so it's often the ideal time to enjoy the last vestiges of the sun as the crowds dwindle.

☆ Dublin Fringe Festival

Upwards of 100 different performances take the stage, the street, the bar and the car in the fringe festival (www.fringefest.com) that is unquestionably more innovative than the main theatre festival that follows it.

☆ All-Ireland Finals

The second and fourth Sundays of the month see the finals of the hurling and Gaelic football championships respectively, with 80,000-plus crowds thronging into Dublin's Croke Park for the biggest sporting days of the year.

October

The weather starts to turn cold so it's time to move the fun indoors again. The calendar is still packed with activities and distractions, especially over the last weekend of the month.

☆ Dublin Theatre Festival

The most prestigious theatre festival in the country (www.dublintheatrefestival.com) sees new work and new versions of old work staged in theatres and venues throughout the capital.

☆ Belfast Festival at Queen's

Northern Ireland's top arts festival (www.belfastfestival.com) attracts performers from all over the world for the second half of the month; on offer is everything from visual arts to dance.

December

Christmas dominates the calendar as the country prepares for the feast with frenzied shopping and after-work drinks with friends and family arrived home from abroad. On Christmas Day nothing is open.

☆ Christmas

This is a quiet affair in the countryside, though on 26 December (St Stephen's Day) the ancient custom of Wren Boys is re-enacted, most notably in Dingle, County Kerry, when groups of children dress up and go about singing hymns.

Plan Your Trip
Get Inspired

RICHARD CUMMINS/GETTY IMAGES ©

Books

Strumpet City (James Plunkett, 1969) Classic portrayal of Dublin during the 1913 Lockout.

The Butcher Boy (Patrick McCabe, 1992) Boy retreats into a violent fantasy life as his small-town world collapses.

Paddy Clarke Ha Ha Ha (Roddy Doyle, 1993) Booker Prize winner about the trials of a Dublin child.

Angela's Ashes (Frank McCourt, 1996) Pulitzer Prize–winning memoir of working-class Limerick.

Reading in the Dark (Seamus Deane, 1996) Young Belfast boy's view of growing up during the Troubles.

Films

Bloody Sunday (Paul Greengrass, 2002) Superb film about the events of 30 January 1972.

The Dead (John Huston, 1987) Based on James Joyce's fantastic story from *Dubliners*.

Garage (Lenny Abrahamson, 2007) A lonely man attempts to come out of his shell.

The Crying Game (Neil Jordan, 1992) A classic that explores violence, gender and the IRA.

The Magdalene Sisters (Peter Mullan, 2002) Harrowing portrayal of life in the infamous asylum.

Music

The Joshua Tree (U2, 1987) A fan-favourite record by the Dublin superstars.

I Do Not Want What I Haven't Got (Sinead O'Connor, 1990) Powerful album by a superb singer.

Becoming a Jackal (Villagers, 2010) The band's knockout debut album.

St Dominic's Preview (Van Morrison, 1972) Lesser known but still brilliant.

Live & Dangerous (Thin Lizzy, 1978) Excellent live album by beloved Irish rockers.

Above: John's Quay and the River Nore, Kilkenny city (p246)

Plan Your Trip
Family Travel

PAUL M O'CONNELL/GETTY IMAGES ©

Ireland is generally a pretty good place to bring kids. The Irish love them – it's not so long ago since the average Irish family numbered four, five, six or more children – and they have a pretty easygoing approach to the noise and mayhem that they often bring in their wake. The quality and availability of services for children vary, however, and can be completely lacking outside of bigger towns and cities.

For further general information see Lonely Planet's *Travel with Children*. Also check out www.eumom.ie for advice for pregnant women and parents with young children, as well as www.babygoes2.com, a travel site about family-friendly accommodation worldwide.

Restaurants & Hotels

On the whole you'll find that restaurants and hotels will go out of their way to cater for you and your children. Hotels will provide cots at no extra charge and most restaurants have highchairs. Bear in mind that under-16s are banned from pubs after 7pm – even if they're accompanied by their parents.

Transport

Under-fives travel free on all public transport and most admission prices have an under-16s reduced fee. It's always a good

SKLA/GETTY IMAGES ©

idea to talk to fellow travellers with (happy) children and locals on the road for tips on where to go.

Car seats (around €50/£25 per week) are mandatory for children in hire cars between the ages of nine months and four years. Bring your own seat for infants under about nine months as only larger, forward-facing child seats are generally available. Remember not to place baby seats in the front if the car has an airbag.

Feeding & Changing

Although breastfeeding is not a common sight (Ireland has one of the lowest rates of it in the world), you can do so with impunity pretty much everywhere without getting so much as a stare. Nappy-changing facilities are generally only found in the newer, larger shopping centres – otherwise you'll have to make do with a public toilet.

Distractions for the Kids

National Museum of Ireland – Natural History (p60)

Titanic Belfast (p230)

Giant's Causeway (p162)

Parks & Gardens

As far as parks, gardens and green spaces, Ireland has an abundance of them but very few amenities such as designated playgrounds and other exclusively child-friendly spots. In Dublin, St Stephen's Green has a popular playground in the middle of it, but it is the exception rather than the rule.

From left: Children playing, Dublin; family hiking, County Kerry

Plan Your Trip
Need to Know

When to Go

Belfast
GO May–Sep

Galway
GO May–Sep

Dublin
GO Any time;
lots of indoor
attractions

Kerry
GO May–Sep

Cork
GO May–Sep

High Season (Jun–mid-Sep)

- Weather at its best.
- Accommodation rates highest (especially in August).
- Tourist peak in Dublin, Kerry, southern and western coasts.

Shoulder (Easter to May, mid-Sep to Oct)

- Weather often good, sun and rain in May; 'Indian summers' and often warm in September.
- Summer crowds and accommodation rates drop off.

Low Season (Nov–Feb)

- Reduced opening hours from October to Easter; some destinations close.
- Cold and wet weather throughout the country; fog can reduce visibility.
- Big city attractions operate as normal.

Language
English, Irish

Visas
Not required by most citizens of Europe, Australia, New Zealand, USA and Canada.

Money
The currency in the Republic of Ireland is the euro (€). The island's peculiar political history means that the six Ulster counties that make up Northern Ireland use the pound sterling (£). Although notes issued by Northern Irish banks are legal tender throughout the UK, many businesses outside of Northern Ireland refuse to accept them and you'll have to swap them in British banks.

Mobile Phones
Phones from most other countries work in Ireland but attract roaming charges. Local SIM cards cost from €10; SIM and basic handsets cost around €40.

Time
Western European Time (UTC/GMT November to March; plus one hour April to October).

Daily Costs

Budget Less than €60

o Dorm bed: €12–20

o Cheap meal in cafe or pub: €6–12

o Inter-city bus travel (200km trip): €12–25

o Pint: €4.50–5 (more expensive in cities)

Midrange €60–€120

o Double room in hotel or B&B (more expensive in Dublin): €80–180

o Main course in midrange restaurant: €12–25

o Car rental (per day): from €25–45

o Three-hour train journey: €65

Top End More than €120

o Four-star hotel stay: from €150

o Three-course meal in good restaurant: around €50

o Top round of golf (midweek): from €90

Useful Websites

Entertainment Ireland (www.entertainment.ie) Countrywide listings for every kind of entertainment.

Fáilte Ireland (www.ireland.com) Official tourist board website – practical info and a huge accommodation database.

Lonely Planet (www.lonelyplanet.com/ireland) Destination information, hotel bookings, traveller forums and more.

Northern Ireland Tourist Board (www.tourismni.com) Official tourist site.

Exchange Rates

For current exchange rates see www.xe.com

Opening Hours

Banks 10am to 4pm Monday to Friday (to 5pm Thursday)

Pubs 10.30am to 11.30pm Monday to Thursday, 10.30am to 12.30am Friday and Saturday, noon to 11pm Sunday (30 minutes 'drinking up' time allowed); closed Christmas Day and Good Friday

Restaurants noon to 10.30pm; many close one day of the week

Shops 9.30am to 6pm Monday to Saturday (until 8pm Thursday in cities), noon to 6pm Sunday

Arriving in Ireland

Dublin Airport Private coaches run every 10 to 15 minutes to the city centre (€7). Taxis take 30 to 45 minutes and cost €20 to €25.

Dun Laoghaire Ferry Port Public bus takes around 45 minutes to the centre of Dublin; DART (suburban rail) takes about 25 minutes.

Dublin Port Terminal Buses are timed to coincide with arrivals and departures; costs €3 to the city centre.

Belfast International Airport/George Best Belfast City Airport A bus runs to the centre every 15 to 20 minutes from both airports; a taxi from the international airport costs around £30, or £10 from George Best City Airport.

Getting Around

Train A limited network links Dublin to all major urban centres, including Belfast in Northern Ireland. Expensive if you're on a budget.

Car The most convenient way to explore Ireland's every nook and cranny. Cars can be hired in every major town and city; drive on the left.

Bus An extensive network of public and private buses make them the most cost-effective way to get around; there's service to and from most inhabited areas.

Bike Dublin operates a bike-share scheme with over 100 stations spread throughout the city.

For more, see the **Survival Guide** (p300) ➡

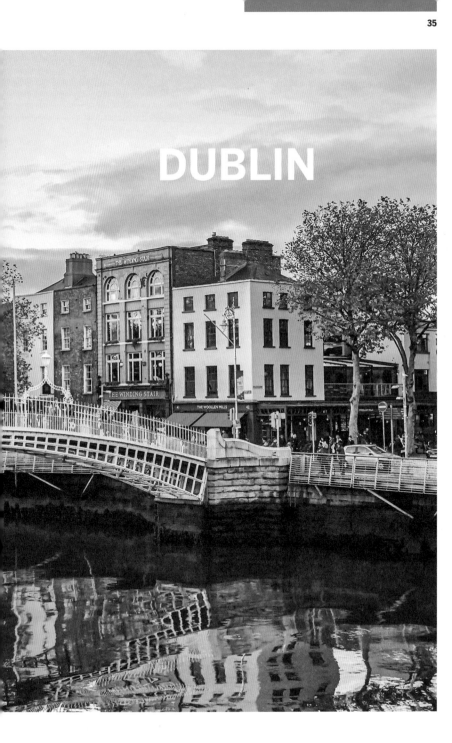

DUBLIN

Discover More
www.lonelyplanet.
com/ireland/dublin

Clockwise from top left:

Buildings at Dublin Castle (p42); woman in Dublin's St Patrick's Day parade (p26); Temple Bar (p61) street; Leinster House (p60); O'Connell Bridge stretching over the River Liffey

BOOK YOUR ACCOMMODATION ON LONELYPLANET.COM/HOTELS

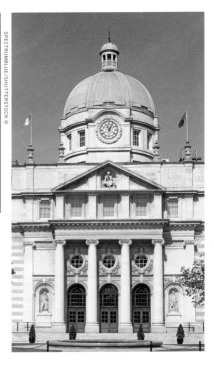

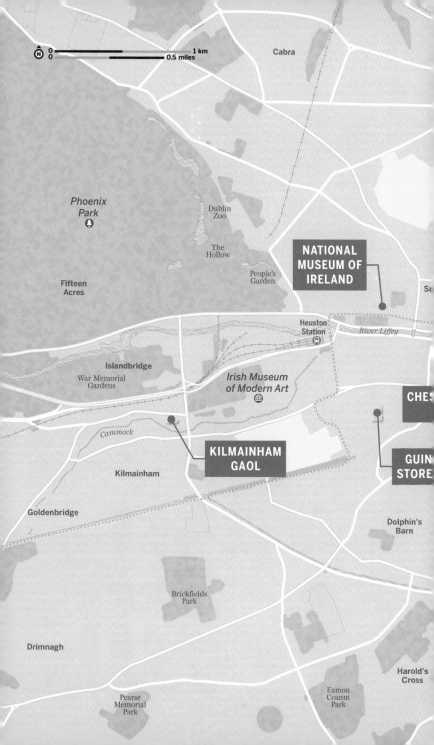

☑ Planning Ahead

Book accommodation, especially in summer. Buy tickets in advance for weekend performances at main theatres, and make reservations for Friday or Saturday nights at the trendiest or most popular restaurants.

❶ Arriving in Dublin

Dublin Airport: Buses to the city centre run every 10 to 15 minutes between 6am and midnight; taxis (€25) take around 45 minutes.

Dun Laoghaire ferry terminal: DART (one way €2.80) to Pearse Station (for south Dublin) or Connolly Station (for north Dublin); bus 46A to St Stephen's Green, or bus 7, 7A or 8 to Burgh Quay.

Dublin Port: terminal Busáras buses (adult/child €2.50/1.25) are timed to coincide with arrivals and departures.

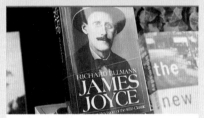

➡ Dublin in Two Days

Start with **Trinity College** (p38) and the Book of Kells before ambling through **St Stephen's Green** (p50) and **Merrion Square** (p51); in the afternoon visit the **National Museum of Ireland – Archaeology** (p46). The next day stop at the **Chester Beatty Library** (p44) on your way to **Dublin Castle** (p42), then spend the afternoon at the **Guinness Storehouse** (p54).

➡ Dublin in Four Days

Follow the two-day itinerary, but stretch it out by refuelling between stops at some of the city's better pubs. Add the **Irish Museum of Modern Art** (p64) and **Kilmainham Gaol** (p40) to your sightseeing list On day four become a whiskey expert at the **Old Jameson Distillery** (p65) and a literary (or beer) one with a **Dublin Literary Pub Crawl** (p66).

From left: O'Connell Bridge; St Patrick's Festival (p26); Guinness Storehouse (p54); Irish literature

Trinity College

The student body here has diversified since those days when a university education was the preserve of a small elite, but Trinity's bucolic charms persist and on a summer's evening it's one of the city's most delightful places to be: a calm retreat from the bustle of contemporary Dublin.

Great For...

☑ Don't Miss

The Long Room, which starred as the Jedi Archive in the movie *Star Wars Episode II: Attack of the Clones*.

The college was established by Elizabeth I in 1592 on land confiscated from an Augustinian priory in an effort to stop the brain drain of young Protestant Dubliners, who were skipping across to continental Europe for an education and becoming 'infected with popery'. Trinity went on to become one of Europe's most outstanding universities, producing a host of notable graduates – how about Jonathan Swift, Oscar Wilde and Samuel Beckett at the same alumni dinner?

It remained completely Protestant until 1793, but even when the university relented and began to admit Catholics, the Catholic Church held firm; until 1970, any Catholic who enrolled here could consider themselves excommunicated.

The campus is a masterpiece of architecture and landscaping beautifully preserved in Georgian aspic. Most of the buildings and statues date from the 18th

Spiral staircase, Long Room

ANDREW MONTGOMERY/O/LONELY PLANET ©

❶ Need to Know

Map p62; ☎01-896 1000; www.tcd.ie; College Green; ⏰8am-10pm; 🚌all city centre) FREE

✕ Take a Break

Fade Street Social (p72) is an excellent lunch spot just a few blocks southwest.

★ Top Tip

The Long Room gets very busy during the summer months, so it's recommended to go online and buy a fast-track ticket (adult/student/family €13/11/26), which gives timed admission to the exhibition and allows visitors to skip the queue.

and 19th centuries, each elegantly laid out on a cobbled or grassy square. The newer bits include the 1978 Arts & Social Science Building, which backs on to Nassau St and forms the alternative entrance to the college. Like the college's Berkeley Library, it was designed by Paul Koralek; it houses the Douglas Hyde Gallery of Modern Art.

To the south of Library Sq is the **Old Library** (⏰9.30am-5pm Mon-Sat year-round, noon-4.30pm Sun Oct-Apr, 9.30am-4.30pm Sun May-Sep), built in a severe style by Thomas Burgh between 1712 and 1732. It is one of five copyright libraries across Ireland and the UK, which means it's entitled to a copy of every book published in these islands – around five million books, of which only a fraction are stored here. You can visit the library as part of a tour of the Long Room, home of the famous Book of Kells.

Trinity's greatest treasures are kept in the Old Library's stunning 65m **Long Room** (adult/student/child €10/9/free), which houses about 200,000 of the library's oldest volumes, including the Book of Kells, a breathtaking illuminated manuscript of the four Gospels of the New Testament, created around AD 800 by monks on the Scottish island of Iona. Other displays include a rare copy of the Proclamation of the Irish Republic, which was read out by Pádraig (Patrick) Pearse at the beginning of the Easter Rising in 1916.

Also here is the so-called harp of Brian Ború, which was definitely not in use when the army of this early Irish hero defeated the Danes at the Battle of Clontarf in 1014. It does, however, date from around 1400, making it one of the oldest harps in Ireland. Your entry ticket also includes admission to temporary exhibitions on display in the East Pavilion.

DESIGN PICS/LJM PHOTO/GETTY IMAGES ©

Kilmainham Gaol

If you have any desire to understand Irish history – especially the juicy bits about resistance to British rule – then a visit to this former prison is an absolute must.

Great For...

☑ **Don't Miss**

Kilmainham houses an outstanding museum dedicated to Irish nationalism and prison life.

This threatening grey building, built between 1792 and 1795, played a role in virtually every act of Ireland's painful path to independence and even today, despite closing in 1924, it still has the power to chill.

It took four years to build, and the prison opened – or rather closed – its doors in 1796. The Irish were locked up for all sorts of misdemeanours, some more serious than others. A six-year-old boy spent a month here in 1839 because his father couldn't pay his train fare, and during the Famine it was crammed with the destitute imprisoned for stealing food and begging. But it is most famous for incarcerating 120 years of Irish nationalists, from Robert Emmet in 1803 to Éamon de Valera in 1923. All of Ireland's botched uprisings ended with the leaders' confinement here, usually before their execution.

Execution site, Kilmainham Gaol

❶ Need to Know

Map p68; www.heritageireland.com; Inchicore Rd; adult/child €7/3; ⊙9.30am-6pm Apr-Sep, 9.30am-5.30pm Mon-Sat, 10am-6pm Sun Oct-Mar; 🚍23, 25, 25A, 26, 68 or 69 from city centre

✕ Take a Break

The **Old Royal Oak** (Map p68; 11 Kilmainham Lane; ⊙10.30am-11.30pm Mon-Thu, to 12.30am Fri & Sat, noon-11pm Sun; 🚍68, 69 & 79 from city centre), a pub that dates from 1845, is just east of Kilmainham Gaol.

★ Top Tip

Tours can sell out and are not bookable in advance – arrive early to avoid disappointment.

It was the treatment of the leaders of the 1916 Easter Rising that most deeply etched the gaol into the Irish consciousness. Fourteen of the rebel commanders were executed in the stone breakers' yard, including James Connolly who was so badly injured at the time of his execution that he was strapped to a chair at the opposite end of the yard.

The gaol's final function was as a prison for the newly formed Irish Free State, an irony best summed up with the story of Ernie O'Malley, who escaped from the gaol when incarcerated by the British but was locked up again by his erstwhile comrades during the Civil War. This chapter is played down on the tour, and even the passing comment that Kilmainham's final prisoner was the future president, Éamon de Valera, doesn't reveal that he had been imprisoned by his fellow Irish citizens. The gaol was decommissioned in 1924.

An excellent audiovisual introduction to the building is followed by a thought-provoking tour of the eerie prison, the largest unoccupied building of its kind in Europe. Sitting incongruously outside in the yard is the *Asgard*, the ship that successfully ran the British blockade to deliver arms to Nationalist forces in 1914. The tour finishes in the gloomy yard where the 1916 executions took place.

JOHN HARPER/GETTY IMAGES ©

Dublin Castle

This mostly 18th-century creation – more hotchpotch palace than medieval castle, though a 13th-century tower survives – was the stronghold of British power in Ireland for 700 years.

Great For...

☑ Don't Miss

The view over Dublin from the top of the Bedford Tower.

The castle is now used by the Irish government for meetings and functions, and can be visited only on a guided tour of the State Apartments and of the excavations of the former Powder Tower.

It was officially handed over to Michael Collins, representing the Irish Free State, in 1922, when the British viceroy is reported to have rebuked Collins on being seven minutes late. Collins replied, 'We've been waiting 700 years, you can wait seven minutes.'

As you walk into the grounds from the main Dame St entrance, there's a good example of the evolution of Irish architecture. On your left is the Victorian **Chapel Royal** (occasionally part of the Dublin Castle tours), decorated with more than 90 heads of various Irish personages and saints carved out of Tullamore limestone. Beside

ⓘ Need to Know

Map p62; 📞01-677 7129; www.dublin castle.ie; Dame St; adult/child €8.50/6.50; 🕘9.45am-4.45pm Mon-Sat, noon-4.45pm Sun; 🚌all city centre

✕ Take a Break

Head across the street to **Queen of Tarts** (Map p62; www.queenoftarts.ie; 4 Cork Hill; mains €5-10; 🕘8am-7pm Mon-Fri, 9am-7pm Sat & Sun; 🚌all city centre) for great cakes and coffee.

★ Top Tip

There's a self-guided tour option, but it only includes the State Apartments.

---

this is the Norman **Record Tower** with its 5m-thick walls. It's currently closed to the public pending a long-awaited revamp. On your right is the Georgian **Treasury Building**, the oldest office block in Dublin, and behind you, yikes, is the uglier-than-sin Revenue Commissioners Building of 1960.

Heading away from that eyesore, you ascend to the Upper Yard. On your right is a figure of Justice with her back turned to the city – an appropriate symbol for British justice, reckoned Dubliners. Next to it is the 18th-century **Bedford Tower**, from which the Irish Crown Jewels were stolen in 1907 and never recovered. Opposite is the entrance for the tours.

The 45-minute **guided tours** (departing every 20 to 30 minutes, depending on numbers) are pretty dry, but you get to visit the **State Apartments**, many of

which are decorated in dubious taste. You will also see **St Patrick's Hall**, where Irish presidents are inaugurated and foreign dignitaries toasted, and the room in which the wounded James Connolly was tied to a chair while convalescing after the 1916 Easter Rising, so that he could be executed by firing squad.

The highlight is a visit to the **medieval undercroft** of the old castle, discovered by accident in 1986. It includes foundations built by the Vikings (whose long-lasting mortar was made of ox blood, egg shells and horse hair), the hand-polished exterior of the castle walls that prevented attackers from climbing them, the steps leading down to the moat and the trickle of the historic River Poddle, which once filled the moat on its way to join the Liffey.

Chester Beatty Library

This breathtaking collection includes more than 20,000 manuscripts, rare books, miniature paintings, clay tablets, costumes and other objects of artistic, historical and aesthetic importance, the legacy of Sir Alfred Chester Beatty (1875–1968).

Great For...

☑ Don't Miss

Fragments of the Christian gospels written on papyrus, dating from around AD 200.

Sir Alfred Chester Beatty

An avid traveller and collector, Beatty was fascinated by different cultures and amassed more than 20,000 manuscripts, rare books, miniature paintings, clay tablets, costumes and any other objets d'art that caught his fancy and could tell him something about the world. Fortunately for Dublin, he also happened to take quite a shine to the city and made it his adopted home. In return, the Irish made him their first honorary citizen in 1957.

Art of the Book

The collection is spread over two levels. On the ground floor you'll find the Art of the Book, a compact but stunning collection of artworks from the Western, Islamic and East Asian worlds. Highlights include the finest

Chester Beatty
Library
Dubhlinn
Garden
Palace St
Great Ship St
S Great George's St

❶ Need to Know

Map p62; ☎01-407 0750; www.cbl.ie;
Dublin Castle; ⊗10am-5pm Mon-Fri, 11am-
5pm Sat, 1-5pm Sun year-round, closed Mon
Nov-Feb, free tours 1pm Wed, 3pm & 4pm Sun;
🚌50, 51B, 77, 78A or 123; FREE

✗ Take a Break

The library's own **Silk Road Café** (Map
p62; Chester Beatty Library, Dublin Castle;
mains €11; ⊗11am-4pm Mon-Fri, closed
Mon Nov-Feb; 🚌50, 51B, 77, 78A or 123) is a
great place for lunch.

★ Top Tip

The library regularly holds specialist
workshops, exhibitions and talks on
everything from origami to
calligraphy.

collection of Chinese jade books in the world
and illuminated European texts featuring
exquisite calligraphy that stand up in comparison with the *Book of Kells*. Audiovisual
displays explain the process of bookbinding,
paper-making and printing.

Sacred Traditions

The 2nd floor is home to Sacred Traditions,
a wonderful exploration of the world's
major religions through decorative and
religious art, enlightening text and a cool
cultural-pastiche video at the entrance. The
collection of Korans dating from the 9th
to the 19th centuries (the library has more
than 270 of them) is considered by experts
to be the best example of illuminated
Islamic texts in the world. There are also
outstanding examples of ancient papyri,
including renowned Egyptian love poems

from the 12th century, and some of the
earliest illuminated gospels in the world,
dating from around AD 200. The collection
is rounded off with some exquisite scrolls
and artwork from China, Japan, Tibet and
Southeast Asia, including the two-volume
Japanese *Chogonka Scroll*, painted in the
17th century by Kano Sansetu.

The Building

As if all of this wasn't enough for one visit,
the library also hosts temporary exhibits
that are usually too good to be missed.
Not only are the contents of the museum
outstanding, but the layout, design and
location are also unparalleled, from the
marvellous Silk Road Café and gift shop, to
the Zen rooftop terrace and the beautiful
landscaped garden out the front. These
features alone would make this an absolute
Dublin must-do.

STEVEN ALLAN/GETTY IMAGES ©

National Museum of Ireland

The mother of all Irish museums and the country's most important cultural institution was established in 1977 as the primary repository of the nation's treasures.

Great For...

☑ **Don't Miss**

The extraordinary hoard of prehistoric gold objects in the archaeology museum.

The collection is so big, however, that it is spread across three separate museums – the archaeology museum in Kildare St, the decorative arts museum at Collins Barracks and a country life museum in County Mayo, on Ireland's west coast. They're all fascinating, but the star attractions are to be found in the archaeology museum that includes Europe's finest collection of Bronze- and Iron Age gold artefacts, the most complete collection of medieval Celtic metalwork in the world, fascinating prehistoric and Viking artefacts, and a few interesting items relating to Ireland's fight for independence. If you don't mind groups, the themed guided tours will help you wade through the myriad exhibits.

NMI Archaeology

NMI Decorative Arts

River Liffey

NMI Archaeology

ℹ️ Need to Know

NMI Archaeology: Map p62; www.
museum.ie; Kildare St; ⏰10am-5pm Tue-Sat,
2-5pm Sun; 🚌all city centre; FREE
NMI Decorative Arts: Map p68; www.
museum.ie; Benburb St; ⏰10am-5pm Tue-
Sat, 2-5pm Sun; 🚌25, 66, 67 or 90 from city
centre, 🚋Smithfield; FREE

✕ Take a Break

There are several good eateries on Merrion Row, just south of the archaeology
museum.

★ Top Tip

You can travel between the two museum locations on a hop-on, hop-off
tour bus.

NMI Archaeolology

Treasury

The Treasury is perhaps the most famous
part of the collection, and its centrepieces
are Ireland's two most famous crafted
artefacts, the **Ardagh Chalice** and the **Tara
Brooch**. The 12th-century Ardagh Chalice
is made of gold, silver, bronze, brass, copper and lead; it measures 17.8cm high and
24.2cm in diameter and, put simply, is the
finest example of Celtic art ever found. The
equally renowned Tara Brooch was crafted
around AD 700, primarily in white bronze,
but with traces of gold, silver, glass, copper,
enamel and wire beading, and was used
as a clasp for a cloak. It was discovered
on a beach in Bettystown, County Meath,
in 1850, but later came into the hands of
an art dealer who named it after the hill of

Tara, the historic seat of the ancient high
kings. It doesn't have quite the same ring
to it, but it was the Bettystown Brooch that
sparked a revival of interest in Celtic jewellery that hasn't let up to this day. There are
many other pieces that testify to Ireland's
history as the land of saints and scholars.

Ór-Ireland's Gold

Elsewhere in the Treasury is the Ór-Ireland's
Gold exhibition, featuring stunning jewellery
and decorative objects created by Celtic
artisans in the Bronze and Iron Ages. Among
them are the **Broighter Hoard**, which
includes a 1st-century-BC large gold collar,
unsurpassed anywhere in Europe, and an ex-
traordinarily delicate gold boat. There's also
the wonderful **Loughnasade bronze war
trumpet**, which dates from the 1st century
BC. It is 1.86m long and made of sheets of
bronze, riveted together, with an intricately
designed disc at the mouth. It produces a

sound similar to the Australian didgeridoo, though you'll have to take our word for it. Running alongside the wall is a **15m log boat**, which was dropped into the water to soften, abandoned and then pulled out 4000 years later, almost perfectly preserved in the peat bog.

Other Exhibits

If you can cope with any more history, upstairs are **Medieval Ireland 1150–1550**, **Viking Age Ireland** – which features exhibits from the excavations at Wood Quay, the area between Christ Church Cathedral and the river – and our own favourite, the aptly named **Clothes from Bogs in Ireland**, a collection of 16th- and 17th-century woollen garments recovered from the bog. Enthralling stuff!

NMI Decorative Arts

Once the world's largest military barracks, this splendid early-neoclassical grey-stone building on the Liffey's northern banks was completed in 1704 according to the design of Thomas Burgh, whose CV also includes the Old Library in Trinity College and St Michan's Church. It is now home to the Decorative Arts & History collection of the National Museum of Ireland.

The Building

The building's central square held six entire regiments and is a truly awesome space, surrounded by arcaded colonnades and blocks linked by walking bridges. Following the handover to the new Irish government in 1922, the barracks was renamed to honour Michael Collins, a hero of the struggle for independence, who was killed that year

Interior of NMI Archaeology (p47)

in the Civil War; to this day most Dubliners refer to the museum as the **Collins Barracks**. Indeed, the army coat he wore on the day of his death (there's still mud on the sleeve) is part of the **Soldiers and Chiefs** exhibit, which covers the history of Irish soldiery at home and abroad from 1550 to the 21st century. In the same case is the cap purportedly also worn by Collins on that fateful day, complete with a bullet hole in its side

★ Top Tip

The Curator's Choice exhibition in the decorative arts museum is a collection of 25 objects hand-picked by different curators, with an account of why they were chosen.

The Exhibits

The museum's exhibits include a treasure trove of artefacts ranging from silver, ceramics and glassware to weaponry, furniture and folk-life displays – and an exquisite exhibition dedicated to iconic Irish designer **Eileen Gray** (1878–1976). The fascinating **Way We Wore** exhibit displays Irish clothing and jewellery from the past 250 years. An intriguing sociocultural study, it highlights the symbolism jewellery and clothing had in bestowing messages of mourning, love and identity. An exhibition chronicling Ireland's **1916 Easter Rising** is on the ground floor. Visceral memorabilia, such as firsthand accounts of the violence of the Black and Tans and post-Rising hunger strikes, the handwritten death certificates of the Republican prisoners and their postcards from Holloway prison, bring to life this poignant period of Irish history.

✕ Take a Break

A 10-minute walk east along the Liffey from the decorative arts museum is the atmospheric **Brazen Head** (Map p68; 📞01-679 5186; www.brazenhead.com; 20 Lower Bridge St; 🕙10am-midnight Mon-Thu, 10am-12.30am Fri-Sat, 11am-midnight Sun; 🚌51B, 78A or 123 from city centre), reputedly Dublin's oldest pub.

RICHARD WAREHAM FOTOGRAFIE/ALAMY STOCK PHOTO ©

CEZARY ZAREBSKI/GETTY IMAGES ©

Dublin Greenery

Dublin is blessed with plenty of green spaces, from the manicured lawns of St Stephen's Green to the sprawling acres of Phoenix Park, home to deer, the zoo, the president and the US ambassador.

Great For...

☑ Don't Miss

The famous statue of Oscar Wilde in Merrion Square.

St Stephen's Green

As you watch the assorted groups of friends, lovers and individuals splaying themselves across the nine elegantly land-scaped hectares of Dublin's most popular green lung, **St Stephen's Green** (Map p62; ☉dawn-dusk; 🚌all city centre, 🚊St Stephen's Green) FREE, consider that those same hectares once formed a common for public whippings, burnings and hangings. These days, the harshest treatment you'll get is the warden chucking you off the grass for playing football or Frisbee.

Spread across the green's lawns and walkways are some notable artworks; the most imposing of these is a monument to Wolfe Tone, the leader of the abortive 1798 rebellion. Occupying the northeast-ern corner of the green, the vertical slabs

St Stephen's Green

Just inside the northwestern corner of the square is a flamboyant statue of Oscar Wilde, who grew up across the street at No 1 (now used exclusively by the American University Dublin); Wilde wears his customary smoking jacket and reclines on a rock. Atop one of the plinths, daubed with witty one-liners and Wildean throwaways, is a small green statue of Oscar's pregnant mother.

Phoenix Park

Dubliners are rightly proud of this humungous **park** (www.phoenixpark.ie; ⊙24hr; 🚌10 from O'Connell St, 25 & 26 from Middle Abbey St) FREE at the northwestern edge of the city centre, a short skip from Heuston Station and the Liffey quays. The hugely impressive 709 hectares that comprise the park make up one of the largest sets of inner-city green lungs in the world. To put it into perspective, it dwarfs the measly 337 hectares of New York's Central Park and is larger than all of the major London parks put together. The park is home to the Irish president's residence, **Áras an Uachtaráin** (www.president.ie; Phoenix Park; ⊙guided tours hourly 10am-4pm Sat; 🚌10 from O'Connell St, 25 & 26 from Middle Abbey St) FREE, as well as the American ambassador and a shy herd of fallow deer who are best observed –

serving as a backdrop to the statue have been dubbed 'Tonehenge'. At this entrance is a memorial to all those who died in the Potato Famine (1845–51).

Merrion Square

Arguably the most elegant of Dublin's Georgian squares, **Merrion Square** (Map p68; ⊙dawn-dusk; 🚌7 & 44 from city centre) FREE is also the most prestigious. It's well-kept lawns and beautifully tended flower beds are flanked on three sides by gorgeous Georgian houses with colourful doors, peacock fanlights, ornate door knockers and, occasionally, foot-scrapers, used to remove mud from shoes before venturing indoors.

from a distance – during the summer months. It is also where you'll find Europe's oldest **zoo** (Map p68; www.dublinzoo.ie; Phoenix Park; adult/child/family €16.80/12/47; ☺9.30am-6pm Mar-Sep, to dusk Oct-Feb; 🚌10 from O'Connell St, 25 & 26 from Middle Abbey St), not to mention dozens of playing fields for all kinds of sport. How's that for a place to stretch your legs?

Chesterfield Ave runs northwest through the length of the park from the Parkgate St entrance to the Castleknock Gate. Near the Parkgate St entrance is the 63m-high **Wellington Monument** obelisk, completed in 1861. Nearby is the People's Garden, which dates from 1864, and the bandstand in the Hollow. Across Chesterfield Ave from Áras an Uachtaráin – and easily visible

from the road – is the massive **Papal Cross** (Phoenix Park; 🚌10 from O'Connell St, 25 & 26 from Middle Abbey St), which marks the site where Pope John Paul II preached to 1¼ million people in 1979. In the centre of the park the Phoenix Monument, erected by Lord Chesterfield in 1747, looks so unlike a phoenix that it's often referred to as the Eagle Monument.

Bus 10 from O'Connell St or buses 25 and 26 from Middle Abbey St will get you here.

Iveagh Gardens

These beautiful gardens may not have the sculpted elegance of the other city parks, but they never get too crowded and the warden won't bark at you if you walk on

Deer, Phoenix Park

the grass. They were designed by Ninian Niven in 1863 as the private grounds of Iveagh House and include a rustic grotto, cascade, fountain, maze and rosarium. Enter the gardens from Clonmel St, off Harcourt St.

National Botanic Gardens

Founded in 1795, the 19.5-hectare **botanic gardens** (Botanic Rd; ◷ 9am-6pm Mon-Sat, 11am-6pm Sun Apr-Oct, 10am-4.30pm Mon-Sat, 11am-4.30pm Sun Nov-Mar; ▣ 13, 13A or 19 from O'Connell St, or 34 or 34A from Middle Abbey St) FREE are located well north of the city centre. They are home to a series of curvilinear glasshouses, dating from 1843 to 1869, created by Richard Turner, who was also responsible for the glasshouses at Belfast Botanic Gardens and the Palm House in Lond's Kew Gardens. Within these Victorian masterpieces you will find the latest in botanical technology, including a series of computer-controlled climates reproducing environments of different parts of the world.

Among the pioneering botanical work conducted here was the first attempt to raise orchids from seed, back in 1844.

DESIGN PICS/PATRICK SWAN/GETTY IMAGES ©

FORGET PATRICK/SAGAPHOTO.COM/ALAMY STOCK PHOTO ©

Guinness Storehouse

More than any beer produced anywhere in the world, Guinness has transcended its own brand. This beer-lover's Disneyland is a multimedia homage to Ireland's most famous export.

Great For...

☑ Don't Miss

Enjoying the view from the Gravity Bar with your pint of Guinness (price included with admission).

The mythology of Guinness is remarkably durable: it doesn't travel well; its distinctive flavour comes from Liffey water; it is good for you – not to mention the generally held belief that you will never understand the Irish until you develop a taste for the black stuff. All absolutely true, of course, so it should be no surprise that the Guinness Storehouse, in the heart of the St James's Gate Brewery, is the city's most visited tourist attraction, an all-singing, all-dancing extravaganza that combines sophisticated exhibits, spectacular design and a thick, creamy head of marketing hype.

Grain Storehouse & Brewery

The old grain storehouse, the only part of the massive, 26-hectare St James's Gate Brewery open to the public, is a suitable cathedral in which to worship the black

gold: shaped like a giant pint of Guinness, it rises seven impressive storeys high around a stunning central atrium. At the top is the head, represented by the Gravity Bar, with a panoramic view of Dublin.

Immediately below it is the brewery itself, founded in 1759 by Arthur Guinness and once the employer of over 5000 people; the gradual shift to greater automatisation has reduced the workforce to around 300.

The Perfect Pour

As you work your way to the top and your prize of arguably the nicest Guinness you could drink anywhere, you'll explore the various elements that made the beer the brand that it is and perhaps understand a little better the efforts made by the company to ensure its quasi-mythical status. From the (copy of) the original 9000-year lease (in a glass box embedded in the ground floor) to the near-scientific lesson in how to pour the perfect pint, everything about this place is designed to make you understand that Guinness isn't just any other beer.

Arthur Guinness

One fun fact you will learn is that genius can be inadvertent: at some point in the 18th century, a London brewer accidentally burnt his hops while brewing ale, and so created the dark beer we know today. It's name of 'porter' came because the dark beer was very popular with London porters. In the 1770s, Arthur Guinness, who had until then only brewed ale, started brewing the dark stuff to get a jump on all other Irish brewers. By 1799 he decided to concentrate all his efforts on this single brew. He died four years later, aged 83, but the foundations for world domination were already in place.

Dublin Crawl Walking Tour

If there's one constant about life in Dublin, it's that Dubliners will always take a drink. Come hell or high water, the city's pubs will never be short of customers, and we suspect that exploring a variety of Dublin's legendary pubs and bars ranks pretty high on the list of reasons you're here.

Distance: 2.5km
Duration: One hour to two days

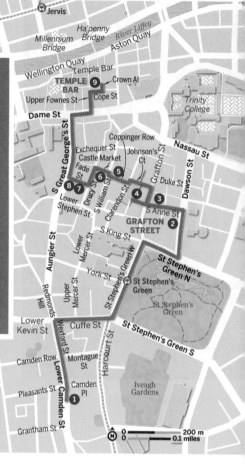

Start Lower Camden St

❶ Anseo

Start in the always excellent **Anseo** (Map p68; 18 Lower Camden St; ⊙10.30am-11.30pm Mon-Thu, to 12.30am Fri & Sat, 11am-11pm Sun; ▣all city centre) on Lower Camden St, where hipsters rub shoulders with the hoi polloi and everyone toe-taps to the great bag of DJ tunes.

❷ 37 Dawson St

Head deep into the city centre and become a character in *Mad Men* at the whiskey bar at the back of one of Dublin's trendiest bars, **37 Dawson St** (Map p62; ☎01-902 2908; www.37dawsonstreet.ie; 37 Dawson St; ⊙10.30am-11.30pm Mon-Thu, to 12.30am Fri & Sat, noon-11pm Sun; ▣all city centre).

❸ Kehoe's

Sink an equally glorious pint of plain (Guinness) in the snug at South Anne St's **Kehoe's** (p75), one of the city centre's most atmospheric bars and a must-stop for all visitors to the city.

❹ Bruxelles

Find a spot out the front of **Bruxelles** (Map p62; 7-8 Harry St; ⊙9.30am-1.30am; ▣all city centre): the bronze statue of Thin Lizzy's Phil Lynott outside is testament to the bar's reputation as a great spot for rock music.

Temple Bar

AITORMMFOTO/SHUTTERSTOCK ©

⑤ Pygmalion

Directly across the street in the basement of the Powerscourt Townhouse Centre is **Pygmalion** (Map p62; 📞01-674 6712; www. bodytonicmusic.com; Powerscourt Townhouse Shopping Centre, 59 South William St; ⊙to 1.30am Tue-Sat; 🚌all city centre), a favourite haunt of cool kids.

⑥ Grogan's Castle Lounge

Discuss the merits of that unwritten masterpiece with a clutch of frustrated writers and artists in **Grogan's Castle Lounge** (Map p62; www.groganspub.ie; 15 South William St; ⊙10.30am-11.30pm Mon-Thu, to 12.30am Fri & Sat, 12.30-11pm Sun) on Castle Market.

⑦ No Name Bar

A couple of streets away is the appropriately named **No Name Bar** (Map p62; 3 Fade St; ⊙to 1.30am Tue-Sat; 🚌all city centre). Occupying the upstairs floor of an old townhouse, this is one of the city centre's most pleasant and handsome watering holes.

⑧ Hogan's

At the corner with South Great George's St, **Hogan's** (p76) has been one of the most popular watering holes in the city for longer than most of its clientele has been alive.

⑨ Vintage Cocktail Club

Finally, make your way into Temple Bar and ring the doorbell to access the **Vintage Cocktail Club** (Map p62; Crown Alley; ⊙5pm-1.30am Mon-Fri, from 12.30pm Sat & Sun; 🚌all city centre), which is upstairs behind a plain steel door on Crown Alley. If you've followed the tour correctly, it's unlikely that you'd now be referring to this guide. How many fingers?

Finish Crown Alley

Ha'Penny Bridge

Take a Walk on the North Side

Grittier than its more genteel south-side counterpart, the neighbourhoods immediately north of the River Liffey offer a fascinating mix of 18th-century grandeur, traditional city life and the multicultural melting pot that is contemporary Dublin. Beyond its widest, most elegant boulevard you'll find art museums and whiskey museums, bustling markets and some of the best ethnic eateries in town.

Distance: 2.5km
Duration: 2 hours

Start Mountjoy Sq

❶ Mountjoy Square

Take a left at the northwestern corner of Mountjoy Sq and walk down Gardiner Pl, turning right onto North Temple St. Up ahead is the fine, but now deconsecrated Georgian **St George's Church** (Map p68; Hardwicke Pl; 🚌11, 16 or 41 from city centre), designed by architect Francis Johnston.

❷ Abbey Presbyterian Church

Take a left onto Hardwicke St and left again onto North Frederick St. On your right you'll spot the distinctive Abbey Presbyterian Church, built in 1864.

❸ Northern Parnell Square

The northern slice of Parnell Sq houses the **Garden of Remembrance** (Map p72; Parnell Sq; ⊘8.30am-6pm Apr-Sep, 9.30am-4pm Oct-Mar; 🚌3, 10, 11, 13, 16, 19 or 22 from city centre), opened in 1966 to commemorate the 50th anniversary of the 1916 Easter Rising.

❹ The Hugh Lane

North of the square, facing the park, is the excellent **Dublin City Gallery – The Hugh Lane** (p64), home to some of the best modern art in Europe.

❺ Southern Parnell Square

In the southern part of Parnell Sq is the **Rotunda Hospital** (Map p72; 📞01-873 0700; Parnell Sq; ⊘visiting hours 6-8pm; 🚌3, 10, 11, 13, 16, 19 or 22 from city centre), a wonderful example of public architecture in the Georgian style. The southeastern corner of

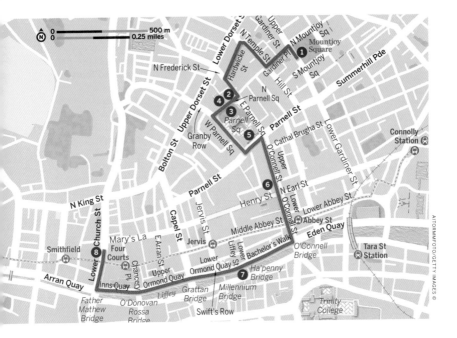

the square has the Gate Theatre (p71), one of the city's most important cultural institutions.

❻ Iconic Sights

Head south down O'Connell St, passing by the 120m-high **Spire** (p66). Erected in 2001, it is an iconic symbol of the city. On the western side of O'Connell St, the stunning neoclassical **General Post Office** (Map p72; 📞01-705 7000; www.anpost.ie; Lower O'Connell St; 🕗8am-8pm Mon-Sat; 🚇all city centre, 🚇Abbey) towers over the street.

❼ The Liffey

When you hit the river, turn right and walk along the boardwalk until you reach the city's most distinctive crossing point, the Ha'Penny Bridge (named for the charge levied on those who used it).

❽ St Michan's Church

Continue west along Ormond Quay to one of James Gandon's Georgian masterpieces, the **Four Courts** (p65), home to the most important law courts in Ireland. Finally take a right onto Church St to admire **St Michan's Church** (Map p68; www.stmichans.com; Lower Church St; adult/child/student €5/3.50/4; 🕗10am-12.45pm & 2-4.45pm Mon-Fri, 10am-12.45pm Sat; 🚇Smithfield), a beautiful Georgian construction with grisly vaults populated by the remains of the long departed.

Finish St Michan's Church

◎ SIGHTS

◎ Grafton Street & Around

National Gallery Museum

A magnificent Caravaggio and a breath-taking collection of works by Jack B Yeats – William Butler's younger brother – are the main reasons to visit the National Gallery, but not the only ones. Its excellent collection is strong in Irish art and there are also high-quality collections of every major European school of painting. The gallery is open but it's in the middle of a major reno-vation, so until at least 2016 the entrance is on Clare St. (Map p30; www.nationalgallery.ie; West Merrion Sq; ◐9.30am-5.30pm Mon-Wed, Fri & Sat, to 8.30pm Thu, noon-5.30pm Sun; ◙7 & 44 from city centre) FREE

Leinster House Notable Building

All the big decisions are made at the Oireachtas (parliament). This magnifi-cent Palladian mansion was built as a city residence for James Fitzgerald, the Duke of Leinster and Earl of Kildare, by Richard Cassels between 1745 and 1748 – hence its name. Pre-arranged **guided tours** (www.oireachtas.ie; ◐10.30am, 11.30am, 2.30pm & 3.30pm Mon-Fri) FREE are available when parliament is in session (but not sitting). You can get an entry ticket to the lower- or upper-house observation galleries from the Kildare St entrance on production of photo identification. (Map p62; Oireachtas Éireann; ☏01-618 3271; www.oireachtas.ie; Kildare St; ◐observation galleries 2.30-8.30pm Tue, 10.30am-8.30pm Wed, 10.30am-5.30pm Thu Nov-May; ◙all city centre)

Museum of Natural History Museum

Dusty, weird and utterly compelling, this window into Victorian times has barely changed since Scottish explorer Dr David Livingstone opened it in 1857 – before disappearing into the African jungle for a meeting with Henry Stanley. It is a beautifully preserved example of Victorian charm and scientific wonderment, and its enormous collection is a testament to the

> *Dublin has all the baubles of a major international metropolis.*

Christ Church Cathedral

DRAGOS COSMIN PHOTOS/GETTY IMAGES ©

rich diversity of the natural world and the skill of taxidermy. (Map p62; National Museum of Ireland – Natural History; www.museum.ie; Upper Merrion St; ⊙10am-5pm Tue-Sat, 2-5pm Sun; ☐7 & 44 from city centre) FREE

Little Museum of Dublin   Museum

The idea is ingeniously simple: a museum, spread across two rooms of an elegant Georgian building, devoted to the history of Dublin in the 20th century, made up of memorabilia contributed by the general public. You don't need to know anything about Irish history or Dublin to appreciate it: visits are by guided tour and everyone is presented with a handsome booklet on the history of the city. (Map p62; ☑01-661 1000; www.littlemuseum.ie; 15 St Stephen's Green N; adult/student €7/4.50, guided tours €12; ⊙9.30am-5pm Mon-Fri, to 8pm Thu; ☐all city centre, ☐St Stephen's Green)

◎ Temple Bar

National
Photographic Archive   Museum

What should be a wonderful resource putting a face on all facets of Irish history is actually a sadly disappointing archive of photographs taken from the 19th century onwards. Its visitor-friendly catalogue is computer accessible and the eager staff are always willing to help with queries, but the available material is not nearly as extensive as we'd hoped. (Map p62; Meeting House Sq; ⊙10am-4.45pm Mon-Sat, noon-4.45pm Sun; ☐all city centre) FREE

Gallery of Photography   Gallery

This small gallery devoted to the photograph is set in an airy three-level space overlooking Meeting House Square. It features a constantly changing menu of local and international work, and while it's a little too small to be considered a really good gallery, the downstairs shop is well stocked with all manner of photographic tomes and manuals. (Map p62; www.galleryofphotography.ie; Meeting House Sq; ⊙11am-6pm Mon-Sat; ☐all city centre) FREE

Friends'
Meeting House   Historic Building

The Dublin branch of the Society of United Irishmen, who sought Parliamentary reform and equality for Catholics, was first convened in 1791 in the Eagle Tavern, now the Friends' Meeting House. (This should not be confused with the other Eagle Tavern, which is on Cork St.) (Map p62; Eustace St; ☐all city centre)

◎ The Liberties & Kilmainham

St Patrick's Cathedral   Church

Ireland's largest church is St Patrick's Cathedral, built between 1191 and 1270 on the site of an earlier church that had stood here since the 5th century. It was here that St Patrick himself reputedly baptised the local Celtic chieftains, making this bit of ground some fairly sacred turf: the well in question is in the adjacent **St Patrick's Park**, which was once a slum but is now a lovely spot to sit and take a load off. (Map p62; www.stpatrickscathedral.ie; St Patrick's Close; adult/student/child €6/5/free; ⊙9.30am-5pm Mon-Fri, 9am-6pm Sat, 9-10.30am & 12.30-2.30pm Sun; ☐50, 50A or 56A from Aston Quay, 54 or 54A from Burgh Quay)

Christ Church Cathedral   Church

Its hilltop location and eye-catching flying buttresses make this the most photogenic of Dublin's cathedrals. It was founded in 1030 and rebuilt from 1172, mostly under the impetus of Richard de Clare, Earl of Pembroke (better known as Strongbow), the Anglo-Norman noble who invaded Ireland in 1170 and whose monument has pride of place inside. **Guided tours** (www.christchurchcathedral.ie; adult/family €4/10; ⊙11.30am & 1.15pm Sat, 1.15pm Sun;) include the belfry, where a campanologist explains the art of bell-ringing and you can even have a go. (Church of the Holy Trinity; Map p62; www.christchurchcathedral.ie; Christ Church Pl; adult/student/child €6/4.50/2; ⊙9.00am-5pm Mon-Sat, 12.30-2.30pm Sun year-round, longer hours Jun-Aug; ☐50, 50A or 56A from Aston Quay, 54 or 54A from Burgh Quay)

Temple Bar, Grafton St & St Stephen's Green

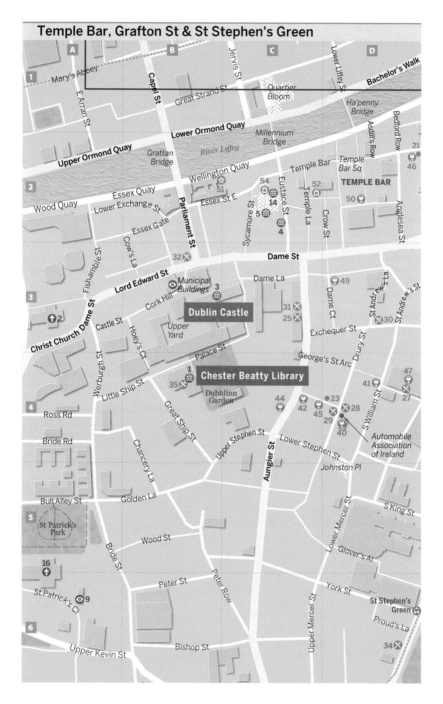

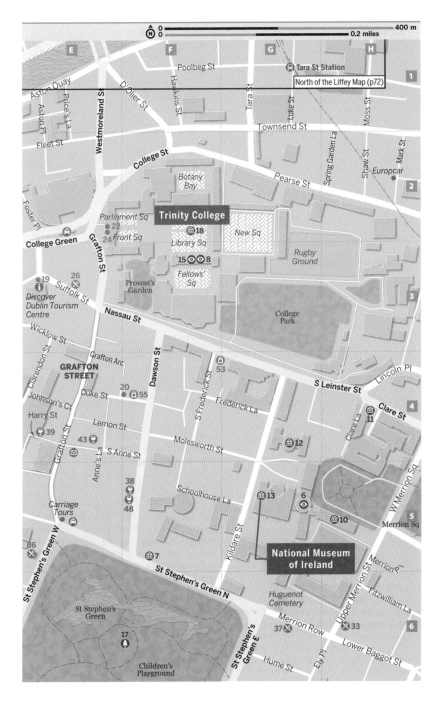

0 400 m
0 0.2 miles

E **F** **G** **H**

1

Poolbeg St

Aston Quay

Price's La

D'Olier St

Hawkins St

Tara St

Tara St Station

North of the Liffey Map (p72)

Aston Pl

Fleet St

Westmoreland St

Townsend St

Luke St

Moss St

Spring Garden La

Shaw St

Mart St

Europcar

College St

Foster Pl

Botany Bay

Pearse St

2

Parliament Sq

22

24 Front Sq

Trinity College

18

New Sq

College Green

Grafton St

Library Sq

15 8

Rugby Ground

3

19

26

Suffolk St

Discover Dublin Tourism Centre

Provost's Garden

Fellows' Sq

Nassau St

College Park

Wicklow St

Clarendon St

Grafton Arc

GRAFTON STREET

Dawson St

S Frederick St

53

S Leinster St

Lincoln Pl

Johnson's Ct

20

55 Duke St

Frederick La

Clare La

Clare St

4

Harry St

39

Lemon St

43

S Anne St

Molesworth St

12

11

Anne's La

Grafton St

38

48

Schoolhouse La

13

6

W Merrion Sq

10

Merrion Sq

5

Carriage Tours

36

St Stephen's Green W

7

Kildare St

National Museum of Ireland

Merrion Sq

St Stephen's Green N

Huguenot Cemetery

Merrion St

Fitzwilliam La

St Stephen's Green

17

Merrion Row

37

33

Upper Merrion St

6

Children's Playground

St Stephen's Green E

Hume St

Ely Pl

Lower Baggot St

Temple Bar, Grafton St & St Stephen's Green

◉ Sights
1 Chester Beatty Library	B4
2 Christ Church Cathedral	A3
3 Dublin Castle	B3
4 Friends' Meeting House	C2
5 Gallery of Photography	C2
6 Leinster House	G5
7 Little Museum of Dublin	F5
8 Long Room	F3
9 Marsh's Library	A6
10 Museum of Natural History	H5
11 National Gallery	H4
12 National Library	G4
13 National Museum of Ireland – Archaeology	G5
14 National Photographic Archive	C2
15 Old Library	F3
16 St Patrick's Cathedral	A5
17 St Stephen's Green	F6
18 Trinity College	F2

◉ Activities, Courses & Tours
19 Dublin Bus Tours	E3
20 Dublin Literary Pub Crawl	F4
21 Dublin Musical Pub Crawl	D2
Guided Tour of Oireachtas	(see 6)
22 Historical Walking Tour	E2
23 See Dublin by Bike	D4
24 Trinity College Walking Tour	E2

◉ Eating
25 777	C3
26 Avoca	E3
27 Coppinger Row Market	D4
28 Drury Buildings	D4
29 Fade Street Social	D4
30 Green Hen	D3
31 Pitt Bros BBQ	C3
32 Queen of Tarts	B3
33 Restaurant Patrick Guilbaud	H6
34 Shanahan's on the Green	D6
35 Silk Road Café	B4
36 Thornton's	E5
37 Unicorn	G6

◉ Drinking & Nightlife
38 37 Dawson Street	F5
39 Bruxelles	E4
40 Drury Buildings Cocktail Bar	D4
41 Grogan's Castle Lounge	D4
42 Hogan's	C4
43 Kehoe's	E4
44 Long Hall	C4
45 No Name Bar	C4
46 Oliver St John Gogarty	D2
47 Pygmalion	D4
48 Sam's Bar	F5
49 Stag's Head	D3
50 Vintage Cocktail Club	D2

◉ Entertainment
51 Workman's Club	B2

◉ Shopping
Avoca Handweavers	(see 26)
52 Claddagh Records	C2
53 Kilkenny Shop	F4
54 Temple Bar Farmers Market	C2
55 Ulysses Rare Books	F4

Irish Museum of Modern Art
Museum

Ireland's most important collection of modern and contemporary Irish and international art is housed in the elegant, airy expanse of the Royal Hospital Kilmainham, designed by Sir William Robinson and built between 1684 and 1687 as a retirement home for soldiers. It fulfilled this role until 1928, after which it languished for nearly 50 years until a 1980s restoration saw it come back to life as this wonderful repository of art. (IMMA; Map p68; www.imma.ie; Military Rd; ⏱11.30am-5.30pm Tue-Fri, 10am-5.30pm Sat, noon-5.30pm Sun, tours 1.15pm Wed, 2.30pm Sat & Sun; 🚇Heuston) FREE

◉ North of the Liffey

Dublin City Gallery – The Hugh Lane
Gallery

Whatever reputation Dublin has as a repository of world-class art has a lot to do with the simply stunning collection at this exquisite gallery, housed in the equally impressive Charlemont House, designed by William Chambers in 1763. Within its walls you'll find the best of contemporary Irish art, a handful of impressionist classics and the complete reconstruction of Francis Bacon's studio. (Map p72; 📞01-222 5550; www.hughlane.ie; 22 North Parnell Sq; ⏱10am-6pm Tue-Thu, to 5pm Fri & Sat, 11am-5pm Sun; 🚌3, 7, 10, 11, 13, 16, 19, 46A, 123) FREE

Four Courts
Historic Building

This masterpiece of James Gandon (1743–1823) is a mammoth complex stretching 130m along Inns Quay, as fine an example of Georgian public architecture as there is in Dublin. Despite the construction of a brand new criminal courts building further west along the Liffey, the Four Courts is still the enduring symbol of Irish law going about its daily business. Visitors are allowed to wander through the building, but not to enter courts or other restricted areas. (Map p68; Inns Quay; ⊙9am-5pm Mon-Fri; ☐25, 66, 67 or 90 from city centre, ☐Four Courts) FREE

Old Jameson Distillery
Museum

Smithfield's biggest draw is devoted to *uisce beatha* (ish-kuh ba-ha, 'the water of life'): that's Irish for whiskey. To its more serious devotees, that is precisely what whiskey is, although they may be put off by the slickness of the museum (occupying part of the old distillery that stopped production in 1971), which shepherds visitors through a compulsory tour of the re-created factory (the tasting at the end is a lot of fun) and into the ubiquitous gift shop. (Map p68; www.jamesonwhiskey.com; Bow St; adult/student/child €15/12/8; ⊙9am-6pm Mon-Sat, 10am-6pm Sun; ☐25, 66, 67 or 90 from city centre, ☐Smithfield)

◉ Docklands

Custom House
Museum

Georgian genius James Gandon (1743–1823) announced his arrival on the Dublin scene with this magnificent building (1781–91), constructed just past Eden Quay at a wide stretch in the River Liffey. It's a colossal, neoclassical pile that stretches for 114m topped by a copper dome, beneath which the **visitor centre** (Map p72; Custom House Quay; admission €1.50; ⊙10am-12.30pm Mon-Fri, 2-5pm Sat & Sun mid-Mar–Oct, closed Mon, Tue & Sat Nov–mid-Mar; ☐all city centre) features a small museum on Gandon and the history of the building. (Map p72; Custom House Quay; ⊙10am-5pm Mon-Fri, 2-5pm Sat & Sun; ☐all city centre)

📖 Literary Dublin

Dublin Writers Museum (Map p72; www.writersmuseum.com; 18 North Parnell Sq; adult/child €8/5; ⊙10am-5pm Mon-Sat, 11am-5pm Sun; ☐3, 7, 10, 11, 13, 16, 19, 46A, 123) Memorabilia aplenty and lots of literary ephemera line the walls and display cabinets of this elegant museum devoted to preserving the city's rich literary tradition up to 1970. The building, comprising two 18th-century houses, is worth exploring on its own; Dublin stuccodore Michael Stapleton decorated the upstairs gallery.

Marsh's Library (Map p62; www.marsh library.ie; St Patrick's Close; adult/child €3/ free; ⊙9.30am-5pm Mon & Wed-Fri, 10am-5pm Sat; ☐50, 50A or 56A from Aston Quay, 54 or 54A from Burgh Quay) This magnificently preserved scholars' library, virtually unchanged in three centuries, is one of Dublin's most beautiful open secrets, and an absolute highlight of any visit. Atop its ancient stairs are beautiful, dark-oak bookcases, each topped with elaborately carved and gilded gables, and crammed with 25,000 books, manuscripts and maps dating back to the 15th century.

National Library (Map p62; www.nli. ie; Kildare St; ⊙9.30am-7.45pm Mon-Wed, to 4.45pm Thu & Fri, 10am-12.45pm Sat; ☐all city centre) FREE Suitably sedate and elegant, the library's extensive collection has many valuable early manuscripts, first editions and maps. Parts of the library are open to the public, including the domed reading room where Stephen Dedalus expounded his views on Shakespeare in James Joyce's *Ulysses*.

Dublin Writers Museum

Look Up...
and Keep Looking

The city's most visible landmark, the **Spire** (Map p72; O'Connell St; ⊞all city centre, ⊞Abbey), soars over O'Connell St and is an impressive bit of architectural engineering that was erected in 2001: from a base only 3m in diameter, it reaches more than 120m into the sky and tapers into a 15cm-wide beam of light...it's tall and shiny and it does the trick rather nicely.

The brainchild of London-based architect Ian Ritchie, it is apparently the highest sculpture in the world, but much like the Parisian reaction to the construction of the Eiffel Tower, Dubliners are divided as to its aesthetic value and have regularly made fun of it. Among other names, we like 'the erection in the intersection', the 'stiletto in the ghetto', and the altogether brilliant 'eyeful tower'.

The Spire
DAVE G KELLY/GETTY IMAGES ©

🕝 TOURS

A plethora of tours offer a range of exploring options; you can walk (or crawl, if you opt for a drinking tour), get a bus or hop aboard an amphibious vehicle. There are lots of themed tours too, while some companies will combine a city tour with trips further afield. You'll save a few euro booking online.

Dublin Bus Tours   Bus Tour
Offers a variety of tours, including the hop-on-hop-off Dublin City Tour, Ghost Bus Tour, Coast and Castles Tour, and South Coast and Gardens Tour. (Map p72; www.dublinsight seeing.ie; 59 Upper O'Connell St; tours €22-27; ⊗tours daily; ⊞all city centre, ⊞Abbey)

Historical Walking Tour   Walking Tour
Trinity College history graduates lead this 'seminar on the street' that explores the Potato Famine, Easter Rising, Civil War and Partition. Sights include Trinity, City Hall, Dublin Castle and Four Courts. In summer, themed tours on architecture, women in Irish history and the birth of the Irish state are also held. Tours depart from the College Green entrance. (Map p62; ☎01-878 0227; www. historicalinsights.ie; Trinity College Gate; adult/child €12/free; ⊗11am & 3pm May-Sep, 11am Apr & Oct, 11am Fri-Sun Nov-Mar; ⊞all city centre)

Dublin Literary
Pub Crawl   Walking Tour
A tour of pubs associated with famous Dublin writers is a sure-fire recipe for success, and this 2½-hour tour/performance by two actors – which includes them acting out the funny bits – is a riotous laugh. There's plenty of drink taken, which makes it all the more popular. It leaves from the Duke on Duke St; get there by 7pm to reserve a spot for the evening tour. (Map p62; ☎01-670 5602; www.dublinpubcrawl.com; 9 Duke St; adult/student €12/10; ⊗7.30pm daily Apr-Oct, 7.30pm Thu-Sun Nov-Mar; ⊞all city centre)

Dublin Musical
Pub Crawl   Walking Tour
The story of Irish traditional music and its influence on contemporary styles is explained and demonstrated by two expert musicians in a number of Temple Bar pubs over 2½ hours. Tours meet upstairs in the **Oliver St John Gogarty** (Map p62; 58-59 Fleet St; ⊗10.30am-11.30pm Mon-Thu, to 12.30am Fri & Sat, noon-11pm Sun; ⊞all city centre) pub and are highly recommended. (Map p62; ☎01-478 0193; www.discoverdublin.ie; 58-59 Fleet St; adult/student €12/10; ⊗7.30pm daily Apr-Oct, 7.30pm Thu-Sat Nov-Mar; ⊞all city centre)

See Dublin by Bike   Cycling Tour
Three-hour themed tours that start outside Cafe Rothar on Fade St and take in the city's highlights and not-so-obvious sights. The Taste of Dublin is the main tour, but

Tour group on the Dublin Musical Pub Crawl

you can also take a U2's Dublin tour and a literary Dublin tour. Bikes, helmets and high-visibility vests included. (Map p62; 01-280 1899; www.seedublinbybike.ie; Fade St; tours €25-30; all city centre)

🔒 SHOPPING

If it's made in Ireland – or pretty much anywhere else – you can find it in Dublin. Grafton Street is home to a range of largely British-owned high-street chain stores, but you'll find the best local boutiques in the surrounding streets, selling everything from cheese to Irish designer clothing and streetwear.

Avoca Handweavers   Handicrafts
Combining clothing, homewares, a basement food hall and an excellent top-floor **cafe** (Map p62; www.avoca.ie; mains €11-14), Avoca promotes a stylish but homey brand of modern Irish life – and is one of the best places to find an original present. Many of the garments are woven, knitted and naturally dyed at its Wicklow factory. There's a

terrific kids' section. (Map p62; 01-677 4215; www.avoca.ie; 11-13 Suffolk St; 9.30am-6pm Mon-Wed & Sat, to 7pm Thu & Fri, 11am-6pm Sun; all city centre)

Ulysses Rare Books   Books
Our favourite bookshop in the city stocks a rich and remarkable collection of Irish-interest books, with a particular emphasis on 20th-century literature and a large selection of first editions, including rare ones by the big guns: Joyce, Yeats, Beckett and Wilde. (Map p62; 01-671 8676; www.rarebooks.ie; 10 Duke St; 9.30am-5.45pm Mon-Sat; all city centre)

Claddagh Records   Music
An excellent collection of good-quality traditional and folk music is the mainstay at this centrally located record shop. The profoundly knowledgeable staff should be able to locate even the most elusive recording for you. (Map p62; 01-677 0262; 2 Cecilia St; 10am-6pm Mon-Sat, noon-6pm Sun; all city centre)

Central Dublin

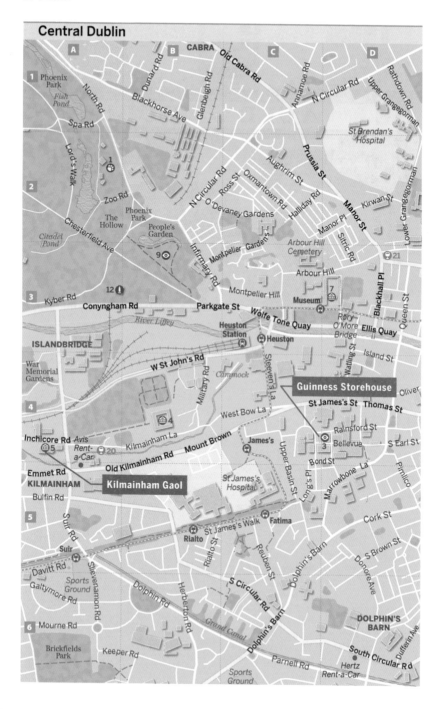

Phoenix Park

Fish Pond

North Rd

Dunard Rd

CABRA

Old Cabra Rd

Glenbeigh Rd

Annamoe Rd

N Circular Rd

Upper Grangegorman

Rathdown Rd

Spa Rd

Blackhorse Ave

St Brendan's Hospital

Lord's Walk

Zoo Rd

The Hollow

Phoenix Park

People's Garden

Prussia St

Aughrim St

N Circular Rd

Ross St

Oxmantown Rd

O'Devaney Gardens

Halliday Rd

Manor St

Kirwan St

Lower Grangegorman

Chesterfield Ave

Manor Pl

Sitric Rd

Citadel Pond

Montpelier Gardens

Arbour Hill Cemetery

Kyber Rd

Infirmary Rd

Montpelier Hill

Arbour Hill

Blackhall Pl

Queen St

Conyngham Rd

Parkgate St

Wolfe Tone Quay

Museum

Rory O'More Bridge

Ellis Quay

River Liffey

Heuston Station

Heuston

Island St

ISLANDBRIDGE

W St John's Rd

Steeven's La

Watling St

Oliver

War Memorial Gardens

Military Rd

Cammock

Guinness Storehouse

St James's St

Thomas St

West Bow La

Rainsford St

S Earl St

Inchicore Rd

Avis Rent-a-Car

Kilmainham La

Mount Brown

James's

Bellevue

Pimlico

Emmet Rd

Old Kilmainham Rd

Upper Basin St

Bond St

Marrowbone La

KILMAINHAM

Kilmainham Gaol

St James's Hospital

Long's Pl

Bulfin Rd

Suir Rd

St James's Walk

Fatima

Cork St

Rialto

Rialto St

Reuben St

Dolphin's Barn

S Brown St

Suir

Davitt Rd

Slievenamon Rd

Sports Ground

Dolphin Rd

S Circular Rd

Donore Ave

Galtymore Rd

Herberton Rd

Dolphin's Barn

DOLPHIN'S BARN

Mourne Rd

Dufferin Ave

Brickfields Park

Keeper Rd

Grand Canal

Parnell Rd

South Circular Rd

Sports Ground

Hertz Rent-a-Car

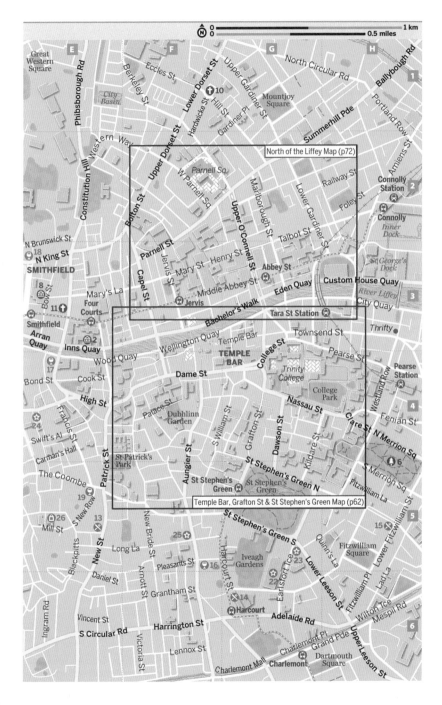

Central Dublin

◉ ENTERTAINMENT

Workman's Club — Live Music
A 300-capacity venue and bar in the former workingmen's club of Dublin, this new spot puts the emphasis on keeping away from the mainstream, which means a broad range of performers, from singer-songwriters to electronic cabaret. When the live music at the Workman's Club (Twitter: @WorkmansClubs) is over, DJs take to the stage, playing everything from rockabilly to hip hop and indie to house. (Map p62; ☎01-670 6692; www.theworkmans-club.com; 10 Wellington Quay; ⊒all city centre)

Evensong at the Cathedrals
In a rare coming together, the choirs of St Patrick's Cathedral and Christ Church Cathedral both participated in the first-ever performance of Handel's *Messiah* in nearby Fishamble St in 1742, conducted by the great composer himself. Both houses of worship carry on their proud choral traditions, and visits to the cathedrals during evensong will provide enchanting and atmospheric memories. In St Patrick's, the choir performs evensong at 5.45pm Monday to Friday (not on Wednesday in July and August), while the Christ Church choir competes at 5.30pm on Sunday, 6pm on Wednesday and Thursday, and 5pm Saturday. If you're going to be in Dublin around Christmas, do not miss the carols at St Patrick's; call ahead for the hard-to-get tickets on ☎01-453 9472.

Vicar Street — Live Music
Smaller performances take place at this intimate venue near Christ Church Cathedral. It has a capacity of 1000, between its table-serviced group seating downstairs and theatre-style balcony. Vicar Street offers a varied program of performers, with a strong emphasis on soul, folk, jazz and foreign music. (Map p68; ☎01-454 5533; www.vicarstreet.com; 58-59 Thomas St; ⊒13, 49, 54a, 56a from city centre)

3 Arena — Live Music
The premier indoor venue in the city has a capacity of 23,000 and plays host to the brightest touring stars in the firmament. Fleetwood Mac, The Who, Neil Diamond and Taylor Swift performed here in 2015. (☎01-819 8888; www.3arena.ie; East Link Bridge, North Wall Quay; ⊒Point Village)

Whelan's — Live Music
Perhaps the city's most beloved live venue is this midsized room attached to a tradi-

tional bar. This is the singer-songwriter's spiritual home: when they're done pouring out the contents of their hearts on stage, you can find them filling up in the bar along with their fans. (Map p68; ☎01-478 0766; www.whelanslive.com; 25 Wexford St; 🚌16, 122 from city centre)

Sugar Club
Live Music

There's live jazz, cabaret and soul music at weekends in this comfortable theatre-style venue on the corner of St Stephen's Green. (Map p68; ☎01-678 7188; www.thesugarclub. com; 8 Lower Leeson St; 🚌St Stephen's Green)

Bord Gáis Energy Theatre
Theatre

Forget the uninviting sponsored name: Daniel Libeskind's masterful design is a three-tiered, 2000-capacity auditorium where you're as likely to be entertained by the Bolshoi or a touring state opera as you are to see Disney on Ice or Barbra Streisand. It's a magnificent venue – designed for classical, paid for by the classics. (☎01-677 7999; www.grandcanaltheatre.ie; Grand Canal Sq; 🚌Grand Canal Dock)

National Concert Hall
Live Music

Ireland's premier orchestral hall hosts a variety of concerts year-round, including a series of lunchtime concerts from 1.05pm to 2pm on Tuesdays, June to August. (Map p68; ☎01-417 0000; www.nch.ie; Earlsfort Tce; 🚌all city centre)

Gate Theatre
Theatre

The city's most elegant theatre, housed in a late-18th-century building, features a generally unflappable repertory of classic American and European plays. Orson Welles and James Mason played here early in their careers. Even today it is the only theatre in town where you might see established international movie stars work on their credibility with a theatre run. (Map 72; ☎01-874 4045; www.gatetheatre.ie; 1 Cavendish Row; 🚌all city centre)

Abbey Theatre
Theatre

Ireland's national theatre was founded by WB Yeats in 1904 and was a central player in the development of a consciously native cultural identity. Its relevance has waned dramatically in recent decades, but it still provides a mix of Irish classics (Synge,

Bord Gáis Energy Theatre

DKPHOTO/GETTY IMAGES ©

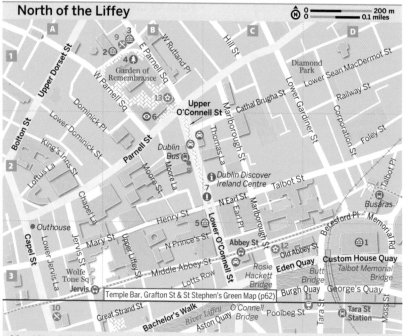

North of the Liffey

◎ Sights
1 Custom House	D3
Custom House Visitor Centre	(see 1)
2 Dublin City Gallery – The Hugh Lane	B1
3 Dublin Writers Museum	B1
4 Garden of Remembrance	B1
5 General Post Office	C3
6 Rotunda Hospital	B2
7 Spire	C2

◎ Activities, Courses & Tours
8 Dublin Bus Tours	B2

◎ Eating
9 Chapter One	B1
10 Musashi Noodles & Sushi Bar	A3

◎ Drinking & Nightlife
11 John Mulligan's	D3

◎ Entertainment
12 Abbey Theatre	C3
13 Gate Theatre	B1

O'Casey), established international names (Shepard, Mamet) and contemporary talent (O'Rowe, Carr).

Debate over the theatre's home – an ugly, purpose-built box from 1966 – has been silenced by economic realities, and so the city's theatregoers have had to make do with an acoustic makeover that has improved the experience of going to a play. Monday performances are cheaper. (Map p72; ☎01-878 7222; www.abbeytheatre.ie; Lower Abbey St; ▣all city centre, ▣Abbey)

◎ EATING

◎ Grafton Street & Around

Fade Street Social Modern Irish €€

Two eateries in one, courtesy of renowned chef Dylan McGrath: at the front, the buzzy tapas bar, which serves up gourmet bites from a beautiful open kitchen. At the back, the more muted restaurant specialises in Irish cuts of meat – from veal to rabbit – served with home-grown, organic vegetables. There's a bar upstairs too. Reservations suggested. (Map p62; 📞01-604 0066; www.fadestreetsocial.com; 4-6 Fade St; mains €19-32, tapas €5-12; ⏱12.30-10.30pm Mon-Fri, 5pm-10.30pm Sat & Sun; 📶; 🚇all city centre) 🍴

Restaurant Patrick Guilbaud French €€€

Ireland's only Michelin two-star is understandably considered the best in the country by its devotees, who proclaim Guillaume Lebrun's French haute cuisine the most exalted expression of the culinary arts. If you like formal dining, this is as good as it gets: the lunch menu is an absolute steal, at least in this stratosphere. The food is innovative without being fiddly, beautifully cooked and superbly presented. (Map p62; 📞01-676 4192; www.restaurantpatrickguilbaud.ie; 21 Upper Merrion St; 2-/3-course set lunch €45/55, dinner menus €90-185; ⏱12.30-2.30pm & 7.30-10.30pm Tue-Sat; 🚌7 & 44 from the city centre)

Drury Buildings Italian €€

An elegant, 1st-floor restaurant in a converted rag trade warehouse...sounds like New York's SoHo, and that's exactly what it's trying to emulate. The food – Italian dishes made with local produce and infused with an international twist – is excellent. The ground-floor **cocktail bar** (mains €10; ⏱noon-3pm) has an Italian lunch menu of sandwiches, salads and other titbits. (Map p62; 📞01-960 2095; drurybuildings.com; 52-55 Drury St; mains €17.50-32; ⏱5-10.30pm daily, noon-3pm Sat & Sun; 🚇all city centre)

777 Mexican €€

You won't eat better, more authentic Mexican cuisine – the *tostados* (crispy corn tortillas with various toppings) and *taquitos* (filled, soft corn tortillas) are great nibbles and the perfect accompaniment for a tequila fest (they serve 22 different types). On Sunday all dishes are €7.77. (Map p62; www.777.ie; 7 Castle House, South Great George's St; mains €19-36; ⏱5.30-10pm Mon-Wed, 5.30-11pm Thu, 5pm-midnight Fri & Sat, 2-10pm Sun; 🚇all city centre)

🖼 Top Spots for Culture

● Abbey Theatre (p71)

● National Gallery (p60)

● Whelan's (p70)

● Gate Theatre (p71)

● Irish Museum of Modern Art (p64)

Irish Museum of Modern Art
GABRIELA INSURATELU/SHUTTERSTOCK ©

Green Hen French €€

New York's Soho meets Parisian brasserie at this stylish eatery, where elegance and economy live side-by-side. If you don't fancy gorging on oysters or tucking into a divine Irish Hereford rib-eye, you can opt for the *plat du jour* or avail yourself of the early-bird menus; watch out for their killer cocktails. Reservations recommended for dinner. (Map p62; 📞01-670 7238; www. greenhen.ie; 33 Exchequer St; mains €18-26; ⏱noon-3pm daily, 5-11pm Mon-Thu & Sun, 5pm-1am Fri & Sat; 🚇all city centre)

L'Ecrivain French €€€

Head chef Derry Clarke is considered a gourmet god for the exquisite simplicity of his creations, which put the emphasis on flavour and the best local ingredients – all given the French once over and turned into something that approaches divine dining. The Michelin people like it too and awarded it one of their stars. (Map p68; 📞01-661 1919; www.lecrivain.com; 109a Lower Baggot St; 3-course lunch menus €40, 8-course tasting menus €75, mains €40-47; ⏱12.30-2pm Thu & Fri, 6.30-10pm Mon-Sat; 🚌38 & 39 from city centre)

Pitt Bros BBQ   Barbecue €€

Delicious, Southern-style barbecue – you have a choice of pulled pork, brisket, ribs, sausage or half a chicken – served amid loud music and a hipster-fuelled atmosphere that says Brooklyn, New York, rather than Birmingham, Alabama. For dessert, there's a DIY ice-cream dispenser. Locals grumble that it's a straight rip-off of Bison Bar, but the happy clientele doesn't care. (Map p62; www.pittbrosbbq.com; Unit 1, Wicklow House, South Great George's St; mains €14; ⏱noon-midnight Mon-Fri, 12.30pm-late Sat & Sun; 🚌all city centre)

❌ The Liberties & Kilmainham

Fumbally Cafe   Cafe €

The unofficial home of Dublin's hipster crowd is this warehouse cafe drenched in daylight from the floor-to-ceiling windows, where couples in skinny jeans and worn-in high-tops pore over a laptop, working out the finer details of their start-up pitch, their energy fuelled by excellent coffee and de-

licious sandwiches. (Map p68; Fumbally Lane; mains €5-8; ⏱8am-5pm Mon-Sat; 🚌49, 54a & 77x from city centre)

❌ North of the Liffey

Musashi Noodles & Sushi Bar   Japanese €€

A lovely, low-lit room, this is the most authentic Japanese restaurant in the city, serving up freshly crafted sushi to a city once starved of it. The lunch bento deals are a steal, and if you don't fancy raw fish they also do a wide range of other Japanese specialties. It's BYOB (corkage charged). Evening bookings recommended. (Map p72; ☎01-532 8057; www.musashidublin.com; 15 Capel St; mains €13-17; ⏱noon-10pm; 🚌all city centre, 🚆Jervis)

Chapter One   Modern Irish €€€

Flawless haute cuisine and a relaxed, welcoming atmosphere make this Michelin-starred restaurant in the basement of the Dublin Writers Museum our choice for best dinner experience in town. The food is French-inspired contemporary Irish, the menus change regularly and the service is

John Mulligan's

top-notch. The three-course pre-theatre menu (€37.50) is great if you're going to the Gate (p71) around the corner. (01-873 2266; www.chapteronerestaurant.com; 18 North Parnell Sq; 2-course lunch €50, 4-course dinner €85; 12.30-2pm Tue-Fri, 7.30-10.30pm Tue-Sat; 3, 10, 11, 13, 16, 19 or 22 from city centre)

DRINKING & NIGHTLIFE

Grafton Street & Around

John Mulligan's Pub

This brilliant old boozer has barely changed since its establishment in 1782. It has one of the finest pints of Guinness in Dublin and a colourful crew of regulars. It's just off Fleet St, outside the eastern boundary of Temple Bar. (Map p72; 8 Poolbeg St; 10.30am-11.30pm Mon-Thu, to 12.30am Fri & Sat, noon-11pm Sun; all city centre)

Kehoe's Pub

This is one of the most atmospheric pubs in the city centre and a favourite with all kinds of Dubliners. It has a beautiful Victorian bar, a wonderful snug, and plenty of other little nooks and crannies. Upstairs, drinks are served in what was once the publican's living room – and looks it! (Map p62; 9 South Anne St; 10.30am-11.30pm Mon-Thu, to 12.30am Fri & Sat, noon-11pm Sun; all city centre)

Stag's Head Pub

The Stag's Head was built in 1770, remodelled in 1895 and thankfully not changed a bit since then. It's a superb pub: so picturesque that it often appears in films and also featured in a postage-stamp series on Irish bars. A bloody great pub, no doubt. (Map p62; www.louisfitzgerald.com/stagshead; 1 Dame Ct; 10.30am-1am Mon-Sat, to midnight Sun; all city centre)

Long Hall Pub

Luxuriating in full Victorian splendour, this is one of the city's most beautiful and best-loved pubs. Check out the ornate carvings in the woodwork behind the bar and the

Dublin's Best Fine Dining

Thornton's Chef Kevin Thornton's culinary genius is to take new French cuisine and give it a theatrical, Irish revamp: the result is a Michelin-starred, wonderful mix of succulent seafood dishes and meatier fare like noisette of milk-fed Wicklow lamb. A nice touch is when Kevin himself comes out to greet his guests and explain his creations. Reservations are essential. (Map p62; 01-478 7000; www.thorntonsrestaurant.com; 128 St Stephen's Green W; 2/3-course lunch €35/45, dinner tasting menus €75-85; 12.30-2pm & 7-10pm Tue-Sat; all city centre)

Shanahan's on the Green You could order seafood or a plate of vegetables, but you'd be missing the point of this supremely elegant steakhouse: the finest cuts of juicy and tender Irish Angus beef you'll find anywhere. The ambience is upscale Americana – the bar downstairs is called the Oval Office and pride of place goes to a rocking chair owned by JFK. (Map p62; 01-407 0939; www.shanahans.ie; 119 St Stephen's Green W; mains €35-49; from 6pm Mon-Thu, Sat & Sun, from noon Fri; all city centre)

Unicorn Saturday lunch at this Italian restaurant in a laneway off Merrion Row is a tradition for Dublin's media types, socialites, politicos and their cronies who guffaw and clink glasses in conspiratorial rapture. The extensive lunchtime antipasto bar is popular, but we still prefer the meaty á la carte menu. There are pasta and fish dishes to cater to all palates. (Map p62; 01-662 4757; www.theunicorn.restaurant; 12b Merrion Ct, Merrion Row; mains €18-34; 12.30-2.30pm & 5-11pm Mon-Wed, 12.30-11pm Thu-Sat, 1-9pm Sun; all city centre)

elegant chandeliers. The bartenders are experts at their craft, an increasingly rare attribute in Dublin these days. (Map p62;

 **Top Organic &
Farmers Markets**

Dublin Food Co-op A buzzing community market specialising in organic veg, homemade cheeses and organic wines. There's also a bakery and even baby-changing facilities. (Map p68; www. dublinfoodcoop.com; 12 Newmarket; ⊙noon-8pm Thu-Fri, 9.30am-4.30pm Sat, 11am-5pm Sun; ☐49, 54a & 77x from city centre)

Coppinger Row Market It's small – only a handful of stalls – but it packs a proper organic punch, attracting punters with the waft of freshly baked breads, delicious hummus and other goodies. (Map p62; Coppinger Row; ⊙9am-7pm Thu; ☐all city centre)

Harcourt Street Food Market Organic veggies, cheeses, olives and meats made into dishes from all over the world. (Map p68; www.irishfarmers-markets.ie; Park Pl, Station Bldgs, Upper Hatch St; ⊙10am-4pm Thu; ☐all city centre)

Temple Bar Food Market This great little market is a fabulous place to while away a Saturday morning, sampling and munching on organic gourmet goodies bound by the market's only rule: local producers only. From cured meats to wildflowers, you could fill an entire pantry with their selection of delights. (Map p62; Meeting House Sq; ⊙9am-4.30pm Sat; ☐all city centre)

For more info on local markets, check out www.irishfarmersmarkets.ie, www.irishvillagemarkets.com or local county council sites such as www.dlrcoco.ie/markets.

Temple Bar Food Market

51 South Great George's St; ⊙10.30am-11.30pm Mon-Thu, to 12.30am Fri & Sat, noon-11pm Sun; ☐all city centre)

Sam's Bar · Bar
A posh Dawson St's drinking spot, Sam's decor is Middle Eastern (a hangover of its previous incarnation as an Asian-themed bar) meets art-college graffiti. None of which seems to bother the young professional clientele, who come to share tales of success over fancy cocktails. (Map p62; 36 Dawson St; ⊙4pm-2am Mon-Thu, 1pm-2.30am Fri-Sun; ☐all city centre, ☐St Stephen's Green)

Hogan's · Bar
Midweek this big contemporary bar is a relaxing hang-out for young professionals, and restaurant and bar workers on a night off. But come the weekend the sweat bin downstairs pulls them in for some more serious music courtesy of the usually excellent DJs. (Map p62; 35 South Great George's St; ⊙1pm-11.30am Mon-Wed, to 1am Thu, to 2.30am Fri & Sat, 4-11pm Sun; ☐all city centre, ☐St Stephen's Green)

🍺 The Liberties & Kilmainham

Fallon's · Traditional Pub
Just west of the city centre, in the heart of medieval Dublin, this is a fabulously old-fashioned bar that has been serving a great pint of Guinness since the end of the 17th century. Prize fighter Dan Donnelly, the only boxer ever to be knighted, was head bartender here in 1818. It's a genuine Irish bar filled with Dubs. (Map p68; ☎01-454 2801; 129 The Coombe; ⊙10.30am-11.30pm Mon-Thu, to 12.30am Fri & Sat, noon-11pm Sun; ☐123, 206 or 51B from city centre)

🍺 North of the Liffey

Cobblestone · Pub
This pub in the heart of Smithfield has a great atmosphere in its cosy upstairs bar, where there are superb nightly music sessions performed by traditional musicians (especially Thursday) and up-and-coming folk acts. (Map p68; North King St; ⊙10.30am-

11.30pm Mon-Thu, to 12.30am Fri & Sat, noon-11pm Sun; Smithfield)

Walshe's
Pub

If the snug is free, a drink in Walshe's is about as pure a traditional experience as you'll have in any pub in the city; if it isn't, you'll have to make do with the old-fashioned bar, where the friendly staff and brilliant clientele (a mix of locals and hipster imports) are a treat. A proper Dublin pub. (Map p68; 6 Stoneybatter; 10.30am-11.30pm Mon-Thu, to 12.30am Fri & Sat, noon-11pm Sun; 25, 25A, 66, 67 from city centre, Museum)

INFORMATION

You'll find everything you need to kick-start your visit at the **Visit Dublin Centre** (Map p62; www.visitdublin.com; 25 Suffolk St; 9am-5.30pm Mon-Sat, 10.30am-3pm Sun; all city centre). Besides general visitor information on Dublin and Ireland, it also has a free accommodation booking service, a concert-booking agent, local and national bus information, rail information, and tour information and bookings. There are also branches at Dublin Airport and **O'Connell St** (Map p72; 14 Upper O'Connell St; 9am-5pm Mon-Sat; all city centre).

GETTING THERE & AWAY

AIR

Dublin Airport (01-814 1111; www.dublin airport.com), 13km north of the centre, is Ireland's major international gateway airport. It has two terminals: most international flights (including all US flights) use the new Terminal 2; Ryanair and select others use Terminal 1. Both terminals have the usual selection of pubs, restaurants, shops, ATMs and car-hire desks.

BOAT

Dublin has two ferry ports: the **Dun Laoghaire ferry terminal** (01-280 1905; Dun Laoghaire; 7A or 8 from Burgh Quay, or 46A from Trinity College, Dun Laoghaire), 13km east of the city, serves Holyhead in Wales and can be reached by DART to Dun Laoghaire, or bus 7, 7A or 8 from

---

Best Pubs for Guinness

- Kehoe's (p75)
- Stag's Head (p75)
- John Mulligan's (p75)
- Walshe's (p77)

Burgh Quay or bus 46A from Trinity College; and the **Dublin Port terminal** (01-855 2222; Alexandra Rd), 3km northeast of the city centre, serves Holyhead and Liverpool.

Buses from Busáras are timed to coincide with arrivals and departures: for the 9.45am ferry departure from Dublin Port, buses leave Busáras at 8.30am. For the 9.45pm departure, buses depart from Busáras at 8.30pm. For the 1am sailing to Liverpool, the bus departs from Busáras at 11.45pm. All bus trips cost adult/child €3/1.50.

BUS

Busáras (Map p72; 01-836 6111; www.buseireann.ie; Store St; Connolly), the main bus station, is just north of the river behind Custom House, and serves as the main city stop for Bus Éireann (www.buseireann.ie), which has a countrywide network.

CAR & MOTORCYCLE

The main rental agencies, which also have offices at the airport, include the following:

Avis Rent-a-Car (Map p68; 01-605 7500; www.avis.ie; 35 Old Kilmainham Rd; 23, 25, 25A, 26, 68 or 69 from city centre)

Budget Rent-a-Car (01-837 9611; 151 Lower Drumcondra Rd; 41 from O'Connell St)

Europcar (Map p62; 01-648 5900; www.europcar.com; 1 Mark St; all city centre)

Hertz Rent-a-Car (Map p68; 01-709 3060; www.hertz.com; 151 South Circular Rd; 9, 16, 77 & 79 from city centre)

Thrifty (Map p68; 01-844 1944; www.thrifty.ie; 26 Lombard St E; all city centre)

TRAIN

Dublin has two main train stations: **Heuston Station** (☎01-836 5421; 🚊Heuston Station), on the western side of town near the Liffey, which serves the southern half of the country; and **Connolly Station** (☎01-836 3333; 🚊Connolly Station, 🚊Connolly Station), a short walk northeast of Busáras, behind the Custom House, which covers the west and north.

Connolly Station is a stop on the DART line into town; the Luas Red Line serves both Connolly and Heuston stations.

ⓘ GETTING AROUND

TO/FROM THE AIRPORT

There is no train service to/from the airport, but there are bus and taxi options.

BUS

Aircoach (www.aircoach.ie) Private coach service with two routes from the airport to 18 destinations throughout the city, including the main streets of the city centre. Coaches run every 10 to 15 minutes between 6am and midnight, then hourly from midnight until 6am.

Airlink Express Coach (☎01-873 4222; www.dublinbus.ie; one way/return €6/3) Bus 747 runs every 10 to 20 minutes from 5.45am to 11.30pm between the airport, the central bus station (Busáras) and the Dublin Bus office on Upper O'Connell St; bus 748 runs every 15 to 30 minutes from 6.50am to 10.05pm between the airport and Heuston and Connolly stations.

Dublin Bus (☎01-873 4222; www.dublinbus.ie) A number of buses serve the airport from various points in Dublin, including buses 16A (Rathfarnham), 746 (Dun Laoghaire) and 230 (Portmarnock); all cross the city centre on their way to the airport.

TAXI

There is a taxi rank directly outside the arrivals concourse. A taxi should cost about €20 from the airport to the city centre, including a supplementary charge of €2.50 (not applied going to the airport). Make sure the meter is switched on.

BICYCLE

One of the most popular ways to get around the city is with the blue bikes of Dublinbikes (www.dublinbikes.ie), a pay-as-you-go service similar to the Parisian Vélib system: cyclists purchase a €10 Smart Card (as well as pay a credit-card deposit of €150) – either online or at any of the 40 stations throughout the city centre – before 'freeing' a bike for use, which is then free of charge for the first 30 minutes and €0.50 for each half-hour thereafter.

CAR & MOTORCYCLE

Traffic in Dublin is a nightmare and parking is an expensive headache. There are no free spots to park anywhere in the city centre during business hours (7am to 7pm Monday to Saturday), but there are plenty of parking meters, 'pay & display' spots (€2.50 to €5 per hour) and over a dozen sheltered and supervised car parks (around €5 per hour).

Clamping of illegally parked cars is thoroughly enforced, and there is an €80 charge for removal. Parking is free after 7pm Monday to Saturday, and all day Sunday, in most metered spots and on single yellow lines.

Car theft and break-ins are a problem, and the police advise visitors to park in a supervised car park. Cars with foreign number plates are prime targets; never leave your valuables behind. When you're booking accommodation, check on parking facilities.

The **Automobile Association of Ireland** (AA; Map p62; ☎01-617 9999, breakdown 1800 667 788; www.aaireland.ie; 56 Drury St; 🚊all city centre) is located in the city centre.

PUBLIC TRANSPORT

BUS

The office of **Dublin Bus** (Map p72; ☎01-873 4222; www.dublinbus.ie; 59 Upper O'Connell St; ⏰9am-5.30pm Mon-Fri, to 2pm Sat; 🚊all city centre) has free single-route timetables of all its services.

PETER UNGER/GETTY IMAGES ©

Dublin city streets

Buses run from around 6am (some start at 5.30am) to 11.30pm. Fares are calculated according to stages:

- one to three stages: €1.95
- four to seven stages: €2.55
- eight to 13 stages: €2.80
- over 13 stages: €3.30

You must tender exact change when boarding; anything more and you will be given a receipt for reimbursement, only possible at the Dublin Bus main office. Avoid this by getting a Leap Card (www.leapcard.ie), a plastic smart card available in most newsagents. Once you register it online, you can top it up with whatever amount you need. When you board a bus, Luas or suburban train, just swipe your card and the fare – usually 20% less than a cash fare – is automatically deducted.

TRAIN

The **Dublin Area Rapid Transport** (DART; ☎01-836 6222; www.irishrail.ie) provides quick train access to the coast as far north as Howth (about 30 minutes) and as far south as Greystones in County Wicklow. Pearse Station is convenient for central Dublin south of the Liffey, and Connolly Station for north of the Liffey. There are services every 10 to 20 minutes, sometimes even more frequently, from around 6.30am to midnight Monday to Saturday; services are less frequent on Sunday. Dublin to Dun Laoghaire takes about 15 to 20 minutes. A one-way DART ticket from Dublin to Dun Laoghaire or Howth costs €3.15; to Bray it's €3.70.

There are also suburban rail services north as far as Dundalk, inland to Mullingar and south past Bray to Arklow.

LUAS

The Luas light-rail system has two lines: the green line (running every five to 15 minutes) connects St Stephen's Green with Sandyford in south Dublin via Ranelagh and Dundrum; the red line (every 20 minutes) runs from Lower Abbey St to Tallaght via the north quays and Heuston Station. There are ticket machines at every stop or you can buy a ticket from newsagents in the city centre; a typical short-hop fare (around four stops) is €2. Services run from 5.30am to 12.30am Monday to Friday, from 6.30am to 12.30am Saturday and from 7am to 11.30pm Sunday.

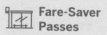

Fare-Saver Passes

A range of fare-saver passes are available.

10 Journey Travel 90 (adult €29.50) Valid for ten 90-minute journeys on all Dublin Bus and Airlink services, except Nitelink.

Freedom Ticket (adult/child €30/14) Three-day unlimited travel on all bus services, including Airlink and Dublin Bus hop-on, hop-off tours.

Rambler Pass (five/30 days €29.50/132) Valid for unlimited travel on all Dublin Bus and Airlink services, except Nitelink.

TAXI

All taxi fares begin with a flagfall fare of €3.60 (€4 from 8pm to 8am), followed by €1.10 per km thereafter from 8am to 10pm (€1.40 per km from 8pm to 8am). In addition to these there are a number of extra charges – €1 for each extra passenger and €2 for telephone bookings. There is no charge for luggage.

Taxis can be hailed on the street and found at taxi ranks around the city, including on the corner of Abbey and O'Connell Sts (Map p72); College Green (Map p62), in front of Trinity College; and St Stephen's Green at the end of Grafton St. There are numerous taxi companies that will dispatch taxis by radio including **City Cabs** (☏01-872 2688) and **National Radio Cabs** (☏01-677 2222; www.radiocabs.ie).

Phone the **Garda Carriage Office** (☏01-475 5888) if you have any complaints about taxis or queries regarding lost property.

UBER & HAILO

Although Uber is available in Dublin, it's not nearly as effective as Hailo (www.hailoapp.com), which works virtually the same as Uber but is largely supported by the taxi industry (many members of which have signed up to the service).

Where to Stay

Like most cities, the closer to the city centre you want to stay, the more you'll pay – and the room sizes get smaller accordingly. Although there are some good midrange options north of the Liffey, the biggest spread of accommodations is south of the river. Prices go up dramatically at peak times.

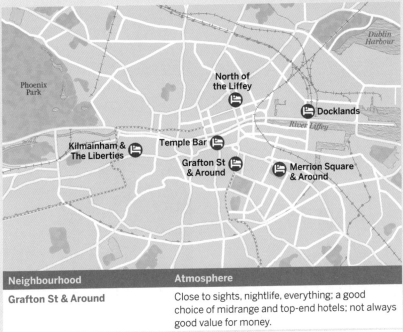

Neighbourhood	Atmosphere
Grafton St & Around	Close to sights, nightlife, everything; a good choice of midrange and top-end hotels; not always good value for money.
Merrion Square & Around	Lovely neighbourhood, elegant hotels and townhouse accommodation; virtually no budget accommodation.
Temple Bar	In the heart of the action; close to everything; noisy and touristy; not especially good value for money.
Kilmainham & The Liberties	Close to the old city; no good accommodations.
North of the Liffey	Good range of choice; within walking distance of sights and nightlife; some locations not especially comfortable after dark.
Docklands	Excellent contemporary hotels with good service; isolated in neighbourhood that doesn't have a lot of life after dark.

COUNTIES
MEATH & LOUTH

Counties Meath & Louth

Meath's rich soil, laid down during the last ice age, drew settlers as early as 8000 BC. They worked their way up the banks of the River Boyne, transforming the landscape from forest to farmland. One of the five provinces of ancient Ireland, Meath played a crucial part in Irish politics for centuries.

Across the Boyne, Louth – Ireland's smallest county – was at the centre of ecclesiastical Ireland during the 5th and 6th centuries, with wealthy religious communities at the monastery at Monasterboice and the Cistercian abbey at Mellifont. In recent times, Louth has prospered greatly during the Celtic Tiger era thanks to its proximity to Dublin, and is slowly but steadily recovering from the subsequent economic crash.

For visitors, there are numerous must-see attractions here, including many tangible reminders of Meath's and Louth's absorbing histories, such as Brú na Bóinne and Monasterboice.

☑ In This Section

ℹ Arriving in Counties Meath & Louth

Bus Éireann runs regular services to Drogheda from Dublin (€8, one hour, one to four hourly) and Dundalk (€7, 30 minutes, hourly). Matthews (p93) also runs a bus service to Dublin (€9) at least every hour.

The train station is just off Dublin Rd. Drogheda is on the main Belfast–Dublin line (Dublin €14, 45 minutes; Belfast €20, 1½ hours).

★ **Classic Photo**
Don't miss taking close-up shots of the kerbstones at Brú na Bóinne (p86) to give a sense of site's incredible history.

Mullary

Collon

Monasterboice

LOUTH

Termonfeckin

Irish Sea

Old Mellifont Abbey

Tullyallen

River Boyne

MEATH

Battle of the Boyne Site

Drogheda

Mornington

Slane

Rathmullan

River Boyne

Donore

Johnstown

★ **Brú na Bóinne**

Hill of Tara (14km)

Dublin (37km)

0 — 5 km
0 — 2.5 miles

From left: Hill of Tara (p92); Gravestone, Drogheda (p93); Irish countryside, County Louth
GEORGE MUNDAY/DESIGN PICS/GETTY IMAGES ©; DESIGN PICS/THE IRISH IMAGE COLLECTION/GETTY IMAGES ©; SABRINA PINTUS/GETTY IMAGES ©

Knowth burial mound

DESIGN PICS/STUART WESTMORLAND/GETTY IMAGES ©

Brú na Bóinne

The vast Neolithic necropolis known as Brú na Bóinne (the Boyne Palace) is one of the most extraordinary sites in Europe. A thousand years older than Stonehenge, it's a powerful and evocative testament to the mind-boggling achievements of prehistoric humankind.

Great For...

☑ Don't Miss

The beautifully carved stone decoration in the passage entrance to Newgrange tomb.

The complex was built to house the remains of those who were at the top of the social heap and its tombs were the largest artificial structures in Ireland until the construction of the Anglo-Norman castles 4000 years later. The area consists of many different sites; the three principal ones are Newgrange, Knowth and Dowth.

Over the centuries the tombs decayed, were covered by grass and trees, and were plundered by everybody from Vikings to Victorian treasure hunters, whose carved initials can be seen on the great stones of Newgrange. The countryside around the tombs is home to countless other ancient tumuli (burial mounds) and standing stones.

Harpist at Knowth

ADSTOCK/UNIVERSAL IMAGES GROUP/GETTY IMAGES ©

Drogheda

Brú na Bóinne

ⓘ Need to Know

Bus Éireann has a service linking the Brú na Bóinne Visitor Centre with Drogheda's bus station (one way/return €4/7, 20 minutes, two daily Monday to Saturday), with connections to Dublin (one hour). You can stay overnight in Drogheda if you plan on visiting other sights.

✕ Take a Break

The cafe in the visitor centre (p88) serves excellent food, including extensive vegetarian options.

★ Top Tip

Tours are primarily outdoors so wear comfortable hiking shoes or boots and bring rain gear.

Newgrange

A startling 80m in diameter and 13m high, the white, round stone walls of **Newgrange** (www.newgrange.com; adult/child incl visitor centre €6/3; ⊙9am-7pm Jun–mid-Sep, to 6.30pm May & mid–end Sep, to 5pm Nov-Jan, 9.30am-5.30 Feb-Apr & Oct), topped by a grass dome, look eerily futuristic. Underneath lies the finest Stone Age passage tomb in Ireland – one of the most remarkable prehistoric sites in Europe. Dating from around 3200 BC, it predates Egypt's pyramids by some six centuries.

The tomb's precise alignment with the sun at the time of the winter solstice suggests it was also designed to act as a calendar.

Newgrange Winter Solstice

At 8.20am on the winter solstice (between 18 and 23 December), the rising sun's rays shine through the roof-box above the entrance, creep slowly down the long passage and illuminate the tomb chamber for 17 minutes. There is little doubt that this is one of the country's most memorable, even mystical, experiences.

There's a simulated winter sunrise for every group taken into the mound. To be in with a chance of witnessing the real thing on one of six mornings around the solstice, enter the free lottery that's drawn in late September; 50 names are drawn and each winner is allowed to take one guest. Fill out the form at the Brú na Bóinne Visitor Centre or email brunaboinne@opw.ie.

Knowth

Northwest of Newgrange, the burial mound of **Knowth** (adult/child incl visitor centre €5/3; ⊙9am-7pm Jun–mid-Sep, to 6.30pm May & mid–end Sep, to 5pm Nov-Jan, 9.30am-5.30 Feb-Apr & Oct) was built around the same time. It has the greatest collection of passage-grave art ever uncovered in Western Europe, and has been under intermittent excavation since 1962 (you may see archaeologists at work when you visit).

Early excavations soon cleared a passage leading to the central chamber which, at 34m, is much longer than the one at Newgrange. In 1968 a 40m passage was unearthed on the opposite side of the mound.

Dowth

The circular mound at **Dowth** (⊙24hr) FREE is similar in size to Newgrange – about 63m in diameter – but is slightly taller at 14m high. Due to safety issues, Dowth's tombs are closed to visitors, though you can visit the mound (and its resident grazing sheep) from the L1607 road between Newgrange and Drogheda.

North of the tumulus are the ruins of **Dowth Castle** and **Dowth House**.

Visiting Brú na Bóinne

In an effort to protect the tombs and their mystical surroundings, all visits to Brú na Bóinne start at the **Brú na Bóinne Visitor Centre** (☑041-988 0300; www.heritage ireland.ie; Donore; adult/child €3/2, visitor centre

Kerbstone 52, Newgrange

& Newgrange €6/3, visitor centre & Knowth €5/3, all 3 sites €11/6; ⊘9am-7pm Jun–mid-Sep, to 6.30pm May & mid–end Sep, to 5pm Nov-Jan, 9.30am-5.30pm Feb-Apr & Oct) from where there is a shuttle bus to the tombs. Built in a spiral design echoing Newgrange, the centre houses interactive exhibits on prehistoric Ireland and its passage tombs, and has regional tourism info, an excellent cafeteria, plus a book and souvenir shop. Upstairs, a glassed-in observation mezzanine looks out over Newgrange.

> ★ **Top Tip**
>
> Allow plenty of time: an hour's visit for the visitor centre alone, two hours to include a trip to Newgrange or Knowth, and half a day to see all three (Dowth's chambers are closed to tourists).

ADSTOCK/UNIVERSAL IMAGES GROUP/GETTY IMAGES ©

In summer, particularly at weekends, Brú na Bóinne can be very crowded; on peak days over 2000 people can show up. As there are only 750 tour slots, you may not be guaranteed a visit to either of the passage tombs. Tickets are sold on a first-come, first-served basis (no advance booking) so the best advice is to arrive early in the morning or visit midweek and be prepared to wait.

The Brú na Bóinne Visitor Centre is well signposted from all directions.

Tours

Brú na Bóinne is one of the most popular tourist attractions in Ireland, and there are plenty of organised tours. Most depart from Dublin.

Mary Gibbons Tours   Guided Tour
Tours depart from numerous Dublin hotels, beginning at 9.30am Monday to Friday, 7.50am Saturday and Sunday, and take in the whole of the Boyne Valley including Newgrange and the Hill of Tara. The expert guides offer a fascinating insight into Celtic and pre-Celtic life in Ireland. No credit cards; pay cash on the bus. (☑086 355 1355; http://newgrangetours.com; tour per adult/child €35/30)

Over the Top Tours   Guided Tour
Offers a Celtic Experience day tour that concentrates on the Boyne Valley, as well as an intriguing 'Mystery' Tour. (☑01-860 0404; www.overthetoptours.com; tour per adult/student €28/25)

Brú na Bóinne

All visits start at the visitor centre ❶, which has a terrific exhibit that includes a short context-setting film. From here, you board a shuttle bus that takes you to Newgrange ❷, where you'll go past the kerbstone ❸ into the main passage ❹ and the burial chamber ❺. If you're not a lucky lottery winner for the solstice, fear not – there's an artificial illumination ceremony that replicates it. If you're continuing on to tour Knowth ❻, you'll need to go back to the visitor centre and get on another bus; otherwise, you can drive directly to Dowth ❼ and visit, but only from outside (the information panels will tell you what you're looking at).

Newgrange interior passage
The passage is lined with 43 orthostats, or standing stones, averaging 1.5m in height: 22 on the left (western) side, 21 on the right (eastern) side.

Newgrange

Knowth
Roughly one third of all megalithic art in Western Europe is contained within the Knowth complex, including more than 200 decorated stones. Alongside typical motifs like spirals, lozenges and concentric circles are rare crescent shapes.

TOP TIP
Best time to visit is early morning mid-week during summer, when there are fewer tourists and no school tours.

Newgrange entrance kerbstone
Newgrange is surrounded by 97 kerbstones (24 of which are still buried), numbered sequentially from K1, the beautifully decorated entrance stone.

Dowth
Like Newgrange, Dowth's passage grave is designed to allow for a solar alignment during the winter solstice. The crater at the top was due to a clumsy attempt at excavation in 1847.

(7)

Newgrange burial chamber
The corbelled roof of the chamber has remained intact since its construction, and is considered one of the finest of its kind in Europe.

(1)

Brú na Bóinne Visitor Centre
Opened in 1997, the modern visitor centre was heavily criticised at first as being unsuitable, but then gained plaudits for the way it was integrated into the landscape.

Around Brú na Bóinne

Tara

The **Hill of Tara** is Ireland's most sacred stretch of turf, occupying a place at the heart of Irish history, legend and folklore. It was the home of the mystical druids, the priest-rulers of ancient Ireland, who practised their particular form of Celtic paganism under the watchful gaze of the all-powerful goddess Maeve (Medbh). Later it was the ceremonial capital of the high kings, all 142 of them, who ruled until the arrival of Christianity in the 5th century. It is also one of the most important ancient sites in Europe, with a Stone Age passage tomb and prehistoric burial mounds that date back some 5000 years.

Although little remains other than humps and mounds on the hill (named from ancient texts), its historic and folkloric significance is immense.

> *Tara's historic and folkloric significance is immense.*

Druid at the Hill of Tara

Battle of the Boyne

Battle of the Boyne Site Historic Site

More than 60,000 soldiers of the armies of King James II and King William III fought in 1690 on this patch of farmland on the border of Counties Meath and Louth. William ultimately prevailed and James sailed off to France. The battle site has an informative visitor centre and parkland walks. It's 3km north of Donore off the N51 and 3.5km west of Drogheda along Rathmullan Rd (follow the river). Buses run to/from Drogheda (€4.10, 15 minutes, two daily).

At the visitor centre you can watch a short show about the battle, see original and replica weaponry of the time and explore a laser battlefield model. Self-guided walks through the parkland and battle site allow time to ponder the events that saw Protestant interests remain in Ireland. Costumed reenactments take place in summer. (www.battleoftheboyne.ie; adult/child €4/2; ⏲10am-5pm May-Sep, 9.30am-4.30pm Mar & Apr, 9am-4pm Oct-Feb)

ANDREW MCCONNELL/ROBERTHARDING/GETTY IMAGES ©

Drogheda

Just 48km north of Dublin, Drogheda is a historic fortified town straddling the River Boyne. A clutch of fine old buildings, a handsome cathedral and a riveting museum provide plenty of cultural interest, while its atmospheric pubs, fine restaurants, numerous sleeping options and good transport links make it an excellent base for exploring the region.

⊗ EATING

Stockwell Artisan Foods Café   Cafe €

Stripped wooden floors, daily newspapers and chunky furniture add to the cosy welcome of this place that serves healthy wraps, salads, soups and hot dishes such as fish cakes. (www.stockwellartisanfoods.ie; 1 Stockwell Lane; mains €6-9; ⊙9am-4pm Mon-Sat)

Kitchen   Mediterranean €€

Sage-green on the outside and cranberry-coloured inside, Drogheda's best restaurant is aptly named for its shiny open kitchen. Organic local produce is used along with worldly ingredients such as Cypriot haloumi and Spanish Serrano ham. Breads are made on-site and there's an excellent choice of wine by the glass. Don't miss the salted-caramel baked Alaska for dessert. (✐041-983 4630; http://kitchenrestaurant.ie; 2 South Quay; mains €17-28; ⊙11am-9pm Wed, 11am-10pm Thu-Sat, noon-9pm Sun; 🔊🛗📶)

❶ GETTING THERE & AWAY

BUS

Bus Éireann regularly serves Drogheda from Dublin (€8, one hour, one to four hourly) and Dundalk (€7, 30 minutes, hourly).

Matthews (✐042-937 8188; http://matthews.ie) also run an hourly-or-better service to Dublin (€9).

TRAIN

The train station is just off Dublin Rd. Drogheda is on the main Belfast–Dublin line (Dublin €14,

🛍 Where to Stay

While there are some B&Bs, hotels and hostels near Brú na Bóinne and Tara, Drogheda and Trim have a more comprehensive range of sleeping options and offer good transport links. Counties Louth and Meath can also be explored as a day trip from Dublin.

45 minutes; Belfast €20, 1½ hours). There are six express trains (and many slower ones) each way.

Around Drogheda

A number of historic sites lie close to Drogheda, but you'll need your own transport.

◎ SIGHTS

Old Mellifont Abbey   Ruins

In its Anglo-Norman prime, this abbey, 1.5km off the main Drogheda–Collon road (R168), was the Cistercians' first and most magnificent centre in Ireland. Although the ruins are highly evocative and well worth exploring, they belie the site's former splendour. Mellifont's most recognisable building and one of the country's finest examples of Cistercian architecture is the 13th-century lavabo, the monks' octagonal washing room. There's good picnicking next to the rushing stream. The visitor centre describes monastic life in detail. (✐041-982 6459; www.heritageireland.ie; Tully-allen; site free, visitor centre adult/student €4/2; ⊙site 24hr year-round, visitor centre 10am-6pm Jun-Aug)

Monasterboice   Historic Site

Crowing ravens lend an eerie atmosphere to Monasterboice, an intriguing monastic site down a leafy lane in sweeping farmland, which contains a cemetery, two ancient church ruins, one of the finest and tallest round towers in Ireland, and two of the most important high crosses. Come early or late in the day to avoid the crowds. It's just off the M1 motorway, about 8km north of Drogheda. (⊙sunrise-sunset) FREE

COUNTY WICKLOW

County Wicklow

Just south of Dublin, Wicklow (Cill Mhantáin) is the capital's favourite playground, a wild pleasure garden of coastline, woodland and a daunting mountain range through which runs the country's most popular walking trail.

Stretching 132km from Dublin's southern suburbs to the rolling fields of County Carlow, the Wicklow Way leads walkers along disused military supply lines, old bog roads and nature trails. Along the way you can explore monastic ruins, handsome gardens and some magnificent 18th-century mansions.

☑ **In This Section**

ⓘ **Arriving in County Wicklow**

Enniskerry is 18km south of Dublin, just 3km west of the M11 along the R117. From here, getting to Powerscourt Estate on foot is not a problem (it's 500m from the town).

St Kevin's Bus (p103) runs twice daily from Dublin and Bray to Roundwood and Glendalough. Dublin Bus 65 runs regularly as far as Blessington.

From left: Powerscourt Estate (p98); lambs, County Wicklow; forest stream, Enniskerry (p106)

BRUNO_IL_SEGRETARIO/GETTY IMAGES © ANDREW TOPPING/EYEEM/GETTY IMAGES © MELISSA DONAGHER/EYEEM/GETTY IMAGES ©

Powerscourt Estate

Wicklow's most visited attraction is this magnificent 64-sq-km estate. At the heart of it is a 68-room mansion, but the real draws are the formal gardens and the stunning views.

Great For...

☑ Don't Miss

The animal cemetery in the estate gardens, final resting place of the Wingfield pets and horses.

History

The estate has existed more or less since 1300, when the LePoer (later anglicised to Power) family built themselves a castle here. The property changed Anglo-Norman hands a few times before coming into the possession of Richard Wingfield, newly appointed Marshall of Ireland, in 1603. His descendants were to live here for the next 350 years. In 1730 the Georgian wunderkind Richard Cassels (or Castle) was given the job of building a 68-room Palladian-style mansion around the core of the old castle.

The Wingfields left during the 1950s, after which the house had a massive restoration. Then, on the eve of its opening to the public in 1974, a fire gutted the whole building. The estate was eventually bought by the Slazenger sporting-goods family who have overseen a second restoration as

BRUNO_IL_SEGRETARIO/GETTY IMAGES ©

Bray
Enniskerry
Powerscourt Estate

ⓘ Need to Know

www.powerscourt.ie; near Enniskerry; house admission free, gardens adult/child €8.50/5; 🕑9.30am-5.30pm Mar-Oct, to dusk Nov-Feb

✕ Take a Break

Enjoy lunch on the terrace at the cafe in Powerscourt House, with lovely views towards Sugarloaf Mountain.

★ Top Tip

If you're driving, plan a picnic lunch at nearby Powerscourt Waterfall.

well as the addition of all the amenities the estate now has to offer, including the two golf courses and the fabulous hotel, now part of Marriott's Autograph collection.

The Gardens

The star of the show is the 20-hectare garden, originally laid out in the 1740s but redesigned in the 19th century by gardener Daniel Robinson. Robinson was one of the foremost horticulturalists of his day and his passion for growing things was matched only by his love of booze: the story goes that by a certain point in the day he was too drunk to stand and so insisted on being wheeled around the estate in a barrow.

Perhaps this influenced his largely informal style, which resulted in a magnificent blend of landscaped gardens, sweeping terraces, statuary, ornamental lakes, secret hollows, rambling walks and walled enclosures replete with more than 200 types of trees and shrubs, all beneath the stunning natural backdrop of the Great Sugarloaf Mountain to the southeast. Tickets come with a map laying out 40-minute and hour-long tours of the gardens.

The Mansion

The house itself is every bit as grand, but the ongoing renovation means there's not much to see beyond the bustle of the ground-floor Avoca cafe and craft shop. The sole exception is the **Museum of Childhood** (Tara's Palace; www.taraspalace.ie; adult/child/family €5/3/12; 🕑10am-5pm Mon-Sat, noon-5pm Sun), full of period miniature dolls and dolls' houses, including Tara's Palace, a 22-room house designed to one-twelfth scale and inspired by the Palladian piles of Castletown House, Leinster House and Carton House. Each of the rooms is decorated in exquisite, hand-crafted miniatures.

Cemetery and round tower, Glendalough

PETER ZELEI/GETTY IMAGES ©

Glendalough

If you've come to Wicklow, chances are that a visit to Glendalough (Gleann dá Loch, 'Valley of the Two Lakes') is one of your main reasons for being here. And you're not wrong, for this is one of the most beautiful corners of the whole country.

Great For...

☑ **Don't Miss**

The 33m-tall, 1000-year-old Round Tower at the heart of the site.

History

In AD 498 a young monk named Kevin arrived in the valley looking for somewhere to kick back, meditate and be at one with nature. He pitched up in what had been a Bronze Age tomb on the southern side of the Upper Lake and for the next seven years slept on stones, wore animal skins, maintained a near-starvation diet and – according to the legend – became bosom buddies with the birds and animals. Kevin's ecofriendly lifestyle soon attracted a bunch of disciples, all seemingly unaware of the irony that they were flocking to hang out with a hermit who wanted to live as far away from other people as possible. Over the next couple of centuries, his one-man operation mushroomed into a proper settlement and by the 9th century Glendalough rivalled Clonmacnoise as the

DAVID GRIBBIN/EYEEM/GETTY IMAGES ©

ℹ Need to Know

Glendalough is approximately 50km south of Dublin (via the N11).

✕ Take a Break

Wicklow Heather (☎0404-45157; www. wicklowheather.ie; Glendalough Rd, Laragh; mains €15-28, r from €70; ⊗noon-8.30pm) is the best place for anything substantial.

★ Top Tip

Take a look around the visitor centre to get a feel for the history before touring the monastic site itself.

island's premier monastic city. Thousands of students studied and lived in a thriving community that was spread over a considerable area.

Inevitably, Glendalough's success made it a key target for Viking raiders, who sacked the monastery at least four times between 775 and 1071. The final blow came in 1398, when English forces from Dublin almost destroyed it. Efforts were made to rebuild and some life lingered on here as late as the 17th century when, under renewed repression, the monastery finally died.

Upper Lake

The original site of St Kevin's settlement, Teampall na Skellig is at the base of the cliffs towering over the southern side of the Upper Lake and is accessible only by boat; unfortunately, there's no boat service to the site and you'll have to settle for looking at it across the lake. The terraced shelf has the reconstructed ruins of a church and early graveyard. Rough wattle huts once stood on the raised ground nearby. Scattered around are some early grave slabs and simple stone crosses.

Just east of here and 10m above the lake waters is the 2m-deep artificial cave called St Kevin's Bed, said to be where Kevin lived. The earliest human habitation of the cave was long before St Kevin's era – there's evidence that people lived in the valley for thousands of years before the monks arrived. In the green area just south of the car park is a large circular wall thought to be the remains of an early Christian stone fort (caher).

Follow the lakeshore path southwest of the car park until you come to the considerable remains of Reefert Church above the tiny River Poulanass. It's a small, plain, 11th-century Romanesque nave-and-chancel church with some reassembled arches and walls. Traditionally, Reefert (literally 'Royal Burial Place') was the burial site of the chiefs of the local O'Toole family. The surrounding graveyard contains a number of rough stone crosses and slabs, most made of shiny mica schist.

Climb the steps at the back of the churchyard and follow the path to the west and you'll find, at the top of a rise overlooking the lake, the scant remains of **St Kevin's Cell** (West of Reefert Churchyard), a small beehive hut.

Lower Lake

While the Upper Lake has the best scenery, the most fascinating buildings lie in the lower part of the valley east of the Lower Lake, huddled together in the heart of the ancient monastic site.

Just round the bend from the Glendalough Hotel is the stone arch of the monastery gatehouse, the only surviving example of a monastic entranceway in the country. Just inside the entrance is a large slab with an incised cross.

Beyond that lies a graveyard, which is still in use. The 10th-century round tower is 33m tall and 16m in circumference at the base. The upper storeys and conical roof were reconstructed in 1876. Near the tower, to the southeast, is the Cathedral of St Peter and St Paul with a 10th-century nave. The chancel and sacristy date from the 12th century.

At the centre of the graveyard to the south of the round tower is the Priest's House. This odd building dates from 1170 but has been heavily reconstructed. It may have been the location of shrines of St

Upper Lake

Kevin. Later, during penal times, it became a burial site for local priests – hence the name. The 10th-century St Mary's Church, 140m southwest of the round tower, probably originally stood outside the walls of the monastery and belonged to local nuns. It has a lovely western doorway. A little to the east are the scant remains of St Kieran's Church, the smallest at Glendalough.

Glendalough's trademark is St Kevin's Kitchen or Church at the southern edge of the enclosure. This church, with a miniature round tower-like belfry, protruding sacristy and steep stone roof, is a masterpiece.

☑ Don't Miss

If you have time, don't miss the walk from the monastic site along the south side of the Lower Lake to the Upper Lake.

The oldest parts of the building date from the 11th century – the structure has been remodelled since but it's still a classic early Irish church.

At the junction with Green Rd as you cross the river just south of these two churches is the Deer Stone in the middle of a group of rocks. Legend claims that when St Kevin needed milk for two orphaned babies, a doe stood here waiting to be milked. The stone is actually a *bullaun* (a stone used as a mortar for grinding medicines or food).

The road east leads to St Saviour's Church, with its detailed Romanesque carvings. To the west, a nice woodland trail leads up the valley past the Lower Lake to the Upper Lake.

Getting to Glendalough

St Kevin's Bus (☎ 01-281 8119; www.glendaloughbus.com; one-way/return €13/20) departs from outside the Mansion House on Dawson St in Dublin at 11.30am and 6pm Monday to Saturday, and 11.30am and 7pm Sunday (1½ hours). It also stops at the Town Hall in Bray. Departures from Glendalough are at 7.15am and 4.30pm Monday to Saturday. During the week in July and August the later bus runs at 5.30pm, and there is an additional service at 9.45am.

✕ Take a Break

If the weather's good, pack a picnic basket and head for the gravel beach at the east end of the Upper Lake for lunch with a view.

Glendalough

WALKING TOUR

A visit to Glendalough is a trip through ancient history and a refreshing hike in the hills. The ancient monastic settlement founded by St Kevin in the 5th century grew to be quite powerful by the 9th century, but it started falling into ruin from 1398 onwards. Still, you won't find more evocative clumps of stones anywhere.

Start at the **Main Gateway** ❶ to the monastic city, where you will find a cluster of important ruins, including the (nearly perfect) 10th-century **Round Tower** ❷, the **Cathedral** ❸ dedicated to Sts Peter and Paul, and **St Kevin's Kitchen** ❹, which is really a church. Cross the stream past the famous **Deer Stone** ❺, where Kevin was supposed to have milked a doe, and turn west along the path. It's a 1.5km walk to the **Upper Lake** ❻. On the lake's southern shore is another cluster of sites, including the **Reefert Church** ❼, a plain 11th-century Romanesque church where the powerful O'Toole family buried their kin, and **St Kevin's Cell** ❽, the remains of a beehive hut where Kevin is said to have lived.

ST KEVIN

St Kevin came to the valley as a young monk in AD 498, in search of a peaceful retreat. He was reportedly led by an angel to a Bronze Age tomb now known as St Kevin's Bed. For seven years he slept on stones, wore animal skins, survived on nettles and herbs and – according to legend – developed an affinity with the birds and animals. One legend has it that, when Kevin needed milk for two orphaned babies, a doe stood waiting at the Deer Stone to be milked.

Kevin soon attracted a group of disciples and the monastic settlement grew, until by the 9th century Glendalough rivalled Clonmacnoise as Ireland's premier monastic city. According to legend, Kevin lived to the age of 120. He was canonised in 1903.

St Kevin's Cell
This beehive hut is reputedly where St Kevin would go for prayer and meditation; not to be confused with St Kevin's Bed, a cave where he used to sleep.

Deer Stone
The spot where St Kevin is said to have truly become one with the animals is really just a large mortar called a *bullaun*, used for grinding food and medicine.

St Kevin's Kitchen
This small church is unusual in that it has a round tower sticking out of the roof – it looks like a chimney, hence the church's nickname.

Reefert Church

Its name derives from the Irish *righ fearta*, which means 'burial place of the kings'. Seven princes of the powerful O'Toole family are buried in this simple structure.

Upper Lake

The site of St Kevin's original settlement is on the banks of the Upper Lake, one of the two lakes that give Glendalough its name – the 'Valley of the Lakes'.

Round Tower

Glendalough's most famous landmark is the 33m-high Round Tower, which is exactly as it was when it was built a thousand years ago except for the roof; this was replaced in 1876 after a lightning strike.

8

7

6

2

3

1

NORTH

INFORMATION

At the eastern end of the Upper Lake is the National Park Information Point, which has leaflets and maps on the site, local walks etc. The grassy spot in front of the office is a popular picnic spot in summer.

Cathedral of Sts Peter & Paul

The largest of Glendalough's seven churches, the cathedral was built gradually between the 10th and 13th centuries. The earliest part is the nave, where you can still see the *antae* (slightly projecting column at the end of the wall) used for supporting a wooden roof.

Main Gateway

The only surviving entrance to the ecclesiastical settlement is a double arch; notice that the inner arch rises higher than the outer one in order to compensate for the upward slope of the causeway.

TOURS

Bus Éireann   Bus
Admission to the visitor centre and a visit to Powerscourt Estate are included in this whole-day tour, which returns to Dublin at about 5.45pm. The guides are good but impersonal. (01-836 6111; www.buseireann. ie; Busáras; adult/child/student €28/19/26; departs 10am mid-Mar–Oct)

Wild Wicklow Tour   Bus
Award-winning tours of Glendalough, Avoca and the Sally Gap that never fail to generate rave reviews for atmosphere and all-round fun. The first pick-up is at the Shelbourne and then the tourist office (Map p72), but there are a variety of pick-up points throughout Dublin; check the point nearest you when booking. The tour returns to Dublin about 5.30pm. (01-280 1899; www.wildwicklow.ie; adult €28, student & child €25; departs 9am)

> *Wicklow is the capital's favourite playground.*

Enniskerry

At the top of the '21 Bends', as the winding R117 from Dublin is known, the handsome village of Enniskerry is home to art galleries and the kind of all-organic gourmet cafes that would treat you as a criminal if you admitted to eating battery eggs. Such preening self-regard is a far cry from the village's origins, when Richard Wingfield, Earl of nearby Powerscourt, commissioned a row of terraced cottages for his labourers in 1760. These days, you'd want to have laboured pretty successfully to get your hands on one of them.

TOURS

All tours that take in Powerscourt start in Dublin.

Dublin Bus Tours   Bus
A visit to Powerscourt is included in the four-hour South Coast & Gardens tour, which takes in the stretch of coastline between Dun Laoghaire and Killiney before turning inland to Wicklow and on to Ennis-

Forest surrounding Glendalough

DACOWLEY/GETTY IMAGES ©

kerry. Admission to the gardens is included. (☎01-872 0000; www.dublinsightseeing.ie; adult/child €27/12; ⊙11am)

✕ EATING

Johnnie Fox   Seafood €€
Busloads of tourists fill this place nightly throughout the summer, mostly for the knees-up, faux-Irish Hooley Show of music and dancing. But there's nothing contrived about the seafood, which is so damn good we'd happily sit through yet another chorus of *Danny Boy* and even consider joining in the jig. The pub is 3km northwest of Enniskerry in Glencullen. (☎01-295 5647; www.jfp.ie; mains €12-20; ⊙noon-10pm)

ⓘ GETTING THERE & AWAY

Enniskerry is 18km south of Dublin, just 3km west of the M11 along the R117. Getting to Powerscourt Estate under your own steam is not a problem (it's 500m from the town), but getting to the waterfall is tricky.

Dublin Bus (☎01-872 0000, 01-873 4222; www.dublinbus.ie) Service 44 (€3.30, hourly) takes about 1¼ hours to get to Enniskerry from Hawkins St in Dublin.

Blessington

Lined with pubs, shops and 17th- and 18th-century townhouses, Blessington makes a convenient exploring base for the surrounding area. The main attraction is Russborough House.

⊙ SIGHTS

Russborough House   Historic Building
Magnificent Russborough House is one of Ireland's finest stately homes, a Palladian palace built for Joseph Leeson (1705–83), later the first Earl of Milltown and, later still, Lord Russborough. Since 1952 the house has been owned by the Beit family, who founded the DeBeers diamond-mining company and stocked the mansion

🏨 Where to Stay

Enniskerry is the best base from which to explore Powerscourt, while both Enniskerry and Blessington are good options for visiting Glendalough. If you're planning on visiting Glendalough or Powerscourt on a tour, most of them leave from Dublin, which is approximately one hour's drive away.

Country Houses

A special Irish experience is to spend a night or two in one of the nearby stately homes. Here are some of our nearby favourites:
Ballyknocken House & Cookery School (☎0404-44627; www.ballyknock-en.com; Glenealy, Ashford; s/d from €90/160, 4-course tasting menus €49)

Ghan House (☎042-937 3682; www.ghanhouse.com; Main Rd, Carlingford; d from €150; @🛜)

Tinakilly Country House & Restaurant (☎0404-69274; www.tinakilly.ie; Rathnew; r €130-200)

Blessington
RIGANMC/SHUTTERSTOCK ©

with a remarkable art collection, including masterpieces by Velázquez, Vermeer, Goya, Rubens and others. The admission price includes a 45-minute tour of the house and begins with a 3D exhibition on the life of Sir Alfred Beit (1903–94), who bought the house. (☎045-865 239; www.russborough-house.ie; Blessington; adult/child guided tours €12/9; ⊙10am-6pm daily Mar 17–Dec)

Events in Wicklow

Wicklow Gardens Festival (www.wick-lowgardens.com) If you want unfettered access to more than 40 of Wicklow's famed public and private gardens, visit during the yearly Wicklow Gardens Festival, which runs from Easter through to the end of August. The obvious advantage for green thumbs and other garden enthusiasts is access to beautiful gardens that would ordinarily be closed to the public.

Wicklow Arts Festival (✆086-033 3906; www.wicklowartsfestival.ie) A five-day extravaganza of music, poetry, comedy and workshops that usually takes place in mid to late May.

Wicklow Regatta Festival (✆0404-68354; www.wicklowregatta.com) Held every year for 10 days from late July into early August. The extensive program of events and activities includes swimming, rowing, sailing and raft races, singing competitions, concerts and the Festival Queen Ball.

County Wicklow flora
RON EVANS/GETTY IMAGES ©

EATING

Grangecon Café International €€
Salads, home-baked dishes and a full menu of Irish cheeses are the staples at this tiny, terrific cafe in a converted schoolhouse. Everything here – from the pasta to the delicious apple juice – is made on the premises and many of the ingredients are organic. A short but solid menu represents the best of Irish cooking. (✆045-857 892; Tullow Rd; mains €12-18; ⏲10am-5pm Tue-Sat)

❶ GETTING THERE & AWAY

Blessington is 35km southwest of Dublin on the N81. There are regular daily services by **Dublin Bus** (✆01-873 4222, 01-872 0000); catch bus 65 from Eden Quay in Dublin (€3.30, 1½ hours, every 1½ hours). Bus Éireann operates express bus 005 to and from Waterford, with stops in Blessington two or three times daily; from Dublin it's pick-up only and from Waterford drop-off only.

Rathdrum

The quiet village of Rathdrum at the foot of the Vale of Clara comprises little more than a few old houses and shops, but in the late 19th century it had a healthy flannel industry and a poorhouse. It's not what's in the town that's of interest to visitors, however, but what's just outside it.

The small **tourist office** (✆0404-46262; 29 Main St; ⏲9am-5.30pm Mon-Fri) has leaflets and information on the town and surrounding area, including the Wicklow Way.

◎ SIGHTS

Avondale House House
This fine Palladian mansion surrounded by a marvellous 209-hectare estate was the birthplace and Irish headquarters of Charles Stewart Parnell (1846–91), the 'uncrowned king of Ireland' and unquestionably one of the key figures in the Irish independence movement. Designed by James Wyatt in 1779, the house's many highlights include a stunning vermilion-hued library and the American Room, dedicated to Parnell's eponymous grandfather, admiral of the USS *Constitution* during the War of 1812. Tours are self-guided. (✆0404-46111; adult/student/child €7/6.50/4.50; ⏲11am-6pm Easter-Oct)

Avondale House

EATING

Bates Inn Pub Food €€

Housed in a coaching inn that first opened its doors in 1785, this outstanding restaurant puts a premium on exquisitely prepared meat dishes (the chargrilled beef options are particularly good). One of the better options in southern Wicklow. Bookings recommended for weekend evenings. (www. batesrestaurant.com; 3 Market Sq, Rathdrum; mains €17-25; ⊙6-9.30pm Tue-Sat, 12.30-8pm Sun)

ⓘ GETTING THERE & AWAY

Bus Éireann (✆01-836 6111; www.buseireann. ie) Service 133 goes to Rathdrum from Dublin (one way/return €14/19, 2¼ hours, 10 daily) on its way to Arklow.

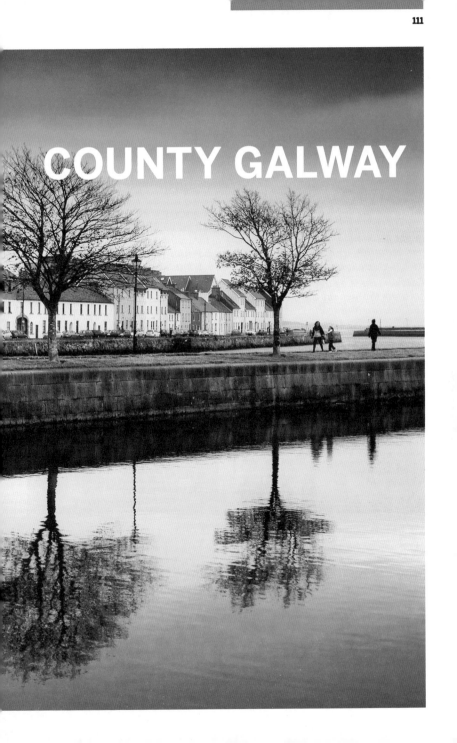

COUNTY GALWAY

County Galway

County Galway is a problem: its namesake city is such a charmer that you might not manage to tear yourself away to the countryside. Conversely, the wild and beautiful Aran Islands and Connemara Peninsula might keep you captive such that you'll never have time for the city. What to do? Both, of course!

Galway city is a swirl of enticing old pubs that hum with trad music sessions throughout the year. More importantly, there's an addictive vibe of culture, fun and frolic.

In the west, the Wild Atlantic Way and the Connemara Peninsula match the beauty of other Atlantic outcrops such as Dingle. Tiny roads wander along a coastline studded with islands, unexpectedly white beaches and intriguing old villages.

☑ In This Section

❶ Arriving in County Galway

A car is the best option for exploring County Galway. If using public transport, base yourself in Galway city and take guided bus tours to the surrounding attractions.

There are up to nine fast, comfortable trains daily between Dublin's Heuston Station and Galway city (from €35, 2¼ hours). Citylink coaches run between Galway and Killarney twice a day (€30, three hours).

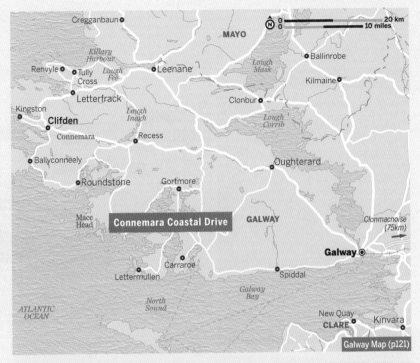

MAYO

Cregganbaun

Killary Harbour
Renvyle • Tully Cross • Lough Fee
Leenane

Ballinrobe
Lough Mask
Kilmaine

Letterfrack
Kingston
Clifden
Lough Inagh
Connemara
Recess
Clonbur
Lough Corrib

Ballyconneely
Roundstone
Gortmore
Oughterard

Mace Head
Connemara Coastal Drive
GALWAY
Clonmacnoise (75km)

Carraroe
Lettermullen
Spiddal
Galway

ATLANTIC OCEAN
North Sound
Galway Bay
New Quay
CLARE
Kinvara

Galway Map (p121)

From left: Thatched cottage, Spiddal (p114); Spanish Arch area, Galway city (p120); Waterfront, Galway city

Galway Bay

Connemara Coastal Drive

The slow coastal route between Galway and Connemara takes you past pretty seascapes and villages, although the fun doesn't really begin until after Spiddal.

Distance: 90km
Duration: 5-7 hours

✗ **Take a Break**
Relax with coffee and cake at the Builín Blasta cafe near Spiddal.

Start Galway

❶ Barna Woods

Opposite the popular Blue Flag beach Silver Strand, 4.8km west of Galway on the R336, are the Barna Woods, a dense, deep green forest preserved for rambling and picnicking. The woods contain the last natural growing oaks in Ireland's west.

❷ Spiddal

Spiddal (An Spidéal) is a refreshingly untouched little village, and the start of the Gaeltacht region. As you approach the village look for the **Ceardlann Spiddal Craft & Design Studios** (www.spiddalcrafts.com; off R336; ⊙hours vary), where you can watch leatherworkers, sculptors and weavers, plus enjoy a cake at the lauded cafe **Builín Blasta** (☎091-558 559; http://builinblasta.ie/; mains €5-15; ⊙10am-5pm Tue-Fri, from 11am Sat & Sun).

❸ Cnoc Suain

Experience life in a 17th-century Connemara hill village at **Cnoc Suain** (☎091-555 703; www.cnocsuain.com; Spiddal), a restored and recreated glimpse of pre-famine life in the countryside. Learn about original dance, language, song and the thatched-roof-cottage lifestyles of the time. It's set amid a large tract of preserved landscape and is 5km north of Spiddal.

❹ Tigh Hughes

Exceptional traditional music sessions take place at the unassuming **Tigh Hughes** (Spiddal; ⊙trad sessions 9pm Tue) – it's not uncommon for major musicians to turn up unannounced and join in the craic (fun). The pub's just adjacent to the main street; turn right at the crossroads next to the bank and it's on your right. Numerous places to stay line the main road.

❺ West of Spiddal

The scenery becomes more dramatic west of Spiddal, with parched fields criss-

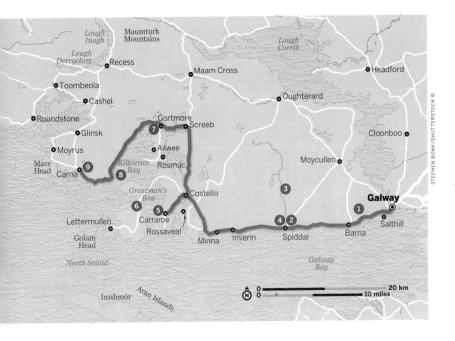

crossed by low stone walls rolling to a ragged shore. Carraroe (An Cheathrú Rua) has fine beaches, including the Coral Strand, which is composed entirely of shell and coral fragments. It's worth wandering the small roads on all sides of Greatman's Bay to discover tiny inlets and little coves, often watched over by the genial local donkeys.

⑥ Islands

Lettermore, Gorumna and Lettermullen islands are low and bleak, with a handful of farmers eking out an existence from minute, rocky fields. Fish farming is big business.

⑦ Patrick Pearse's Cottage

Near Gortmore, along the R340, is **Patrick Pearse's Cottage** (Teach an Phiarsaigh; www.heritageireland.ie; R340; adult/child €4/2; ☺10am-6pm Easter & Jun–Aug). Pádraig Pearse (1879–1916) led the Easter Rising with James Connolly in 1916; after the revolt he was executed by the British. Pearse wrote some of his short stories and plays

in this small thatched cottage with lovely views.

⑧ Kilkieran Bay

The scenic R340 swings south along Kilkieran Bay, an intricate and interlinked system of tidal marshes, bogs, swift-flowing streams and elaborate tidal basins. This environmentally protected area contains an amazing diversity of life.

⑨ Carna

Continuing on, Carna is a small fishing village, with pleasant walks out to Mweenish Island or north to Moyrus and out to the wild headlands at Mace Head.

Finish Carna

★ Top Tip

Rather than rely on an ordinary road map, buy the more detailed Ordnance Survey of Ireland 1:50,000 maps (https://shop.osi.ie/shop).

Tig Cóilí pub

CHRISTOPHER MATTHEWS/ALAMY ©

Pub Crawl in Galway City

Galway's pub selection is second to none, which is why in summer and on weekends they all seem to be pumping. On Saturday nights, the town fills with party-goers from the hinterlands.

Great For...

☑ Don't Miss

Taking in a live *céilidh* at the crowded traditional Irish pub, Tig Cóilí.

Most of Galway's pubs have live music at least a couple of nights a week, whether in an informal trad session or a headline act.

Róisín Dubh   Pub

From the rooftop terrace you can see sweeping views of Galway; inside, emerging acts play here before they hit the big time. It's *the* place to hear bands but comedy's also on the menu. (www.roisindubh.net; Upper Dominick St; ⊙5pm-2am Sun-Thu, till 2.30am Fri & Sat)

Tig Cóilí   Pub

Two live *céilidh* a day draw the crowds to this authentic fire-engine-red pub, just off High St. It's where musicians go to get drunk or drunks go to become musicians... or something like that. A gem. (Mainguard St; ⊙10.30am-11.30pm daily)

NORMAN HOLLANDS/GETTY IMAGES ©

thekingshead.ie; 15 High St; ⊙10.30am-11.30pm Mon-Wed, 10.30am-2am Thu-Sat, 11.30am-11pm Sun)

Quays   Pub
Enormous tavern with endless timber-panelled rooms and passageways, and great vantage points from which to watch live music (ranging from traditional to pop) most nights. Good sidewalk tables. (☑091-568 347; www.louisfitzgerald.com/quaysgalway; 11 Quay St; ⊙10.30am-2am Mon-Sat, from noon Sun)

O'Connell's   Pub
Traditional, seasoned and garrulous pub with a great beer garden, right on Eyre Sq. (www.oconnellsbargalway.com; 8 Eyre Sq; ⊙11am-11.30pm Mon-Sat)

Monroe's Tavern   Pub
Often photographed for its classic black-and-white facade, Monroe's delivers traditional music and ballads, plus it remains the only pub in the city with regular Irish dancing. Live music every night. (www.monroes.ie; Upper Dominick St; ⊙10am-11.30pm Mon-Thu, live music till 2.30am Fri & Sat)

Tí Joe Mac's   Pub
Informal music sessions, peat fires and a broad terrace with harbour views make Tí Joe Mac's a local favourite. Food is limited to a few sandwiches slapped together between pints. (Kilronan)

King's Head   Pub
This vast, ancient pub is often too crowded for its own good. Come mid-afternoon when you can appreciate preserved details that date back to the 14th century. (www.

CORENTIN/SHUTTERSTOCK ©

Clonmacnoise

Gloriously placed overlooking the River Shannon, Clonmacnoise is one of Ireland's most important ancient monastic cities. Although it's located in neighbouring County Offaly, it's easily visited from Galway city.

Great For...

☑ **Don't Miss**

The Cross of the Scriptures, one of Ireland's finest carved stone high crosses.

When St Ciarán founded a monastery here, in AD 548, it was the most important crossroads in the country: the intersection of the north–south River Shannon, and the east–west Esker Riada (Highway of the Kings).

The giant ecclesiastical city had a humble beginning and Ciarán died just seven months after building his first church. Over the years, however, Clonmacnoise grew to become an unrivalled bastion of Irish religion, literature and art and attracted a large lay population. Between the 7th and 12th centuries, monks from all over Europe came to study and pray here, helping to earn Ireland the title of the 'land of saints and scholars'.

The site is enclosed in a walled field and contains several early churches, high crosses, round towers and graves in astonishingly good condition. The surrounding marshy

Celtic cross, Clonmacnoise

TIM DALY/GETTY IMAGES ©

❶ Need to Know

www.heritageireland.ie; adult/child €6/2; ⊙9am–7pm mid-May–mid-Sep, 10am-5.30pm mid-Sep–mid-May, last admission 45min before closing

✕ Take A Break

There's a coffee shop at the visitor centre, but no other source of refreshment nearby.

★ Top Tip

If you plan to visit more than three or four Heritage Ireland sites, save money with an OPW Heritage Card (€25).

area is known as the Shannon Callows, home to many wild plants and one of the last refuges of the seriously endangered corncrake (a pastel-coloured relative of the coot).

Most of what you can see today dates from the 10th to 12th centuries. The monks would have lived in small huts surrounding the monastery. The site was burned and pillaged on numerous occasions by both the Vikings and the Irish. After the 12th century it fell into decline, and by the 15th century it was home solely to an impoverished bishop. In 1552 the English garrison from Athlone reduced the site to a ruin.

Visitor Centre

Three connected conical huts, echoing the design of early monastic dwellings, house the visitors centre museum (☑090-967

4195; www.heritageireland.ie; R444; adult/child €7/3; ⊙9am-6.30pm Jun-Aug, 10am-6pm mid-Mar–May & Sep-Oct, till 5.30pm Nov–mid-Mar, last admission 1hr before closing). A 20-minute audiovisual show provides an excellent introduction to the site.

The exhibition area contains the original high crosses (replicas have been put in their former locations outside) and various artefacts uncovered during excavation, including silver pins, beaded glass and an Ogham stone.

Cathedral

The largest building at Clonmacnoise, the cathedral was originally built in AD 909, but was significantly altered and remodelled over the centuries. Its most interesting feature is the intricate 15th-century Gothic doorway with carvings of Sts Francis, Patrick and Dominic. A whisper carries from one side of the door to the other and this feature was supposedly used by lepers to confess their sins without infecting the priests.

Galway City

Arty, bohemian Galway (Gaillimh) is renowned for its pleasures. Brightly painted pubs heave with live music, while cafes offer front-row seats for observing street performers, weekend parties run amuck, lovers entwined and more.

⊚ SIGHTS & ACTIVITIES

Galway City Museum   Museum
This modern museum has exhibits on the city's history from 1800 to 1950, including an iconic Galway Hooker fishing boat, a collection of *currachs* (boats made from animal hides) and sections covering Galway and the Great War and the city's cinematic connections.

Also check out rotating displays of works by local artists. The ground-floor cafe, with its Spanish Arch views, is a perfect rest stop. (www.galwaycitymuseum.ie; Spanish Pde;

> *Brightly painted pubs heave with live music...*

Spanish Arch

⊙10am-5pm Tue-Sat year-round, noon-5pm Sun Easter-Sep) FREE

Spanish Arch   Historic Site
The Spanish Arch is thought to be an extension of Galway's medieval city walls, designed to protect ships moored at the nearby quay while they unloaded goods from Spain, although it was partially destroyed by the tsunami that followed the 1755 Lisbon earthquake. Today it reverberates to the beat of bongo drums, and the lawns and riverside form a gathering place for locals and visitors on sunny days, as kayakers manoeuvre over the tidal rapids of the River Corrib.

Hall of the Red Earl Archaeological Site
Back in the 13th century when the de Burgo family ran things in Galway, Richard – the Red Earl – erected a large hall as a seat of power. Locals would arrive to curry favour or to grovel as a sign of future fealty. After the 14 tribes took over, the hall fell into ruin, lost until 1997 when expansion of the city's Custom House uncovered its foundations. The Custom House was built on stilts overhead, leaving

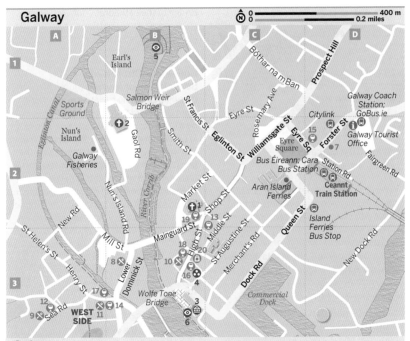

Galway

⊙ Sights

the old foundations open. (www.galwaycivictrust.ie; Druid Lane; ⊙9.30am-4.45pm Mon-Fri, 10am-1pm Sat) FREE

Galway Cathedral   Church

Rising over the River Corrib, imposing Galway Cathedral was dedicated by the late Cardinal Richard Cushing of Boston in 1965. The interior is fantastic, with a beautifully decorated dome, attractive Romanesque arches, lovely mosaics and rough-hewn stonework emblazoned with copious stained glass. A notable side chapel contains a mosaic of the Resurrection with a praying JFK in the tableau. The superb acoustics are best appreciated during a thunderous **organ recital** (program dates are posted on the website).

From the Spanish Arch, a riverside path runs upriver and across the Salmon Weir

Top Galway Festivals

Galway's packed calendar of festivals turns the city and surrounding communities into what feels like one nonstop party – streets overflow with revellers, and pubs and restaurants often extend their opening hours. Highlights include:

Galway Food Festival (www.galwayfood festival.com) Galway's lively food scene is celebrated late March.

Cúirt International Festival of Literature (www.cuirt.ie) Top-name authors converge on Galway in April for one of Ireland's premier literary festivals, featuring poetry slams, theatrical performances and readings.

Galway International Arts Festival (www.giaf.ie) A two-week extravaganza of theatre, music, art and comedy around mid-July.

Galway Film Fleadh (www.galwayfilm fleadh.com) One of Ireland's biggest film festivals, held early July, right before the arts festival.

Galway Race Week (www.galwayraces. com; ⏲late Jul or early Aug) Horse races in Ballybrit, 3km east of the city, are the centrepiece of Galway's biggest, most boisterous festival of all. Thursday is a real knees-up.

Galway International Oyster Festival (www.galwayoysterfest.com) Oysters are washed down with plenty of pints in the last week of September.

Punter at Galway Race Week
HOLGER LEUE/GETTY IMAGES ©

Bridge to the cathedral. (Catholic Cathedral of Our Lady Assumed into Heaven & St Nicholas; www.galwaycathedral.org; Gaol Rd; admission by donation; ⏲8am-6pm)

Collegiate Church of St Nicholas of Myra   Church
Crowned by a pyramidal spire, the Collegiate Church of St Nicholas of Myra is Ireland's largest medieval parish church still in use. Dating from 1320, it has been rebuilt and enlarged over the centuries, while retaining much of its original form. Seafaring has long been associated with the church – St Nicholas, for whom it's named, being the patron saint of sailors. Indeed, Christopher Columbus reputedly worshipped here in 1477. During the day the church is usually all but empty and makes for a welcome escape from Galway's hubbub. (Market St; admission by donation; ⏲9am-5.45pm Mon-Sat, 1-5pm Sun Apr-Sep, 10am-4pm Mon-Sat, 1-5pm Sun Oct-Mar)

Salmon Weir   Landmark
Upstream from Salmon Weir Bridge, which crosses the River Corrib just east of Galway Cathedral, the river cascades down the great weir, one of its final descents before reaching Galway Bay. The weir controls the water levels above it, and when the salmon are running you can often see shoals of them waiting in the clear waters before rushing upriver to spawn. The salmon and sea-trout seasons usually span February to September, but most fish pass through the weir during May and June.

It's naturally a popular spot for anglers, even with **Galway Fisheries**' (Map p121; ☏091-562 388) restriction of one fish per day during May and June – a fish can weigh up to 7kg.

🍴 EATING

Oscar's   Seafood €€
Galway's best seafood restaurant is just west of the tourist bustle. The long and ever-changing menu has a huge range of local specialities, from shellfish to white

fish (which make some superb fish and chips), with some bold flavours. There's a two-course dinner menu from Monday to Thursday (€18.50) before 7.30pm. (☎091-582 180; www.oscarsbistro.ie; Upper Dominick St; mains €14.50-25.50; ⊗6-9.30pm Mon-Sat, 6-9pm Sun)

Kai Cafe   Cafe €€

This fantastic cafe on happening Sea Rd is a delight, whether for a coffee, portions of West Coast Crab or Roscommon hogget and glasses of Galway Hooker Sixty Knots IPA in a relaxed, casual, wholesome and rustic dining environment. Great at any time of the day, but reserve for dinner. (☎091-526 003; www.kaicaferestaurant.com; 20 Sea Rd; lunch/dinner mains from €11.50/18.50; ⊗9.30am-4pm Mon-Fri, 10.30am-4pm Sat, noon-4pm & 6.30-10.30pm Sun; ☎)

McDonagh's   Seafood €€

A trip to Galway isn't complete without a meal here. Divided into two parts, there's a takeaway counter where diners sit elbow to elbow at long communal wooden tables on one side, and a more upmarket restaurant on the other. Galway's best fish-and-chip

Top Five Restaurants

- Aniar (p123)
- Mitchell's (p128)
- O'Dowd's (p127)
- Oscar's (p122)
- Kai Cafe (p123)

shop fries up a haul of battered cod, plaice, haddock, whiting and salmon, accompanied by homemade tartar sauce. (www.mcdonaghs.net; 22 Quay St; takeaway mains from €6, restaurant mains €13.50-26; ⊗cafe & takeaway noon-11pm Mon-Sat, 2-9pm Sun, restaurant 5-10pm Mon-Sat)

Aniar   Modern Irish €€€

Deeply committed to the flavours and food producers of Galway and West Ireland, Aniar wears its Michelin star with pride. There's no fuss here, however. The casual spring-green dining area is a relaxed place to taste from the daily-changing menu. The

Galway market stalls

NEIL SETCHFIELD/GETTY IMAGES ©

Dunguaire Castle

wine list favours small producers. Reserve. (091-535 947; www.aniarrestaurant.ie; 53 Lower Dominick St; mains from €30; 6-10pm Tue-Thu, 5.30-10pm Fri & Sat)

🍺 DRINKING & NIGHTLIFE

Séhán Ua Neáchtain   Pub
Painted a bright cornflower blue, this 19th-century pub, known simply as Neáchtain's (*nock*-tans) or Naughtons, has a wraparound string of tables outside, many shaded by a large tree. It's a place where a polyglot mix of locals plop down and let the world pass them by – or stop and join them

---

📓 **Top Five Historic Sites**

- Clonmacnoise (p118)
- Dunguaire Castle (p125)
- Cnoc Suain (p114)
- Hall of the Red Earl (p120)
- Aughnanure Castle (p126)

---

for a pint. Good lunches. (www.tighneachtain. com; 17 Upper Cross St; noon-11.30pm Mon-Thu, noon-midnight Fri & Sat, noon-11pm Sun)

Crane Bar   Pub
This atmospheric old pub west of the Corrib is the best spot in Galway to catch an informal *céilidh* (traditional music and dancing) most nights. Talented bands play its rowdy, good-natured upstairs bar; downstairs at times it seems straight out of *The Far Side*. (www.thecranebar.com; 2 Sea Rd; 10.30am-11.30pm Mon-Fri, 10.30am-12.30am Sat, 12.30-11pm Sun)

ℹ️ INFORMATION

The large, efficient regional **information centre** (Map p121; www.discoverireland.ie; Forster St; 9am-5.45pm Mon-Sat, 9am-1.15pm Sun) can help arrange local accommodation and tours.

ℹ️ GETTING THERE & AWAY

BUS
Several private bus companies are based at the modern **Galway Coach Station** (New Coach

Station; Map p121; Bothar St), which is located near the tourist office.

Bus Éireann (Map p121; www.buseireann. ie; Station Rd, Cara Bus Station) Services to all major cities in the Republic and the North from just off Eyre Square, near the train station. Hourly services to Dublin (€14.50, three to 3¾ hours). Other services fan out across the region.

Citylink (Map p121; www.citylink.ie; ticket office Forster St; ☺office 9am-6pm; ☎) Services depart from Galway Coach Station for Dublin (from €13, 2½ hours, hourly), Dublin Airport (from €19, 2½ hours, hourly), Cork, Limerick and Connemara. Departures are frequent and fares are as low as €10.

GoBus.ie (www.gobus.ie; Galway Coach Station; ☎) Frequent services to Dublin (2½ hours) and Dublin Airport (three hours). Fares from €12.

TRAIN

From the **train station** (☎091-564 222; www. irishrail.ie), just off Eyre Square, there are up to nine fast, comfortable trains daily to/from Dublin's Heuston Station (one way from €35, 2¼ hours). Connections with other train routes can be made at Athlone (one hour). The line to Ennis is scenic (€19, 1¾ hours, five daily).

Kinvara

The small stone harbour of Kinvara (sometimes spelt Kinvarra) sits smugly at the southeastern corner of Galway Bay, which accounts for its Irish name, Cinn Mhara (Head of the Sea). It's a charming and good-looking village, and makes an excellent pit stop between Galway and Clare. For glorious views of the bay, head out from Kinvara on the N67 towards Ballyvaughan for around 6km, then take the left towards Carron to a **lookout** around 400m up on the right-hand side of the road.

⊙ SIGHTS & ACTIVITIES

Dunguaire Castle   Historic Building
Erected around 1520 by the O'Hynes clan, Dunguaire Castle is widely believed to

occupy the former site of the 6th-century royal palace of Guaire Aidhne, the king of Connaught. Lady Christabel Ampthill restored the castle after buying it for the equivalent of €500 and lived here from the 1950s to the 1970s; her bedroom was in the crafts studio, with her living room at the very top beneath a new pitched roof.

Climb to the roof for glorious views of Galway Bay and Kinvara. Attending a **medieval banquet** (☎061-360 788; banquet adult/child €50/25; ☺5.30pm & 8.45pm Apr-Oct) is the least authentic way to visit the castle. (www.shannonheritage.com; off N67; adult/child €6/3; ☺10am-4pm Apr-early Oct)

❶ GETTING THERE & AWAY

Bus Éireann (www.buseireann.ie) links Kinvara with Galway city (30 minutes) and towns in County Clare, such as Doolin, up to three times daily.

Connemara

The filigreed coast of the Connemara Peninsula is endlessly pleasing, with pockets of sheer delight awaiting discovery. Connemara's interior is a kaleidoscope of rusty bogs, lonely valleys and shimmering black lakes. At its heart are the Maumturk Mountains and the pewter-tinged quartzite peaks of the Twelve Bens mountain range, with a network of scenic hiking and biking trails.

Claddagh Rings

The fishing village of Claddagh has long been subsumed into Galway's city centre, but its namesake rings survive as both a timeless reminder and a timeless source of profits.

Popular with people of real or imagined Irish descent everywhere, the rings depict a heart (symbolising love) between two outstretched hands (friendship), topped by a crown (loyalty). Rings are handcrafted at jewellers around Galway and start from about €20 for a simple band to well over €1000 for a blinged-up diamond-covered version.

Jewellers include Ireland's oldest jewellery shop, **Thomas Dillon's Claddagh Gold** (Map p121; www.claddaghring. ie; 1 Quay St; ⊙10am-6pm), which was established in 1750 and is adorned with Claddagh history placards.

Claddagh ring
GAMARUBA/SHUTTERSTOCK ©

ⓘ INFORMATION

Galway's tourist office has lots of information on the area. Online, Connemara Tourism (www. connemara.ie) and Go Connemara (www.go connemara.com) have region-wide info and links.

ⓘ GETTING THERE & AROUND

BUS

Organised bus tours from Galway are many and offer a good overview of the region, though ideally you'll want more than one day to absorb the area's charms, plus you'll want the freedom to make your own discoveries.

Bus Éireann (☏091-562 000; www.bus eireann.ie) Serves most of Connemara. Services can be sporadic, and many buses operate May to September only, or July and August only. Some drivers will stop in between towns.

Citylink (www.citylink.ie) Has several buses a day linking Galway city with Clifden, with stops in Moycullen, Oughterard, Maam Cross and Recess, and on to Cleggan and Letterfrack. Between towns, you might be able to arrange a drop-off with the driver.

CAR

Your own wheels are the best way to get off this scenic region's beaten track – though watch out for the narrow roads' stone walls.

Oughterard & Around

The village of Oughterard (Uachtar Árd) is one of Ireland's principal angling centres. Immediately west, the countryside opens up to sweeping panoramas of lakes, mountains and bogs, which get more spectacular the further west you travel.

◎ SIGHTS & ACTIVITIES

Aughnanure Castle   Castle
Built around 1500, this beautiful fortress was home to the 'Fighting O'Flahertys', who controlled the region for hundreds of years after they fought off the Normans. The six-storey tower house stands on a rocky outcrop overlooking Lough Corrib and has been extensively restored. Surrounding the castle are the remains of an unusual double *bawn* (area surrounded by walls outside the main castle); there's also the remains of the Banqueting Hall and a small, now isolated watchtower, with a conical roof. (www.heritageireland.com; off N59; adult/child €3/1; ⊙9.30am-6pm Apr–mid-Oct)

Corrib Cruises   Boat Trip
With day cruises from Oughterard to Inchagoill and Ashford Castle near Cong. (☏091-557 798; www.corribcruises.com; adult/

Claddagh village

child €20/10; ☺Easter-Oct, see website for sailing times)

ℹ️ GETTING THERE & AWAY

Bus Éireann (www.buseireann.ie) and **Citylink** (www.citylink.ie) have regular buses from Galway to Oughterard.

Roundstone

Clustered around a boat-filled harbour, Roundstone (Cloch na Rón) is the kind of Irish village you hoped to find. Colourful terrace houses and inviting pubs overlook the shimmering recess of Bertraghboy Bay, which is home to dramatic tidal flows, lobster trawlers and traditional *currachs* with tarred canvas bottoms stretched over wicker frames.

🍽️ EATING

O'Dowd's   Seafood €€
This well-worn, comfortable old pub hasn't lost any of its authenticity since it starred in the 1997 Hollywood flick *The Matchmak-*

er. Specialities at its adjoining restaurant include seafood sourced off the old stone dock right across the street, while produce comes from their garden. There's a good

---

🖼️ Spoken Irish

One of the most important Gaeltacht (Irish-speaking) areas in Ireland begins around Spiddal in Connemara and stretches west to Cashel and north into County Mayo.

That spoken Irish is enjoying a renaissance around the country (aspiring Dublin parents compete to enrol their kids in Irish-language schools) can be credited in no small part to several media outlets based in Connemara and Galway. From this last refuge of the language, Ireland's national Irish-language radio station, Radio na Gaeltachta (www.rte.ie/rnag) and its Irish-language TV station, TG4 (www.tg4.ie), sprang up in the 1990s.

list of Irish microbrews and you can get breakfast before noon. (091-35809; www.odowdsseafoodbar.com; Main St; mains €13-27, 2-course dinner 5-7pm €20; restaurant 10am-9.30pm Jun-Sep, to 9pm Oct-May;)

Clifden & Around

Connemara's 'capital', Clifden (An Clochán), is an appealing Victorian-era country town with a vaguely harp-shaped oval of streets offering evocative strolls. It presides over the head of the narrow bay where the River Owenglin tumbles into the sea. The surrounding countryside beckons you to walk through woods and above the shoreline.

◉ SIGHTS & ACTIVITIES

Sky Road   Scenic Route
This 12km route traces a spectacular loop out to the township of Kingston and back to Clifden, taking in some rugged, stunningly beautiful coastal scenery en route. The round trip of about 12km can be easily walked or cycled; timing things to catch the sun dipping into the Atlantic is best, and

there are several lookout points where you can park the car. Head directly west from Clifden's Market Square.

✖ EATING

Mitchell's   Seafood €€
Seafood takes centre stage at this elegant spot. From a velvety chowder right through a long list of ever-changing and inventive specials, the produce of the surrounding waters is honoured. The wine list does the food justice. Book for dinner. (Lunch includes sandwiches and casual fare.) (095-21867; www.mitchellsrestaurantclifden.com; Market St; lunch mains €8-12, dinner mains €15-25; noon-10pm Mar-Oct)

Letterfrack & Around

Founded by Quakers in the mid-19th century, Letterfrack (Leitir Fraic) is a crossroads with a few pubs and B&Bs. But the forested setting and nearby coast are a magnet for outdoor-adventure seekers. A 4km walk to the peak of Tully Mountain takes 40 minutes and affords wonderful ocean views.

Clifden locals take a drink

◎ SIGHTS

Connemara National Park   Park

Immediately southeast of Letterfrack, Connemara National Park spans 2000 dramatic hectares of bog, mountain and heath. The visitor centre is in a beautiful setting off a parking area 300m south of the Letterfrack crossroads. The visitor centre offers an introduction to the park's flora, fauna and geology, and visitors can scrutinise maps and various trails here before heading out into the park. Various types of flora and fauna native to the area are explained, including the elephant hawkmoth and red deer. There's a tearoom. (www.connemaranationalpark.ie; off N59; ☺visitor centre 9am-5.30pm Mar-Oct, park 24hr) FREE

Kylemore Abbey   Historical Building

Photogenically perched on the shores of Pollacapall Lough, this crenulated 19th-century neo-Gothic fantasy was built for a wealthy English businessman, Mitchell Henry, who spent his honeymoon in Connemara. Only a selection of rooms are open to visitors but you can wander down the lake to the Gothic Church, and admission includes the breathtaking and extravagant Victorian walled gardens, around a 20-minute walk away (or take the free shuttle bus, every 15 minutes). A formal composition in the wildness of Connemara, the gardens are sublime. (www.kylemoreabbey.com; off N59; adult/child €13/free; ☺9am-6pm Apr-Sep, 10am-4.30pm Oct-Mar)

❶ GETTING THERE & AWAY

Bus Éireann (www.buseireann.ie) and **Citylink** (www.citylink.ie) buses continue to Letterfrack at least once a day from Clifden, 15km southwest on the N59.

Leenane & Killary Harbour

The small village of Leenane (also spelled Leenaun) drowses on the shore of dramatic Killary Harbour. Dotted with mussel rafts, the long, narrow harbour is Ireland's only

👓 Lough Corrib

The Republic's biggest lake, Lough Corrib, virtually cuts off western Galway from the rest of the country. More than 48km long and covering some 200 sq km, it encompasses more than 360 islands.

The largest island on Lough Corrib, **Inchagoill** is a lonely place dotted with ancient remains. Most fascinating is an obelisk called **Lia Luguaedon Mac Menueh** (Stone of Luguaedon, Son of Menueh), which identifies a burial site. It stands about 75cm tall, near the Saints' Church, and some people claim that the Latin writing on the stone is the second-oldest Christian inscription in Europe, after those in the catacombs in Rome. **Teampall Phádraig** (St Patrick's Church) is a small oratory of a very early design, with some later additions. The prettiest church is the Romanesque **Teampall na Naoimh** (Saints' Church), probably built in the 9th or 10th century, with carvings around its arched doorway.

Corrib Cruises (p126) have day cruises from Oughterard to Inchagoill and Ashford Castle near Cong.

Bridge over Lough Corrib at Ashford Castle
PETER ZOELLER/DESIGN PICS/GETTY IMAGES ©

fjord – maybe. Slicing 16km inland and more than 45m deep in the centre, it certainly looks like a fjord, although some scientific studies suggest it may not actually have been glaciated. Mt Mweelrea (819m) towers to its north.

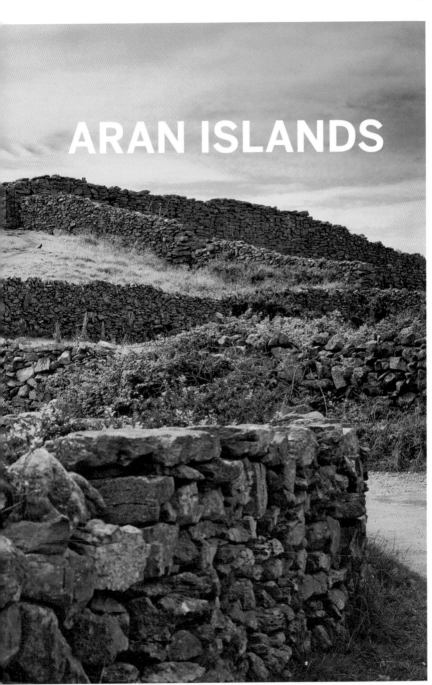

ARAN ISLANDS

Aran Islands

Easily visible from large swaths of coastal Galway and Clare Counties, the Aran Islands sing their own siren song to thousands of Wild Atlantic Way travellers each year who find their desolate beauty beguiling. Day-trippers shuttle through in a daze of rocky magnificence, while those who stay longer find places that, in many ways, seem far further removed from the Irish mainland than the 45-minute ferry ride or 10-minute flight would suggest. Hardy travellers find that the low season showcases the islands at their wildest, windswept best.

An extension of the limestone escarpment that forms the Burren in Clare, the islands have shallow topsoil scattered with wildflowers, grass for grazing and jagged cliffs pounded by surf. Ancient forts such as Dún Aengus on Inishmór and Dún Chonchúir on Inishmaan are some of the oldest archaeological remains in Ireland.

☑ In This Section

❶ Arriving in the Aran Islands

Flights depart from Connemara regional airport, about 35km west of Galway. Aer Arann Islands offers flights to each of the islands several times daily (10 minutes, €49 return, hourly in summer).

Boat Island Ferries services leave from Rossaveal, 40km west of Galway City. Buses from Queen St in Galway (adult/child €7/4) connect with the sailings. From March to October there are also ferries from Doolin (p156).

★ **Classic Photo**
Teampall Bheanáin (Church of St Benen; p135) makes for a quintessential shot of the windswept beauty of the Aran Islands.

North Sound

Port Chorrúch

Kilmurvey Beach

Dún Aengus

Kilmurvy

Dún Eochla

Teampall Chiaráin

Inishmór

Kilronan

Cill Éinne Bay

Aran Islands

Galway Bay

Dún Dúchathair

★ Airport

Teampall Bheanáin (Church of St Benen)

Synge's Chair

Teach Synge

Inishmaan

O'Brien's Castle

Tobar Éinne

Inisheer

South Sound

N
0   5 km
0   2.5 miles

From left: Inisheer (p138); horse and carriage, Inishmore (p136); cottage on Inisheer
DOUG PEARSON/GETTY IMAGES © CARL BRUEMMER/DESIGN PICS/GETTY IMAGES © GAVIN QUIRKE/GETTY IMAGES ©

ARNE KRISTIANSEN/GETTY IMAGES ©

Dún Aengus

Three spectacular prehistoric forts stand guard over Inishmór, each believed to be around 2000 years old. Chief among them is Dún Aengus, with three massive dry-stone walls that run right up to sheer drops to the ocean below.

The fort is protected by remarkable *chevaux de frise*, fearsome and densely packed defensive limestone spikes. A small visitor centre has displays that put everything in context and a slightly strenuous 900m walkway wanders uphill to the fort itself. Dún Aengus is around 7km west of Kilronan.

Powerful swells pound the 60m-high cliff face. A complete lack of railings or other modern additions that would spoil this incredible site means that you can not only go right up to the cliff's edge but also potentially fall to your doom below, so take care.

Great For...

☑ Don't Miss

The stunning view along the cliff tops to the west of Dún Aengus.

Nearby Historic Sites

Between Kilronan and Dún Aengus you'll find the small, perfectly circular fort **Dún Eochla**, which makes for a good walk from the main road.

GAVIN QUIRKE/GETTY IMAGES ©

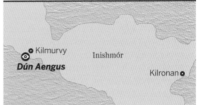

ℹ Need to Know

Dún Aonghasa; www.heritageireland.ie; adult/child €4/2; ⊙9.45am-6pm Apr-Oct, 9.30am-4pm Nov-Mar, closed Mon & Tue Jan & Feb

✕ Take a Break

Refuel with a slap-up meal of fish and chips at Joe Watty's Bar (p136).

★ Top Tip

Hiring a bike makes it easier to explore the myriad sites around the island.

The ruins of numerous stone churches identify the island's monastic history. The small **Teampall Chiaráin** (Church of St Kieran), with a high cross in the churchyard, is near Kilronan.

West of Kilmurvey is the perfect **Clochán na Carraige**, an early Christian stone hut that stands 2.5m tall, and various small early Christian ruins known rather inaccurately as the **Na Seacht dTeampaill** (Seven Churches), comprising a couple of ruined churches, monastic houses and some fragments of a high cross from the 8th or 9th century. To the south of the ruins is **Dún Eoghanachta**, another circular fort.

Along the low-lying northern coast, the sheltered little bay of **Port Chorrúch** is home to up to 50 grey seals, who sun themselves and feed in the shallows. Further on, **Kilmurvey Beach** gets an EU Blue Flag for its clean white-sand beach.

In the southeast, near Cill Éinne Bay, is the early Christian **Teampall Bheanáin** (Church of St Benen). Near the airport are the sunken remains of a church; the spot is said to have been the site of St Enda's Monastery in the 5th century, though what's visible dates from the 8th century onwards.

Dún Dúchathair (Black Fort) is an ancient fort dramatically perched on a south-facing clifftop promontory to the southwest of Kilronan.

📖 Top Five Aran Islands Prehistoric Sites

- Dún Aengus (p134)
- Dún Eochla (p134)
- Dún Dúchathair (p135)
- Dún Chonchúir (p137)
- Dún Eoghanachta (p135)

Inishmór

Most visitors who venture out to the islands don't make it beyond Inishmór (Árainn) and its main attraction, Dún Aengus, the stunning stone fort perched perilously on the island's towering cliffs. The arid landscape west of Kilronan (Cill Rónáin), Inishmór's main settlement, is dominated by stone walls, boulders, scattered buildings and the odd patch of deep-green grass and potato plants.

⚙ ACTIVITIES

Burke's Bicycle Hire   Bicycle Rental
Patrick Burke is an expert on local cycling and can advise on routes that avoid crowds and reach seldom-visited ends of the island. (📞 087 280 8273; www.bikehirearan islands.com; Kilronan; rental per day from €10; ⏱Apr-Oct) 📝

Aran Cycle Hire   Bicycle Rental
Hires out hundreds of sturdy bikes, electric bikes and tandems, which it delivers to your accommodation anywhere on the island. It's at the pier. (www.aranislandsbikehire.com;

Kilronan; rental per day from €10, electric bikes from €30, deposit €10-20; ⏱Apr-Oct)

✖ EATING & DRINKING

Bayview Restaurant   European €€
A short walk west from the pier, this excellent restaurant is a modern, light-filled environment that's decorated with local art and offers a delectable menu capturing impressive Latin flair, thanks to the Guatamalan roots of head chef, Byron. (lunch mains €10-14, dinner mains €10-28; ⏱10am-9pm; 📶)

Pier House   Irish €€
This is the best spot for lunch right in Kilronan – on the large terrace watching the ferries come and go while grazing your way through platters of fish and chips, falafels or steaks. There's a fireplace inside for when the cold winds blow. (Kilronan; mains €13.50-24.95; ⏱noon-9pm May-Aug)

Joe Watty's Bar   Pub
The best local pub, with trad sessions most summer nights and weekends other times. Posh pub food ranges from fish and chips to steaks. Peat fires warm the air on the 50

Beach on Inisheer

weeks a year when this is needed. Book for dinner in summer. (www.joewattys.com; Kilronan; ⊙kitchen 12.30-9pm)

ℹ️ INFORMATION

The useful **tourist office** (☎099-61263; Kilronan; ⊙9am-5pm May & Jun, 9am-5.45pm Jul & Aug, 11am-5pm Sep-Apr) is located on the waterfront west of the ferry pier in Kilronan.

ℹ️ GETTING AROUND

The airstrip is 2km southeast of town; a shuttle to Kilronan costs €5 return (be sure to carefully reconfirm return pick-ups for flights lest you be forgotten).

Year-round, numerous **minibuses** greet each ferry and also prowl the centre of Kilronan. All offer 2½-hour tours of the island (€10) to ad hoc groups. The drive – with commentary – between Kilronan and Dún Aengustakes is about 45 minutes each way. You can also negotiate for private and customised tours.

To see the island at a gentler pace, **pony traps** with a driver are available for trips between Kilronan and Dún Aengus; the return journey costs between €60 and €100 for up to four people.

Inishmaan

The least-visited of the islands, with the smallest population, Inishmaan (Inis Meáin) is a rocky respite. Inishmaan's scenery is breathtaking, with a jagged coastline of startling cliffs, empty beaches and fields where the main crop seems to be stone.

You can easily **walk** to any place on the island, enjoying the stark, rocky scenery and sweeping views on the way.

On a hill, **St Mary's Church** has excellent stained-glass windows from 1939. In the east of the island, about 500m north of the boat-landing stage, is **Trá Leitreach**, a safe, sheltered beach.

◎ SIGHTS & ACTIVITIES

Synge's Chair   Lookout
At the desolate western edge of the island, Synge's Chair is a lookout at the edge of

a sheer limestone cliff with the surf from Gregory's Sound booming below. The cliff ledge is often sheltered from the wind, so do as Synge did and find a comfortable stone seat to take it all in. The formation is two minutes' walk from the parking area; you can leg it around the bleak west side of the island from here in an hour. On the walk out to Synge's Chair, a sign points the way to a **clochán**, hidden behind a house and shed.

Teach Synge   Historic Building
This thatched cottage, on the road just before you head up to the fort Dún Chonchúir, is where the writer JM Synge spent his summers between 1898 and 1902. (☎099-73036; admission €3; ⊙by appointment)

Dún Chonchúir   Fort
Glorious views of Inishmaan's limestone valleys extend from this elliptical stone fort, built sometime between the 1st and 7th centuries AD.

Brídín Tours   Tour
Provides fact-filled, one- to two-hour car tours of the island. (☎099-73993; adult €15)

Island Hopping

It's possible to bounce between the three Aran Islands, allowing you to start at one and return to the mainland from another. However, ferry schedules are geared to return trips to a single island and in order to find ferries between the islands you'll need to consult with Island Ferries as well as the boats operating from Doolin. There will be at least one connection a day between any two islands; just be prepared for ad hoc schedules. Fares should run from €5 to €10.

✖ EATING

Tig Congaile   Irish €
Not far from the pier, Guatemalan-born Vilma Conneely serves guests freshly ground coffee from her native land, but it's her use of local foods that really wins plaudits. Her sea-vegetable soup is famous and best enjoyed – if possible – at a table outside. The dining room is open to nonguests, but you must book. The seven rooms (single/double €50/80) are spacious and have starkly iconic views. (099-73085; www.inismeainbb.com; lunch dishes from €5, dinner from €20)

Inis Meáin   Irish €€
An anomaly on the island, where almost everything is as basic as a rock – or is a rock – this smart boutique inn has five lovely suites crafted from local materials (rocks). The restaurant serves a changing menu of exquisite dishes made from local foods. Open to nonguests, but book. (086 826 6026; www.inismeain.com; dinner mains €15-35; ⏲Apr-Sep; 📶)

Teach Ósta   Pub Food €€
The island's perfect pub hums on summer evenings (grab a table outside for the views) and supplies snacks, sandwiches, soups and seafood platters. Though the pub often keeps going until the wee hours, food service generally stops around 7pm and may not be available in the winter months. (mains from €8)

Inisheer

Inisheer (Inis Oírr), the smallest of the Aran Islands, has a palpable sense of enchantment, enhanced by the island's deep-rooted mythology, its devotion to traditional culture and ethereal landscapes.

◎ SIGHTS

Tobar Éinne   Historic Site
Locals still carry out a pilgrimage known as the Turas to the Well of Enda, an ever-burbling spring in a remote rocky expanse in the southwest. The ceremony involves, over the course of three consecutive Sundays, picking up seven stones from the ground nearby and walking around the small well seven times, putting one stone down each time, while saying the rosary until an elusive eel appears from the well's watery depths.

If, during this ritual, you're lucky enough to see the eel, it's said your tongue will be bestowed with healing powers, enabling you to literally lick wounds.

O'Brien's Castle   Historic Building
A 100m climb to the island's highest point yields dramatic views over clover-covered fields to the beach and harbour. This 15th-century church (Caisleán Uí Bhriain) was built within the remains of a ring fort called Dún Formna, dating from as early as the 1st century AD. Nearby is an 18th-century signal tower.

Plassy   Historic Site
Dating from 1960, this iconic island sight was a freighter that was thrown up on the rocks in bad weather. Miraculously, all on board were saved; Tigh Ned's pub has a collection of photographs and documents detailing the rescue. An aerial shot of the wreck was used in the opening sequence of the iconic TV series *Father Ted*.

TINY-AL/GETTY IMAGES ©

Wreck of the *Plassy*

🍴 EATING

Tigh Ruaírí Pub Food €

Rory Conneely's atmospheric digs host live music sessions in the cosy pub. There are 20 basic rooms (€50 to 90), many with views across the waters. (Strand House; 📞099-75020; www.tighruairi.com; @)

Where to Stay

After the last day trippers have left in summer, the islands assume a lovely serenity and good accommodation options can be found on Inishmór, Inishmaan and Inisheer. Advance bookings are advised, particularly in summer. The Inishmór tourist office offers a room-booking service. Many B&Bs and hotels, such as Inis Meáin on Inishmaan or Fisherman's Cottage & South Aran House on Inisheer, offer excellent evening meals that are available to nonguests.

Tigh Ned Pub Food €

Here since 1897, Tigh Ned is a welcoming, unpretentious place, with lively traditional music and inexpensive lunchtime fare. Tables in the garden have harbour views. (meals €5-10)

Fisherman's Cottage & South Aran House Irish €€

Slow-food enthusiasts run this sprightly B&B and cafe that's a mere five-minute walk from the pier, with lavender growing in profusion at the entrance. Food (nonguests can enjoy cakes by day and dinner at night, but will need to book) celebrates local seafood and organic produce. Kayaking and fishing are among the activities on offer. (📞099-75073; www.southaran.com; Castle Village; dinner mains €12-20; ⏱Apr-Oct)

COUNTY CLARE

County Clare

Clare combines the stunning natural beauty of its long, meandering coastline with unique windswept landscapes and choice dollops of Irish culture.

Rugged nature and the timeless ocean meet on the county's coast. The Atlantic relentlessly pounds year-round, eroding rock into fantastic formations, and fashioning sheer cliffs like those at the iconic Cliffs of Moher and intriguing little islands like those near Loop Head. There are even stretches of beach where surfers flock to the (chilly) waves. The Burren, an ancient region of alien vistas, stretches down to the coast and right out to the Aran Islands.

But if the land is hard, Clare's soul certainly isn't: traditional Irish culture and music flourish here. And it's not just a show for tourists, either. In little villages like Miltown Malbay, Ennistymon, Doolin and Kilfenora, you'll find pubs with year-round sessions of trad music.

☑ In This Section

❶ Arriving in County Clare

Exploring County Clare by public transport is difficult and time-consuming. If you don't have a car, it's best to base yourself in Galway city, and visit the Cliffs of Moher and Doolin as part of a guided coach tour. Operators include: Galway Tour Company, Lally Tours and Burren Wild Tours (p153).

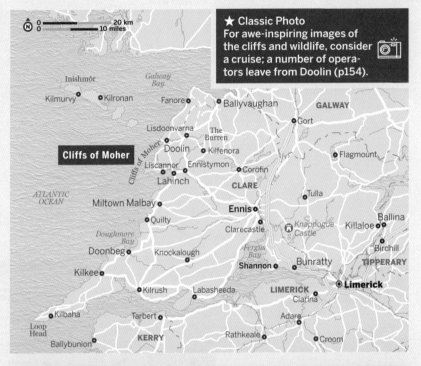

N
0 ———— 20 km
0 ———— 10 miles

★ **Classic Photo**
For awe-inspiring images of
the cliffs and wildlife, consider
a cruise; a number of operators leave from Doolin (p154).

Inishmór
Kilmurvy
Kilronan
Galway Bay
Fanore
Ballyvaughan
GALWAY
Gort
Lisdoonvarna
The Burren
Doolin
Kilfenora
Flagmount
Cliffs of Moher
Cliffs of Moher
Liscannor
Ennistymon
Corofin
Lahinch
CLARE
Tulla
ATLANTIC OCEAN
Miltown Malbay
Ennis
Quilty
Clarecastle
Knappogue Castle
Killaloe
Ballina
Doughmore Bay
Doonbeg
Knockalough
Fergus Bay
Shannon
Bunratty
TIPPERARY
Birdhill
Kilkee
Kilrush
Labasheeda
LIMERICK
⊙ **Limerick**
Kilbaha
Tarbert
Clarina
Loop Head
Ballybunion
KERRY
Rathkeale
Adare
Croom

From left: Surfer, Kilkee (p150); trad music session at O'Connor's (p156), Doolin; cows, Ballyvaughan (p156)

O'Brien's Tower

PETER UNGER/GETTY IMAGES ©

Cliffs of Moher

In good visibility, the Cliffs of Moher (Ailltean Mothair, or Ailltreacha Mothair) are stupefyingly impressive and staggeringly beautiful.

Great For...

☑ Don't Miss

The view west along the cliffs around sunset, when the scenery is at its most spectacular.

The entirely vertical cliffs rise to a height of 203m, their edge falling away abruptly into the constantly churning sea. A series of heads, the dark limestone seems to march in a rigid formation that amazes, no matter how many times you look. On a clear day you'll channel Barbra Streisand as you can see forever; the Aran Islands stand etched on the waters of Galway Bay, and beyond lie the hills of Connemara in western Galway.

Its fame guarantees a steady stream of visitors which can surge to a swell almost as impressive as the raging ocean below, but the tireless Atlantic winds can drown out the chatter and you can shrug off the crowds, even though busloads arrive in summer. A vast visitor centre is set back into the side of a hill, Teletubbies style. As part of the development, however, the

Sunset from the Cliffs of Moher

PATRYK KOSMIDER/SHUTTERSTOCK ©

❶ Need to Know

www.cliffsofmoher.ie; admission to site adult/
child €6/free; ◷9am-9.30pm Jul & Aug, 9am-
7pm May, Jun & Sep, 9am-6pm Mar, Apr & Oct,
9.15am-5pm Nov-Feb; 📶

✕ Take A Break

Escape the overcrowded cafes in the
visitor centre by taking a picnic and
dining on the cliff tops.

★ Top Tip

Bring binoculars – more than 30
species of birds, including darling
little puffins, can be spotted here.

main walkways and viewing areas along
the cliffs have been surrounded by a
1.5m-high wall that's too high and set too
far back from the edge.

Walking Trails

There are good rewards if you're willing to
walk for 10 minutes. Past the end of the
'Moher Wall' south, a trail runs along the
cliffs to Hag's Head (about 5.5km) – few
venture this far, yet the views are unin-
hibited. From here you can continue on to
Liscannor for a total walk of 12km (about
3.5 hours). To the north, you can follow
the Doolin Trail via O'Brien's Tower right
to the village of Doolin (about 7km and
2.5 hours). The entire Liscannor to Doolin
walking path via the cliffs is now signposted; note that there are a lot of ups and
downs and narrow, cliff-edge stretches.

Visitor Centre

The modern **visitor centre** (www.cliffsof-
moher.ie; admission to site adult/child €6/free;
◷9am-9.30pm Jul & Aug, 9am-7pm May, Jun
& Sep, 9am-6pm Mar, Apr & Oct, 9.15am-5pm
Nov-Feb; 📶) contains numerous shops and
a few cafes, plus a rewarding exhibition
regarding the fauna, flora, geology and
climate of the cliffs. There is also an audiovisual virtual reality experience called *The
Ledge*, shown on a loop in an auditorium
through the day. Free information booklets
on the cliffs are available. The soulless
ground-floor Puffin's Nest Cafe seems
designed to urge you up to the pricier
Cliffs View Cafe above.

Trad session, Miltown Malbay (p152)

CARL BRUEMMER/DESIGN PICS/GETTY IMAGES ©

Trad Music Sessions

From atmospheric small pubs in tiny villages where non-instrument-playing patrons are a minority to rollicking urban boozers in Ennis, Clare is one of Ireland's best counties for traditional music.

Great For...

☑ Don't Miss

A session at Vaughan's in Kilfenora, one of Ireland's top trad music venues.

Ennis

You can bounce from one music-filled pub to another on most nights, especially in the summer. Musicians from around the county come here to show off and there are good venues for serious trad pursuits.

O'Dea's   Pub

Unchanged since at least the 1950s, this plain-tile-fronted pub is a hideout for local musicians serious about their trad sessions, drawing some of Clare's best. (66 O'Connell St)

Brogan's   Pub

On the corner of Cooke's Lane, Brogan's is a big pub that rambles from one room to the next with a fine bunch of musicians rattling even the stone floors from about 9pm Monday to Thursday (more nights in summer). (24 O'Connell St)

Bagpiper, Bunratty Castle (p150)

ELAN FLEISHER/GETTY IMAGES ©

Vaughan's Pub Pub Food €€

A pub with a big reputation in Irish music circles, there's seafood, traditional foods and local produce featured on the menu. Have a pint under the big tree out front. There's music in the bar every night during the summer and on many nights at other times. The adjacent barn is the scene of terrific set-dancing sessions on Thursday (10pm) and Sunday (9pm). (www.vaughanspub.ie; Main St; mains €8-15; ⊘kitchen 10am-9pm)

Ennistymon

A charming village inland from Doolin with a couple of ancient pubs attracting top local talent.

Eugene's Pub

With one of the most amazing pub frontages you'll ever see, Eugene's is a classic choice. Intimate and cosy, with a trademark collection of visiting cards covering its walls, it has a great whiskey collection and some fab stained glass. (Main St; ⊘10.30am-11.30pm Mon-Thu, 10.30am-12.30am Fri & Sat, 12.30-11pm Sun)

Doolin

A collection of pubs with nightly trad music sessions. However, tourist crowds can be intense, so sensations of intimacy or enjoyment can evaporate.

McGann's Pub

McGann's has all the classic touches of a full-on Irish music pub, with action often spilling onto the street. The food here (mains €11 to €18) is the best of Doolin's three famous pubs. Inside you'll find locals playing darts in its warren of small rooms, some with peat fires. (www.mcgannspub doolin.com; Roadford; ⊘bar 10am-12.30am, kitchen 10am-9.30pm)

Kilfenora

Small village with a big musical heritage on show at the great local pub Vaughan's.

Ennis

Ennis (Inis) is the busy commercial centre of Clare. It lies on the banks of the smallish River Fergus, which runs east, then south into the Shannon Estuary.

It's short on sights but is the place to stay if you want a bit of urban flair; from Ennis, you can reach any part of Clare in under two hours.

◎ SIGHTS & ACTIVITIES

Ennis Friary   Church
North of the Square, this friary was founded by Donnchadh Cairbreach O'Brien, a king of Thomond, sometime between 1240 and 1249. A mix of structures dating between the 13th and 19th centuries, the friary has a graceful five-section window dating from the late 13th century, a McMahon tomb (1460) with alabaster panels depicting scenes from the Passion and a particularly

> *If the land is hard, Clare's soul certainly isn't: traditional Irish music flourishes here.*

Ennis Friary

fine *Ecce Homo* panel portraying a stripped and bound Christ and objects associated with the Passion. (www.heritageireland.ie; Abbey St; adult €4; ⊙10am-6pm Easter-Sep, to 5pm Oct)

⊗ EATING

Food Heaven   Cafe €
This small cafe-deli lives up to its ambitious name with creative and fresh fare. Sandwiches arrive on renowned brown bread, while soups and salads change daily. Hot specials are just that. Be ready to queue at lunch. (www.food-heaven.ie; 21 Market St; mains €8-10; ⊙8.30am-6pm Mon-Thu, 8.30am-9pm Fri & Sat; 🕾)

⊖ DRINKING & NIGHTLIFE

Cruise's Pub   Pub
With some of Ennis Friary's stonework incorporated into its fabric, this friendly bar has a long side courtyard that's perfect for enjoying a fresh-air pint, with trad music sessions most nights from 9pm. (Abbey St;

🕙 5-11.30pm Mon-Thu, 4pm-2am Fri, 11am-2am Sat, 11am-1am Sun)

Poet's Corner Bar   Pub
The old hotel pub sees trad sessions from Thursday to Sunday. (Old Ground Hotel, O'Connell St; 🕙 11am-11.30pm Mon-Thu, 11am-12.30am Fri & Sat, noon-11pm Sun)

ℹ INFORMATION

The **tourist office** (📞 065-682 8366; www. visitennis.ie; Arthur's Row; 🕙 9am-1pm & 2-5pm Tue-Sat) is very helpful and efficient. Can book accommodation for a €4 fee.

ℹ GETTING THERE & AWAY

The M18 bypass east of the city lets traffic between Limerick and Galway whiz right past, although trips to the coast still take you through the centre.

BUS
Bus Éireann (📞 065-682 4177; www.buseireann. ie) services operate from the bus station beside the train station.

Buses run from Ennis to Cork (€18, three hours, 12 daily); Doolin (€13.90, 1½ hours, four daily) via Corofin, Ennistymon, Lahinch, Liscannor and Cliffs of Moher; Galway (€11.50, 1½ hours, hourly) via Gort; Limerick (€10, 40 minutes, hourly) via Bunratty; and Shannon Airport (€8.40, 50 minutes, hourly).

To reach Dublin (€23), connect through Limerick.

TRAIN
Irish Rail (www.irishrail.ie) trains from **Ennis station** (📞 065-684 0444; Station Rd) serve Limerick (€11.35, 40 minutes, nine daily), where you can connect to trains to places further afield like Dublin. The line to Galway (€19.70, 1¾ hours, five daily) features good Burren scenery.

Bunratty

A crossbow bolt's shot from the N18 motorway, Bunratty (Bun Raite) is home

Traditional Music Festivals

Craiceann Inis Oírr International Bodhrán Summer School   Cultural
The island reverberates to the thunder of traditional drums at the end of June when bodhrán masterclasses, lectures and performances are held. Craiceann takes its name from the Irish word for 'skin', referring to the goat skin used to make these circular drums. The festival features top talent and nightly drumming sessions take place in the pubs. (www.craiceann.com)

Ennis Trad Festival   Music
Traditional music is performed in venues across town. (www.ennistradfest. com; 🕙 Nov)

Fleadh Nua   Cultural
A lively traditional music festival with singing, dancing and workshops. (📞 065-682 4276; www.fleadhnua.com; 🕙 May)

Micho Russell Festival   Music
Held on the last weekend in February, this festival celebrates the work of a legendary Doolin musician and attracts top trad talent. (www.doolin-tourism.com; 🕙 Feb)

Fiddle player
MICHAEL KEVIN DALY/FUSE/GETTY IMAGES ©

to a splendid castle that abuts a theme park recreating an Irish village of yore, a double-act that draws in endless visitors. Groups – disgorged by leviathan buses –

Clare's Best Music Festival

Half the population of Miltown Malbay seems to be part of the annual **Willie Clancy Summer School** (065-708 4148; www.scoilsamhraidhwillieclancy.com; Jul), a tribute to a native son and one of Ireland's greatest pipers. The nine-day festival usually begins in the first or second week in July, when impromptu sessions occur day and night, the pubs are packed and Guinness is consumed by the barrel.

Workshops and classes underpin the event; don't be surprised to attend a recital with 40 noted fiddlers. Asked how such a huge affair has happened for almost four decades, a local who teaches fiddle said: 'No one knows, it just does.'

lay siege to Bunratty from April to October, retreating with all manner of tourist trash and well-fed from medieval banquets.

⊙ SIGHTS & ACTIVITIES

Bunratty Castle & Folk Park   Castle
Square, hulking and imposing Bunratty Castle is only the latest of several edifices to occupy its location beside the River Ratty. Vikings founded a settlement here in the 10th century, and later occupants included the Norman Thomas de Clare in the 1270s. The castle is accessed via a folk park: a reconstructed traditional Irish village with thatched cottages, smoke coiling from chimneys, a forge and working blacksmith, weavers, post office, pub, children's play zones and small cafe. (www.shannonheritage. com; adult/child €15/9; 9am-5.30pm, last admission 4.15pm;)

Traditional Irish Night   Banquet
Traditional Irish nights lift the roof of a corn barn in the folk park. Red-haired servers dish out traditional chow amid music and dancing while servings of wine can get you in the mood for the singalong. (061-360 788; adult/child €48.70/24.75; 7-9.30pm Apr-Oct)

Bunratty Medieval Banquet Castle   Banquet
You can skip the high-jinks in the corn barn for a feisty medieval banquet, replete with harp-playing maidens, court jesters and meaty medieval food, washed down with goblets of mead – a kind of honey wine. The banquets are popular with groups, so book well ahead; you can often find savings online. (061-360 788; adult/child €58.45/29.25; 5.30pm & 8.45pm Apr-Oct, schedule varies Nov-Mar)

Killaloe & Ballina

Facing each other across a narrow channel, Killaloe and Ballina are really one destination, even if they have different personalities (and counties). A fine 1770 13-arch, one-lane bridge spans the river, linking the pair. You can walk it in five minutes or drive it in about 20 (a Byzantine system of lights controls traffic).

Killaloe (Cill Da Lúa) is picturesque Clare at its finest. It lies on the western banks of lower Loch Deirgeirt, the southern extension of Lough Derg, where the lough narrows at one of the principal crossings of the River Shannon. The village lies snugly against the Slieve Bernagh Hills that rise abruptly to the west. The Arra Mountains create a fine balance to the east and all of Lough Derg is at hand.

Not as quaint as Killaloe, Ballina (Béal an Átha) is in County Tipperary and has some of the better pubs and restaurants. It lies at the end of a scenic drive from Nenagh along Lough Derg on the R494.

Kilkee

Kilkee's wide beach and fine, powdery sand is thronged with daytrippers and holiday-makers in warmer months. The sweeping semicircular bay has high cliffs on the north end and weathered rocks to the south, with

PHB.CZ (RICHARD SEMIK)/SHUTTERSTOCK ©

Loop Head Lighthouse

fantastic walks at either extremity. The waters are highly tidal, with wide-open sandy expanses replaced by pounding waves in just a few hours.

🛈 GETTING THERE & AWAY

Bus Éireann has three to four buses daily to Kilkee from Limerick (€22, two hours) and Ennis (€16.50, 1¼ hours). Both routes pass through Kilrush.

Loop Head

As you approach along the R487, sea begins to appear on both flanks as land tapers to a narrow shelf. On a clear day, Loop Head (Ceann Léime), Clare's southernmost point, has gob-smacking views south to the Dingle Peninsula crowned by Mt Brandon (951m), and north to the Aran Islands and Galway Bay. Bracing walks and a long hiking trail runs along the cliffs to Kilkee.

The working **Loop Head Lighthouse** (Kilbaha; admission €5; ⊙10am-5pm May-Sep), complete with Fresnel lens, is the punctuation on the point. On the northern side of

the cliff near the point, a dramatic crevice has been cleaved from the coastal cliffs where you'll first hear and then see a teeming bird breeding area. Guillemots, chough and razorbills are among the squawkers nesting in rocky niches.

The often-deserted wilds of the head are perfect for exploration, but be extra careful near the cliff edge. **Bog Road Bike Tours** (📞086 278 0161; www.bogroadbiketours.com; tours €20-35) cycles laneways denied to cars around Loop Head; bikes and equipment can be rented for a small extra fee. **Long Way Round** (📞086 409 9624; www.thelong wayround.ie; €20) has historical and nature tours led by noted guide Laura Foley.

Kilkee to Lahinch

Doonbeg

Doonbeg (An Dún Beag) is a tiny seaside village about halfway between Kilkee and Quilty. Another Spanish Armada ship, the *San Esteban,* was wrecked on 20 September 1588 near the mouth of the River Doonbeg. The survivors were later executed at

Surfer near the Cliffs of Moher

Spanish Point. The surviving little 16th-century castle tower next to the graceful stone bridge over the Doonbeg River is the sad remains of Doonbeg Castle.

White Strand (Trá Bán) is a quiet beach, 0.5km long and backed by dunes. It's north of town and hard to miss, as it's now been surrounded by the Doonbeg Golf Club. From the public car park, you follow a break in the dunes to a perfect sweep of sand.

A long 2km stretch of sand further to the north of White Strand, Doughmore Bay is popular with horse riders and locals walking their dogs. Doonbeg also has some decent surfing for those who want to get away from the crowds in Lahinch.

✖ EATING

Morrissey's   Seafood €
Opposite the remains of Doonbeg Castle, this old pub is a stylish coastal haven, with six rooms featuring king-size beds and large soaking tubs. The pub's restaurant is renowned for its casual but enticing seafood, from fish and chips to succulent

local crab claws. Outside there's a terrace overlooking the river. (☎065-905 5304; www. morrisseysdoonbeg.com; Main St; ⊗Mar-Oct; @ 🗢)

Miltown Malbay

A classically friendly place in the chatty Irish way, Miltown Malbay has a thriving music scene. Every year it hosts the Willie Clancy Summer School, one of Ireland's great traditional music events.

✖ EATING

Old Bake House   Irish €
In a region awash with fantastic seafood chowder, some of the best is at the Old Bake House, where delightful seafood and classic Irish and international dishes can be enjoyed in a smart yet homely environment. There's blackboard menus on the walls, tapas in the evening and live music on Fridays from 7pm. (www.theoldbakehouse. ie; Main St; mains €5-15; ⊗noon-9pm, to 10pm Fri & Sat)

🍸 DRINKING & NIGHTLIFE

O'Friel's Bar (Lynch's; The Square) is one of a couple of genuine old-style places with occasional trad music sessions. The other is the dapper **Hillery's** (Main St).

ℹ️ GETTING THERE & AWAY

Bus Éireann service is paltry. Expect one or two buses Monday to Saturday north and south along the coast and inland to Ennis.

Lahinch

Coming round the headland on the N67 from Milton Malbay, the sweeping bay at Lahinch is quite a sight. Steeped in the strong aromas of ocean salt and seaweed, this old holiday town is one of the centres of Ireland's hot surfing scene. Surf schools and stores cluster near the seafront, like surfers waiting for the perfect set.

🍴 EATING

Atlantic Hotel   Irish €€

This old-fashioned and lovely town-centre classic has a charming air, from its welcoming reception rooms and cosy bar to its restaurant offering traditional food prepared using local produce. (📞065-708 1049; www.atlantichotel.ie; Main St; @)

Barrtrá Seafood Restaurant   Seafood €€

This rural repose 3.5km south of Lahinch offers views over pastures to the sea from a lovely country cottage, surrounded by pretty kitchen gardens. The lavish €35 set meal is great value. (📞065-708 1280; www. barrtra.com; Miltown Malbay Rd; mains €15-28; 🕐noon-2pm & 6-10pm Thu-Sat Mar-May, Thu-Mon Jun-Oct)

ℹ️ GETTING THERE & AWAY

Bus Éireann runs two to four buses daily through Lahinch on the Doolin–Ennis/Limerick routes and one or two Monday to Saturday south along the coast to Doonbeg in summer.

🔭 Clare's Other Cliffs

On the way to and from Loop Head, take in the jaw-dropping sea visuals and drama of the sensational cliffs along the coast roads. Heading to Loop Head from Carrigaholt, drive south down Church St for around 2km till you reach the junction, then turn right along the L2002. This scenic route is the Coast Rd, hugging the coastline and offering splendid panoramas of the sea, running through the village of Rhinevilla and eventually rejoining the R487 at Kilbaha. Heading west from Loop Head, drive along the R487 to Cavan and then take a left along the Coast Rd (L2000) and follow the signs, making your way to Kilkee. You'll rejoin the R487 but can head north again along small roads north from just after either Oughterard or Cross for stunning vistas of soaring coastal cliffs.

Cliffs at Loop Head
PETER UNGER/GETTY IMAGES ©

The Burren

The Burren region is rocky and windswept, an apt metaphor for the hard-scrabble lives of those who've eked out an existence here. Stretching across northern Clare, from the Atlantic coast to Kinvara in County Galway, it's a unique striated limestone landscape that was shaped beneath ancient seas, then forced high and dry by a great geological cataclysm.

This is not the green Ireland of postcards. But there are wildflowers in spring, giving the 560-sq-km Burren brilliant, if ephemeral, colour amid the arid beauty.

Guided Walks

Burren Guided Walks & Hikes   Walking Tour
Long-time guide Mary Howard leads groups on a variety of rambles, off-the-beaten-track hikes and rugged routes. (☏065-707 6100, 087 244 6807; www.burrenguidedwalks.com)

Burren Wild Tours   Walking Tour
John Connolly offers a broad range of walks, from gentle to more strenuous. (☏087 877 9565; www.burrenwalks.com)

Heart of Burren Walks   Walking Tour
Local Burren author Tony Kirby leads walks and archaeology hikes. (☏065-682 7707; www.heartofburrenwalks.com)

Hikers, Poulnabrone dolmen portal tomb, Burren
HOLGER LEUE/GETTY IMAGES ©

There are also intriguing villages to enjoy. These include the music hub of Doolin on the west coast, a inland and Ballyvaughan in the north, on the shores of Galway Bay.

Flora & Fauna

Soil may be scarce on the Burren, but the small amount that gathers in the cracks is well drained and rich in nutrients. This, together with the mild Atlantic climate, supports an extraordinary mix of Mediterranean, Arctic and alpine plants. Of Ireland's native wildflowers, 75% are found here, including 24 species of beautiful orchids,

the creamy-white burnet rose, the little starry flowers of mossy saxifrage and the magenta-coloured bloody cranesbill.

The Burren is a stronghold of Ireland's most elusive mammal, the rather shy weasel-like pine marten. Badgers, foxes and even stoats are common throughout the region. Otters and seals haunt the shores around Bell Harbour, New Quay and Finavarra Point.

✪ ACTIVITIES

The Burren is a walker's paradise. The bizarre, beautiful landscape, numerous trails and many ancient sites are best explored on foot. 'Green roads' are the old highways of the Burren, crossing hills and valleys to some of the remotest corners of the region. Many of these unpaved ways were built during the Famine as part of relief work, while some date back possibly thousands of years. They're now used mostly by hikers and the occasional farmer. Some are signposted.

The Burren Way is a 123km network of marked hiking routes throughout the region.

Guided nature, history, archaeology and wilderness walks are great ways to appreciate the Burren. Typically the cost of the walks averages €10 to €25 and there are many options, including individual trips. Confirm times and walk locations.

ⓘ GETTING THERE & AWAY

A few Bus Éireann (www.buseireann.ie) services pass through the Burren. The main routes include one from Limerick and Ennis to Corofin, Ennistymon, Lahinch, Liscannor, the Cliffs of Moher, Doolin and Lisdoonvarna; another connects Galway with Ballyvaughan, Lisdoonvarna and Doolin. Usually there are one to four buses daily, with the most in summer.

Doolin

Doolin gets plenty of press and chatter as a centre of Irish traditional music, owing to a trio of pubs that have sessions throughout the year. It's also known for its setting – 6km north of the Cliffs of Moher and down near the ever-unsettled sea, the land is wind-blown, with huge rocks exposed by the long-vanished topsoil.

Given all its attributes, you might be surprised when you realise that Doolin as it's known barely exists. Rather, you might be forgiven for exclaiming, 'There's no there here!' For Doolin is really three infinitesimally small neighbouring villages. Fisherstreet is right on the water, Doolin itself is about 1km east on the little River Aille, and Roadford is another 1km east. None has more than a handful of buildings, which results in a scattered appearance, without a centre.

Still, the area is hugely popular with music-seeking tourists. There are scores of good-value hostels and B&Bs spread about the rough landscape. It's also a place to get boats to the offshore Aran Islands.

🛎 Where to Stay

Ennis is a great base from which to explore: it has a great variety of accommodation, with modest B&Bs on most of the main roads into town, some an easy walk to the centre – and Shannon Airport is less than 30 minutes' drive to the south. There are also some great B&B and hotel options scattered throughout the county which allow you to be closer to sights of interest; traditional music is the main drawcard in Miltown Malbay, while stunning coastal scenery abounds in Lahinch.

🎧 DRINKING & NIGHTLIFE

Doolin's rep is largely based on music. A lot of musicians live in the area, and they have a symbiotic relationship with the tourists: each desires the other and each year things grow a little larger.

Cottage, Doolin

Croagh Patrick

St Patrick couldn't have picked a better spot for a pilgrimage than this conical mountain (also known as 'the Reek'). It was on Croagh Patrick that Ireland's patron saint fasted for 40 days and nights, and where he reputedly banished venomous snakes. Climbing the 772m holy mountain is an act of penance for thousands of pilgrims on the last Sunday of July (Reek Sunday). The truly contrite take the original 40km route from **Ballintubber Abbey** (094-903 0934; www.ballintubberabbey.ie; Ballintubber; 9am-midnight, tours 10am-5pm Jul & Aug) FREE, Tóchar Phádraig (Patrick's Causeway), and ascend the mountain barefoot.

The main trail ascends the mountain from the car park in Murrisk. You can rent walking sticks for €1.50 for the steep trail which is rocky in parts. The average return trip takes three to four hours and it gets crowded on sunny weekends. At the summit you'll find a 1905 whitewashed church and a 9th-century oratory fountain. Views are sublime.

Opposite the car park is the National Famine Memorial, a spine-chilling sculpture of a three-masted ghost ship wreathed in swirling skeletons, commemorating the lives lost on so-called 'coffin ships' employed to help people escape the Famine. A path down past the memorial leads to the scant remains of Murrisk Abbey, founded by the O'Malleys in 1547.

Murrisk is 8km southwest of Westport. The best way to get here is along the lovely bayside bike and walking path. Otherwise there are daily buses.

O'Connor's
Pub

Right on the river as it runs into the sea, this sprawling favourite packs them in and has a rollicking atmosphere when the music is in full swing. On some summer nights you won't squeeze inside. (www.gusoconnors doolin.com; Fisherstreet; 9.30am-midnight)

MacDiarmada's
Pub

Also known as McDermott's, this simple red-and-white traditional pub is a rowdy favourite. The inside is pretty basic, as is the menu of sandwiches and roasts; there's an outside area. (www.mcdermottspubdoolin. com; Roadford; bar 11am-11.30pm, kitchen 9am-9.30pm)

🛈 GETTING THERE & AWAY

BOAT
Doolin is one of two ferry departure points to the Aran Islands from mid-March to October. Sailings are often cancelled due to high seas or tides which make the small dock inaccessible. The boats also offer Cliffs of Moher tours (about €15 for one hour) which are best done late in the afternoon when the light is from the west.

Doolin 2 Aran Ferries (065-707 5949; www. doolin2aranferries.com; Doolin Pier; mid-Mar–Oct) Has a full schedule to the Aran islands plus Cliffs of Moher cruises.

O'Brien Line (065-707 5618; www.obrienline. com) Usually has the most sailings to the Arans; also offers cliff cruises and combo tickets.

BUS
Bus Éireann runs one to four buses daily to Doolin from Ennis (€12, 1½ hours) and Limerick (€18, 2½ hours) via Corofin, Lahinch and the Cliffs of Moher. Buses also go to Galway (€16, 1½ hours, one or two daily) via Ballyvaughan.

In summer, various backpacker shuttles often serve Doolin from Galway and other points in Clare. These are amply marketed in hostels.

Ballyvaughan & Around

Something of a hub for the otherwise dispersed charms of the Burren, Ballyvaughan (Baile Uí Bheacháin) sits between the hard land of the hills and a quiet leafy corner of Galway Bay. It makes an excellent base for visiting the northern reaches of the Burren.

◎ SIGHTS & ACTIVITIES

Aillwee Caves   Caves
The caves were carved out by water some
two million years ago. The main cave pen-
etrates 600m into the mountain, widening
into larger caverns, one with its own waterfall. Near the entrance are the remains of
a brown bear, extinct in Ireland for more
than 10,000 years. Often crowded in
summer, the site has a cafe, and a large
raptor exhibit with captive hawks, owls and
more, accessible on a joint ticket with the
caves or as a standalone. (www.aillweecave.
ie; off R480; combined ticket adult/child €16/9;
⊙10am-5pm, to 6.30pm Jul & Aug)

⊗ EATING & ENTERTAINMENT

Gregan's Castle
Hotel   Modern Irish €€€
This hidden Clare gem is housed in a grand
estate dating to the 19th century, some
6km south of Ballyvaughan at Corkscrew
Hill. Inventive fresh fare sourced locally is
served in the restaurant. (☏065-707 7005;
www.gregans.ie; N67; 🕾)

Ólólainn   Pub
A tiny family-run place on the left as you
head out to the pier, Ólólainn (o-*loch*-lain)
is the place for a timeless moment or two
in old-fashioned snugs. The old whiskey
bottles in the window offer clues to the
amazing selection of rare tipples within.
(Coast Rd)

❶ GETTING THERE & AWAY

Bus Éireann runs one to three buses daily from
Galway through Ballyvaughan and around Black
Head to Lisdoonvarna and Doolin.

THE ANTRIM COAST

The Antrim Coast

Northern Ireland's spectacular north coast is a giant geology classroom. The patient workmanship of the ocean has laid bare the black basalt and white chalk that underlie much of County Antrim, and dissected the rocks into a scenic extravaganza of sea stacks, pinnacles, cliffs and caves. This mystical landscape's extraordinary rock formations, ruined castles and wooded glens have made the region an atmospheric backdrop for the TV series Game of Thrones, *with numerous filming locations here.*

The north coast of County Antrim from Ballycastle west to Portrush is known as the Causeway Coast, one of the most impressively scenic stretches of coastline in all of Ireland. Its grand geological centrepiece is the spectacular rock formation known as the Giant's Causeway, a Unesco World Heritage site.

☑ In This Section

❶ Arriving in the Antrim Coast

As well as the seasonal **Antrim Coaster** (p172) and **Causeway Rambler** (p172) services, bus 217 links Ballycastle with Ballymena where you can connect to Belfast.

Bus 172 from Ballycastle to Coleraine stops at the Giant's Causeway year-round. From Coleraine, trains run to Belfast.

★ Classic Photo
Sunset in spring and autumn is the best time for photos of the Giant's Causeway (p162).

ATLANTIC OCEAN

0 20 km
0 10 miles

Culdaff

Carndonagh
Gleneely

Inishowen Peninsula

Moville

DONEGAL

Lough Foyle

Muff

Limavady

Claudy

Dunnamanagh

TYRONE

Dungiven

Derry/Londonderry

Garvagh

LONDONDERRY

Kilrea

Portglenone

Maghera

Lough Neagh

Portrush

Portstewart

Dunluce Castle

Coleraine

Bushmills

Ballymoney

Giant's Causeway

Dunseverick

Rathlin Island

Carrick-a-Rede Rope Bridge

Murlough Bay

Ballycastle

Armoy

ANTRIM

Waterfoot

Glenariff Forest Park

Clogh

Glenarm

Ballymena

Broughshane

Cushendun

Cushendall

North Channel

River Main

Derry/Londonderry Map (p178)

From left: murals, Derry/Londonderry (p177); Murlough Bay (p174); Giant's Causeway Visitor Experience (p164)

PETER UNGER/GETTY IMAGES ©

Giant's Causeway

This spectacular rock formation – a national nature reserve and Northern Ireland's only Unesco World Heritage Site – is one of Ireland's most impressive and atmospheric landscape features.

Great For...

☑ **Don't Miss**
The cliff-top views from the Chimney Tops headland.

When you first see it you'll understand why the ancients believed the causeway was not a natural feature. The vast expanse of regular, closely packed, hexagonal stone columns beneath the waves looks for all the world like the handiwork of giants.

Visiting the Giant's Causeway itself is free of charge but you pay to use the car park on a combined ticket with the Giant's Causeway Visitor Experience (p164); parking-only tickets aren't available.

The Making of the Causeway

The story goes that the Irish giant Finn McCool built the Causeway so he could cross the sea to fight the Scottish giant Benandonner. Benandonner pursued Finn back across the Causeway, but in

DANIELE MARCHEGIANI/GETTY IMAGES ©

Giant's
Causeway

Portballintrae

ℹ️ Need to Know

www.nationaltrust.org.uk; ⊘ dawn-dusk; FREE

✕ Take A Break

There's a cafe in the visitor centre, but the nearby Nook (p171) offers a more convivial atmosphere.

★ Top Tip

Try to visit midweek or out of season to experience the causeway at its most evocative.

turn took fright and fled back to Scotland, ripping up the causeway as he went. All that remains are its ends – the Giant's Causeway in Ireland, and the island of Staffa in Scotland (which has similar rock formations).

The more prosaic scientific explanation is that the causeway rocks were formed 60 million years ago, when a thick layer of molten basaltic lava flowed along a valley in the existing chalk beds. As the lava flow cooled and hardened – from the top and bottom surfaces inward – it contracted, creating a pattern of hexagonal cracks at right angles to the cooling surfaces (think of mud contracting and cracking in a hexagonal pattern as a lake bed dries out). As solidification progressed towards the centre of the flow, the cracks spread down

from the top and up from the bottom, until the lava was completely solid. Erosion has cut into the lava flow, and the basalt has split along the contraction cracks, creating the hexagonal columns.

Exploring the Causeway

From the car park, it's an easy 10- to 15-minute walk downhill on a tarmac road (wheelchair accessible) to the Giant's Causeway itself (a shuttle bus also plies the route). However, a much more interesting approach on foot is to follow the cliff-top path northeast for 2km to the **Chimney Tops** headland, which has an excellent view of the Causeway and the coastline to the west, including Inishowen and Malin Head.

This pinnacled promontory was bombarded by ships of the Spanish Armada in 1588, who thought it was Dunluce Castle, and the wreck of the Spanish galleon

Girona lies just off the tip of the headland. Return towards the car park and about halfway back descend the **Shepherd's Steps** (signposted) to a lower-level footpath that leads down to the Causeway. Allow 1½ hours for the round trip.

Alternatively, you can visit the Causeway first, then follow the lower coastal path as far as the **Amphitheatre** viewpoint at Port Reostan, passing impressive rock formations such as the **Organ** (a stack of vertical basalt columns resembling organ pipes), and return by climbing the Shepherd's Steps.

You can also follow the cliff-top path east as far as Dunseverick or beyond.

The superb, ecofriendly **Giant's Causeway Visitor Experience** (028-2073 1855; www.nationaltrust.org; adult/child with parking £9/4.50, without parking £7/3.25; 9am-7pm Apr-Sep, to 6pm Feb, Mar & Oct, to 5pm Nov-Jan;) , built into the hillside and walled in by tall black basalt slabs that mimic the basalt columns of the Causeway, houses an exhibition explaining the geology of the region, as well as a tourist information desk, restaurant and shop. It's cheaper if you arrive on foot, bicycle or by public transport; admission includes an audioguide.

Wreck of the Girona

The little bay 1km to the northeast of the Giant's Causeway is called Port na Spaniagh – Bay of the Spaniards. It was here, in October 1588, that the *Girona* – a ship of the Spanish Armada – was driven onto the rocks by a storm.

The *Girona* had escaped the famous confrontation with Sir Walter Raleigh's fleet in the English Channel but, along with many other fleeing Spanish ships, had been driven north around Scotland and Ireland by bad weather. Though designed for a crew of 500, when she struck the rocks she was loaded with 1300 people – mostly survivors gathered from other shipwrecks – including the cream of the Spanish aristocracy. Barely a dozen survived.

Somhairle Buidhe (Sorley Boy) MacDonnell (1505–90), the constable of nearby Dunluce Castle, salvaged gold and cannons from the wreck, and used the money to extend and modernise his fortress – cannons from the ship can still be seen on the castle's landward wall. But it wasn't until 1968 that the wreck site was excavated by a team of archaeological divers. They recovered magnificent treasures of gold, silver and precious stones, as well as everyday sailors' possessions, which are now on display in Belfast's Ulster Museum (p234).

ⓘ Need to Know

As well as the seasonal Antrim Coaster (p172) and Causeway Rambler (p172) services and Giant's Causeway & Bushmills Railway (p169), bus 172 from Ballycastle (£4.40, 30 minutes, eight daily Monday to Friday, three Saturday and Sunday) to Coleraine (£2.80, 25 minutes) and Bushmills (£2.30, five minutes) stops here year-round. From Coleraine, trains run to Belfast or Derry.

White Park Bay

Causeway Coast Way Walking Tour

This spectacular stretch of the Causeway Coast Way is one of the finest coastal walks in Ireland. Be prepared: parts of the walk follow a narrow, muddy path along the top of unfenced cliffs, and can be dangerous in wet and/or windy weather. High tides can temporarily block the way at either end of White Park Bay; check tide times in advance.

Distance: 16.5km
Duration: 4–6 hours

Start Carrick-a-Rede Rope Bridge

① Carrick-a-Rede Rope Bridge

After testing your nerve on the Carrick-a-Rede Rope Bridge (p171), take the path from its Larrybane car park along a cliff top with views of Sheep Island, then cut inland. At Ballintoy church, turn right and follow the road down to Ballintoy Harbour.

② White Park Bay

Continue along the shoreline past a series of conical sea stacks and arches, and scramble around the foot of a limestone crag to reach the 2km-long sandy sweep of White Park Bay. The going here is easiest at low tide, when you can walk on the firm sand.

③ Portbradden

At the far end of the bay, scramble over rocks and boulders at the bottom of a high limestone cliff for 250m (slippery in places) to Portbradden.

④ Dunseverick

Beyond Portbradden white limestone gives way to black basalt, and the path threads through a natural tunnel in the rocks before weaving around several rocky coves. At tiny Dunseverick Harbour you follow a minor road for 200m before descending steps on the right. The path then wanders along the grassy foreshore, rounds a headland and crosses a footbridge above a waterfall before reaching Dunseverick Castle.

⑤ Hamilton's Seat

From here the often-narrow, cliff-top path climbs steadily, passing an old salmon fishery (the little rusty-roofed cottage on

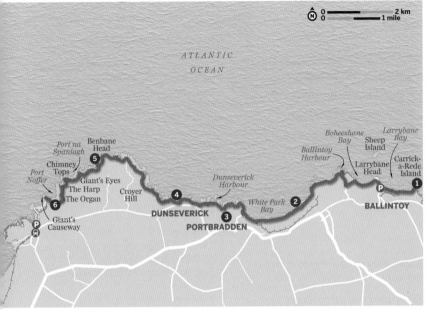

JASON FRIEND PHOTOGRAPHY LTD/GETTY IMAGES ©

the shore far below). Near Benbane Head, the walk's highest and most northerly point, a wooden bench marks the viewpoint known as Hamilton's Seat (after 18th-century clergyman and amateur geologist William Hamilton). Soak up the spectacular panorama of 100m-high sea cliffs, stacks and pinnacles stretching away to the west, before you set off on the final stretch.

⑥ Shepherd's Steps

Descend the Shepherd's Steps (signposted), about 1km before the Giant's Causeway Visitor Experience to reach the Giant's Causeway (p162).

Finish Giant's Causeway

📷 Top Five Photo Opps

- Giant's Causeway (p162)
- Dunluce Castle (p170)
- White Park Bay (p170)
- Carrick-a-Rede Rope Bridge (p171)
- Torr Head Scenic Road (p174)

✕ Take a Break

Bring a picnic lunch with you and stop at one of the viewpoints along the way; if the weather isn't too wild, Dunseverick Castle is the perfect spot for a scenic meal.

🍽 **Top Five**
Places to Eat

○ Bushmills Inn (p170)

○ Morton's Fish & Chips (p173)

○ 55 Degrees North (p169)

○ Cellar Restaurant (p173)

○ The Nook (p171)

Portrush

The seaside resort of Portrush (Port Rois) bursts at the seams with holidaymakers in high season and, not surprisingly, many of its attractions are focused unashamedly on good old-fashioned family fun. However, it's also one of Ireland's top surfing centres and home to the North's most prestigious golf clubs.

◎ SIGHTS & ACTIVITIES

Curran Strand   Beach

Portrush's main attraction is the beautiful sandy beach of Curran Strand that stretch-es for 3km to the east of the town, ending at the scenic chalk cliffs of White Rocks.

Royal Portrush Golf Club   Golf

Spectacularly sited alongside the Atlantic at the town's eastern edge, 1888-founded Royal Portrush is the only golf club in Ireland to have hosted the Open Championship, in 1951, which it will host again in 2019. It's home to two courses, the par 72 Dunluce, with its water's-edge White Rock (5th) and ravine-set Calamity (14th) holes, and the par 70 Valley. (📞028-7082 2311; www.royalportrushgolfclub.com; Dunluce; green fees weekday/weekend £160/180)

✴ EATING

Arcadia   Cafe £

A Portrush landmark, this 1920s art-deco pavilion houses a breezy beach cafe on the ground floor, serving big breakfasts, bagels, salads and ice cream for a post-surf refuel, and a free art gallery on the upper floor, which also hosts workshops and classes (yoga, painting etc). (www.arcadiaportrush. co.uk; East Strand; dishes £3-6; ⏰9am-6pm Apr-Sep, to 5pm Oct-Mar)

Arcadia

DUNE PRINTS BY PETER HOLLOWAY/GETTY IMAGES ©

55 Degrees North International £££
Floor-to-ceiling windows allow you to soak
up a spectacular panorama of sand and
sea from this stylish restaurant. The food
concentrates on clean, simple flavours.
Downstairs, licensed Café North (lunch
mains £6-8, dinner mains £10-14; 9am-9pm
Mon, Tue & Sat, to 6pm Wed-Fri Easter-Sep,
reduced hours Oct-Easter) has a beach-facing
terrace. (028-7082 2811; www.55-north.
com; 1 Causeway St; mains £10-19; 12.30-3pm
& 5-9pm Mon-Fri, noon-10pm Sat, noon-8.30pm
Sun;)

ⓘ GETTING THERE & AROUND

Bus The bus terminal is near the Dunluce Centre.
Bus 140A and 140B link Portrush with Portstewart (£2.30, 10 minutes, every 20 minutes
Monday to Saturday, five Sunday) and Coleraine
(£2.70, 20 minutes). It's also served by seasonal
Antrim Coaster (p172) and Causeway Rambler
(p172) buses.

Train The train station is just south of the harbour. Portrush is served by trains from Coleraine
(£2.30, 12 minutes, hourly Monday to Saturday,
10 Sunday), where there are connections to
Belfast or Derry.

Bushmills

The small town of Bushmills has long been
a place of pilgrimage for connoisseurs of
Irish whiskey.

◎ SIGHTS & ACTIVITIES

Old Bushmills Distillery Distillery
Bushmills is the world's oldest legal
distillery, having been granted a licence by
King James I in 1608. Bushmills whiskey is
made with Irish barley and water from St
Columb's Rill, a tributary of the River Bush,
and matured in oak barrels. During ageing,
the alcohol content drops from around
60% to 40%; the spirit lost through evapo-
ration is known as 'the angels' share'. After
the tour, you can enjoy a free sample of
your choice from Bushmills' range. (028-
2073 3218; www.bushmills.com; Distillery Rd; tour

👍 Portstewart Strand

Just 8km southwest of Portrush is the
broad, 2.5km beach of Portstewart
Strand.
   Bang on the beach, a National Trust–
owned wooden shack houses one of
Northern Ireland's hottest restaurants,
Harry's Shack (028-7083 1783; Portstewart Strand; mains £10-18; 10.30am-
4pm & 5-9pm Tue-Sat, 10.30am-7pm Sun).
Harry's uses fruit, vegetables and
herbs from its own organic farm and
local meat and seafood in simple but
sensational dishes like buttermilk-
battered, saltwater-cured pollock,
brioche burgers, and spiced whitebait
served in a newspaper cone. BYO. Book
way ahead for lunch and dinner.
WWW.DEIRDREGREGG.COM/GETTY IMAGES ©

adult/child £7.50/4; 9.15am-5pm Mon-Sat,
noon-5pm Sun Mar-Oct, 10am-5pm Mon-Sat,
noon-5pm Sun Nov-Feb)

**Giant's Causeway
& Bushmills Railway** Heritage Railway
Brought from a private line on the shores
of Lough Neagh, the narrow-gauge line and
locomotives (two steam and one diesel)
follow the route of a 19th-century tourist
tramway for 3km from Bushmills to below
the Giant's Causeway Visitor Experience.
Seasonal trains run hourly between 11am
and 5.30pm, departing on the hour from
the Causeway, on the half-hour from
Bushmills, daily in July and August, and on
weekends only from Easter to June and
September and October. (028-2073 2844;

Dunluce Castle

The ruins of **Dunluce Castle** (87 Dunluce Rd; adult/child £5/3; ⊙10am-4pm, last admission 30min before closing) perch atop a dramatic basalt crag 5km east of Portrush, a one-hour walk away along the coastal path. A narrow bridge leads from the mainland courtyard across a dizzying gap to the main part of the fortress. Below, a path leads down from the gatehouse to the Mermaid's Cave beneath the castle crag. All coastal buses stop at here.

In the 16th and 17th centuries the castle was the seat of the MacDonnell family (the earls of Antrim from 1620), who built a Renaissance-style manor house within the walls. Part of the castle, including the kitchen, collapsed into the sea in 1639, taking seven servants and that night's dinner with it.

RAINBOW79/GETTY IMAGES ©

www.freewebs.com/giantscausewayrailway; adult/child return £5/3)

⊗ EATING

Bushmills Inn　　　Irish **££**
Set in the old 17th-century stables of the Bushmills Inn, this haven has intimate wooden booths and blazing fires, and uses fresh Ulster produce in dishes like onion and Guinness soup, haunch of venison, and traditional Dalriada Cullen Skink (wood-smoked haddock poached in cream, with poached eggs and new potatoes). Book

ahead. (9 Dunluce Rd; lunch mains £10-15, dinner mains £12.50-23.50; ⊙noon-9.30pm Mon-Sat, 12.30-9pm Sun; 🛜)

Tartine　　　Irish, French **££**
Inside a former pub, with bare boards, exposed stone and glowing fire, Tartine's three interconnecting dining rooms are adorned with Irish art. Local produce is given an inspired French twist: crab crème brûlée; roast pork with cassoulet; and oven-baked rice pudding with date and honey compote. (📞028-2073 1044; www.distillersarms.com; 140 Main St; mains £11-22; ⊙5-9pm Wed-Sat, noon-8.30pm Sun)

Giant's Causeway to Ballycastle

The Antrim coast is at its most scenic between the Giant's Causeway and Bally-castle – a section known as the Causeway Coast – with sea cliffs of contrasting black basalt and white chalk, rocky islands, picturesque little harbours and broad sweeps of sandy beach.

The main attractions can be reached by car or bus, but the 16.5km stretch between the Carrick-a-Rede car park and the Giant's Causeway is best enjoyed on a walk (p166), following the waymarked **Causeway Coast Way** (www.walkni.com).

About 9.5km east of the Giant's Causeway is the tiny seaside hamlet of **Portbrad-den**, with half a dozen harbourside houses. Visible from Portbradden and accessible via the next junction off the A2 is the spectacular **White Park Bay**, with its wide, sweeping sandy beach.

Some 3km further east is **Ballintoy** (Baile an Tuaighe). This pretty village tumbles down the hillside to a picture-postcard harbour, better known to *Game of Thrones* fans as the Iron Islands' Lordsports Harbour (among other scenes filmed here). The restored limekiln on the quayside once made quicklime using stone from the chalk cliffs and coal from Ballymoney.

DAVID SOANES PHOTOGRAPHY/GETTY IMAGES ©

Carrick-a-Rede Rope Bridge

⊚ SIGHTS

Carrick-a-Rede Rope Bridge   Bridge
This 20m-long, 1m-wide bridge of wire rope
spans the chasm between the sea cliffs and
the little island of Carrick-a-Rede, swaying
30m above the rock-strewn water. Crossing
the bridge is perfectly safe, but frightening
if you don't have a head for heights, especially if it's breezy (in high winds the bridge
is closed). From the island, views take in
Rathlin Island and Fair Head to the east.
There's a small National Trust information
centre and cafe at the car park. (www.
nationaltrust.org.uk; Ballintoy; adult/child
£5.90/3; ⊗9.30am-7.30pm Apr-Aug, to 6pm
late Feb-late Mar & Sep-late Oct, to 3.30pm late
Oct-late Feb)

⊗ EATING

Causeway Hotel   Irish £££
A stone's throw from the Giant's Causeway,
this 28-room National Trust–owned hotel is
an ideal base for exploring the coast early
or late in the day without the crowds. The
refurbished restaurant offers new takes on

*Sea cliffs of contrasting black
basalt and white chalk, and
broad sweeps of sandy beach...*

traditional dishes. Parking for guests and
diners at its restaurant is free. (☎028-9073
1210; www.thecausewayhotel.com; 40 Causeway
Rd; 🛜)

The Nook   Pub Food £
At the turn-off to the Giant's Causeway,
this 18th-century former schoolhouse is
now a cosy pub serving open sandwiches,
soup, chowder, Irish stew, scampi, fish and
chips and so on. Inside there are open fires;
outside, a wraparound terrace overlooks
the coast. If you're dining or drinking here,
you can use the free car park. (48 Causeway
Rd; mains £9-12.25; ⊗kitchen 11am-7pm)

ⓘ GETTING THERE & AWAY

Bus 172 between Ballycastle, Bushmills and
Coleraine (eight daily Monday to Friday, three
Saturday and Sunday) is the main, year-round
service along this coast, stopping at the Giant's

Ballintoy harbour (p170)

Causeway, Ballintoy and Carrick-a-Rede. The Antrim Coaster and Causeway Rambler buses cover the route in season.

Seasonal Bus Services

Antrim Coaster   Bus

The Antrim Coaster has two services in each direction on a seasonal schedule between Coleraine and Larne's bus station. Stops include Portstewart, Portrush, Bushmills, the Giants Causeway, Ballintoy, Ballycastle, Cushendun, Cushendall, Glenariff (Waterfoot), Glenarm and Larne's town-centre train station. (Bus 252; www.translink.co.uk; adult/child £9/4.50; ☺Easter, May bank holiday weekends, Jul & Aug; 🛜)

Causeway Rambler   Bus

Seasonal service linking Coleraine with Carrick-a-Rede car park via Portstewart, Portrush, Dunluce Castle, Bushmills, Giant's Causeway, Dunseverick Castle and Ballintoy. There are four services daily in April and May, and eight services daily from June to September. (Bus 402; www.translink.co.uk; adult/child £6.50/3.25; ☺Easter to Sep)

Ballycastle

The harbour town and holiday resort of Ballycastle (Baile an Chaisil) marks the eastern end of the Causeway Coast. It's a pretty town with a good bucket-and-spade beach. Apart from that, there's not a lot to see. Ferries to Rathlin Island depart from here.

◎ SIGHTS

Marconi Memorial   Monument

In the harbour car park, a plaque at the foot of a rock pinnacle commemorates the day in 1898 when Guglielmo Marconi's assistants contacted Rathlin Island by radio from Ballycastle to prove to Lloyds of London that wireless communication was a viable proposition. The idea was to send notice to London or Liverpool of ships arriving safely after a transatlantic crossing – most vessels on this route would have to pass through the channel north of Rathlin.

ALLYSTEWART/GETTY IMAGES ©

✖ EATING

Morton's Fish & Chips   Seafood £

Fish and chips don't come fresher: local
boats unload their daily catch right alongside this little harbourside hut. The cod,
haddock, sea bass, scallops, scampi, as
well as chips made from locally farmed
potatoes, see huge queues in summer
(expect to wait). Gluten-free options,
cooked in separate oil, are also available.
(The Harbour, Bayview Rd; fish £1.90-5.40, chips
£1.20-2.40; ☺3-8pm Mon-Thu, noon-9pm Fri &
Sat, 1-8pm Sun)

Cellar Restaurant   Irish ££

Down a flight of steps from the street,
this cosy little basement restaurant with
intimate wooden booths and a big slate
fireplace is a good place to sample Ulster
produce such as locally caught crab claws
grilled, Carrick-a-Rede salmon and Rathlin
Island lobster, along with Irish beef and
lamb. (☎028-2076 3037; www.cellarballycastle.
com; 11b The Diamond; mains £13-25; ☺noon-
10pm daily Jun-Aug, 5-9.30pm Sun-Fri, noon-
10pm Sat Sep-May)

ⓘ GETTING THERE & AWAY

The bus station is on Station Rd, just east of
the Diamond. Bus 217 links Ballycastle with
Ballymena (£6.70, 50 minutes, hourly Monday
to Friday, five Saturday) where you can connect
to Belfast.

Bus 172 goes along the coast to Coleraine
(£6.70, one hour, eight daily Monday to Friday,
three Saturday and Sunday) via Ballintoy, the
Giant's Causeway and Bushmills.

The seasonal Antrim Coaster also stops here.

Glens of Antrim

The northeastern corner of Antrim is a high
plateau of black basalt lava overlying beds
of white chalk. Along the coast, between
Cushendun (famed for its National Trust
Cornish-style cottages) and Glenarm, the

🐦 Rathlin Island

In spring and summer, rugged Rathlin
Island, 6km offshore from Ballycastle,
is home to hundreds of seals and thousands of nesting seabirds. An L-shaped
island just 6.5km long and 4km wide,
Rathlin is famous for the coastal scenery and bird life at **Kebble National
Nature Reserve** at its western end.

The RSPB's **Rathlin Seabird Centre**
(www.rspb.org.uk; ☺10am-4pm Apr-Aug)
FREE at Rathlin West lighthouse provides
stunning views of the neighbouring sea
stacks, thick with guillemots, kittiwakes,
razorbills and puffins from mid-April to
August.

The **Boathouse Visitor Centre**
(☎07708 869605; www.rathlincommunity.
org; ☺9.30am-12.30pm & 1-5pm Apr-Sep),
south of the harbour, details the history,
culture and ecology of the island.

Getting There & Around

A **ferry** (☎028-2076 9299; www.rathlinbal-
lycastleferry.com; adult/child/bicycle return
£12/6/3.30) operates daily from Ballycastle; advance booking is recommended. From April to mid-September there
are up to 10 crossings a day, half of
which are fast catamaran services (20
minutes), the rest are slower car ferries
(45 minutes); in winter the service is
reduced.

Only residents can take their car to
Rathlin (except for disabled drivers),
but nowhere on the island is more than
6km (about 1½ hours' walk) from the
ferry pier. **McGinn's** (☎028-2076 3451;
per adult/child £5/3) shuttles visitors between the ferry and Kebble Nature Reserve from April to August; contact the
company for other transport requests.

plateau has been dissected by a series of
scenic, glacier-gouged valleys known as the
Glens of Antrim.

👓 Torr Head Scenic Road

A few kilometres east of Ballycastle, a minor road signposted 'Scenic Route' branches north off the A2. This alternative route to Cushendun is not for the faint-hearted driver (nor for caravans), as it clings, precarious and narrow, to steep slopes high above the sea. Side roads lead off to the main points of interest. On a clear day, there are superb views across the sea to Scotland, from the Mull of Kintyre to the peaks of Arran.

The first turn-off ends at the National Trust car park at Coolanlough, the starting point for a waymarked 5km return hike to **Fair Head**. The second turn-off leads steeply down to **Murlough Bay**. From the parking area at the end of this road, you can walk north along the shoreline to some ruined miners' cottages (10 minutes); coal and chalk were once mined in the cliffs above, and burned in a limekiln (south of the car park) to make quicklime.

The third turn-off leads you past some ruined coastguard houses to the rocky headland of **Torr Head**, crowned with a 19th-century coastguard station (abandoned in the 1920s). This is Ireland's closest point to Scotland – the Mull of Kintyre is a mere 19km away across the North Channel. In late spring and summer, a fixed-net salmon fishery operates here. The ancient ice house beside the approach road was once used to store the catch.

Stone wall, Torr Head
MANUEL URREA PACHECO/GETTY IMAGES ©

Cushendun & Cushendall

The pretty seaside village of Cushendun is famous for its distinctive Cornish-style cottages, now owned by the National Trust. Built between 1912 and 1925 at the behest of the local landowner, Lord Cushendun, they were designed by Clough Williams-Ellis, the architect of Portmeirion in north Wales.

Cushendall is a holiday centre (and traffic bottleneck) at the foot of Glenbally-eamon, overlooked by the prominent flat-topped hill of Lurigethan.

◎ SIGHTS & ACTIVITIES

Cushendun has a sandy **beach**, various short **coastal walks** (outlined on an information board beside the car park), and some impressive **caves** – a *Game of Thrones* filming location – cut into the overhanging conglomerate sea cliffs south of the village (follow the trail around the far end of the holiday apartments south of the river mouth).

Some 6km north of the village on the A2 road to Ballycastle is **Loughareema**, also known as the Vanishing Lake. Three streams flow in but none flow out. The lough fills up to a respectable size (400m long and 6m deep) after heavy rain, but the water gradually drains away through fissures in the underlying limestone, leaving a dry lake bed.

The unusual red sandstone **Curfew Tower** at the central crossroads in Cushendall was built in 1817, based on a building the landowner had seen in China. It was originally a prison 'for the confinement of idlers and rioters'.

✕ EATING

Harry's Restaurant   Bistro ££
With its cosy lounge-bar atmosphere and friendly welcome, Harry's is a local institution, serving pub grub staples from noon to 6pm plus an à-la-carte evening menu that ranges from steak to lobster. (📞 028-2177

2022; http://harryscushendall.com; 10 Mill St; mains lunch £8-13, dinner £10-19; ⏱noon-10pm Easter-Sep, to 9pm Oct-Easter; 🛜)

ℹ GETTING THERE & AWAY

Bus 150 runs from Ballymena (£6.70, one hour, six daily Monday to Friday, four Saturday) to Cushendun via Glenariff Forest Park (£6.20, 40 minutes) and Cushendall (£6.30, 50 minutes).

The seasonal Antrim Coaster (p172) stops here.

Glenariff

About 9km south of Cushendun is the village of **Waterfoot**, with a 2km-long sandy beach. From here the A43 Ballymena road runs inland along Glenariff, the loveliest of Antrim's glens.

Glenariff Forest Park   Forest

At the head of the Glenariff Valley is Glenariff Forest Park, where the main attraction is **Ess-na-Larach Waterfall**, an 800m walk from the visitor centre. You can also walk to the waterfall from **Laragh Lodge** (📞028-

2175 8221; 120 Glen Rd; mains £8-12, 4-course Sun lunch £18; ⏱11am-9pm daily Mar-Oct, 11am-9pm Fri-Sun Nov-Feb), 600m downstream. Wonderful hikes in the park include a 10km circular trail. There are plans to build a caravan park here. (www.nidirect.gov.uk; car/motorcycle/pedestrian £5/2.50/2; ⏱10am-dusk)

You can reach Glenariff Forest Park on bus 150 from Cushendun (£4.20, 20 minutes, eight daily Monday to Friday,

Water wheel, Glenariff Forest Park

MNIETEQ/GETTY IMAGES ©

four Saturday) and Ballymena (£6.70, 30 minutes).

The seasonal Antrim Coaster (p172) stops at Waterfoot.

Glenarm

Delightful little Glenarm (Gleann Arma) is the oldest village in the glens.

◉ SIGHTS & ACTIVITIES

Take a stroll into the old village of neat Georgian houses (off the main road, immediately south of the river). Where the street opens into the broad expanse of Altmore St, look right to see the **Barbican Gate** (1682), the entrance to Glenarm Castle grounds.

Up steep Vennel St, turn left after the last house along the Layde Path to the **viewpoint**, which has a grand view of the village and the coast.

Glenarm Castle
& Walled Garden   Castle

Since 1750 Glenarm has been the family seat of the MacDonnell family; the present 14th Earl of Antrim lives in Glenarm Castle, hidden behind an impressive wall. The castle itself is closed to the public – except during the **Tulip Festival** on the May bank holiday weekend, and for two days in July when a **Highland Games** competition takes place – but you can visit the lovely **walled garden**. (www.glenarmcastle.com; walled garden adult/child £5/2.50; ⊙garden 10am-5pm Mon-Sat, 11am-5pm Sun May-Sep)

Steensons   Gallery

Watch craftspeople at work at Steensons, the designer-jewellery workshop that produces the jewellery worn in *Game of Thrones*. (You can't buy copyrighted *Game of Thrones* pieces, but you can buy similarly inspired designs.) (www.thesteensons.com; Toberwine St; ⊙9am-5pm Mon-Sat)

❶ GETTING THERE & AWAY

The seasonal Antrim Coaster (p172) stops in the village.

Glenarm foreshore

DESIGN PICS/SIC/GETTY IMAGES ©

Derry/Londonderry

Northern Ireland's second-largest city continues to flourish as an artistic and cultural hub. Derry's city centre was given a striking makeover for its year as the UK City of Culture 2013, with the new Peace Bridge, Ebrington Square, and the redevelopment of the waterfront and Guildhall area making the most of the city's splendid riverside setting.

There's lots of history to absorb here, along with the burgeoning live-music scene in the city's lively pubs.

◎ SIGHTS

◎ Walled City

Derry's walled city is Ireland's earliest example of town planning. It is thought to have been modelled on the French Renaissance town of Vitry-le-François, designed in 1545 by Italian engineer Hieronimo Marino; both are based on the grid plan of a Roman military camp, with two main streets at right angles to each other, and four city gates, one at either end of each street.

Completed in 1619, Derry's **city walls** (Map p178; www.derryswalls.com; ☾dawn-dusk) FREE are 8m high and 9m thick, with a circumference of about 1.5km, and are the only city walls in Ireland to survive almost intact.

Tower Museum   Museum
Head straight to the 5th floor of this award-winning museum inside a replica 16th-century tower house for a view from the top. Then work your way down through the excellent **Armada Shipwreck** exhibition, and the **Story of Derry**, where well-thought-out exhibits and audiovisuals lead you through the city's history from the founding of the monastery of St Colmcille (Columba) in the 6th century to the Battle of the Bogside in the late 1960s. Allow at least two hours here. (www.derrycity.gov.uk/museums; Union Hall Pl; adult/child £4/2; ☾10am-6pm)

St Columb's Cathedral   Cathedral
Built between 1628 and 1633 from the same grey-green schist as the city walls, this was the first post-Reformation church to be erected in Britain and Ireland, and is Derry's oldest surviving building. In the **porch** (under the spire, by the St Columb's Court entrance) you can see the original foundation stone of 1633 that records the cathedral's completion. The smaller stone inset comes from the original church built here in 1164. (www.stcolumbscathedral.org; 17 London St; admission by donation; ☾9am-5pm Mon-Sat)

◎ Outside the Walls

Guildhall   Notable Building
Standing just outside the city walls, the neo-Gothic Guildhall was originally built in 1890, then rebuilt after a fire in 1908. Its fine stained-glass windows were presented by the London Livery companies, and its clock tower was modelled on London's Big Ben. Inside, there's a historical exhibition on the Plantation of Ulster, and a tourist information point. (☏028-7137 6510; www.derrycity.gov.uk/Guildhall; Guildhall Sq; ☾10am-5.30pm) FREE

◎ Bogside

The Bogside district, to the west of the walled city, developed in the 19th and early 20th centuries as a working-class, predominantly Catholic, residential area.

In August 1969 the three-day 'Battle of the Bogside' – a running street battle between local youths and the Royal Ulster Constabulary (RUC) – prompted the UK government to send British troops into Northern Ireland. The residents of the Bogside and neighbouring Brandywell districts – 33,000 of them – declared themselves independent of the civil authorities and barricaded the streets to keep the security forces out. 'Free Derry', as it was known, was a no-go area for the police and army, its streets patrolled by IRA volunteers. In January of 1972 the area around Rossville St witnessed the horrific events

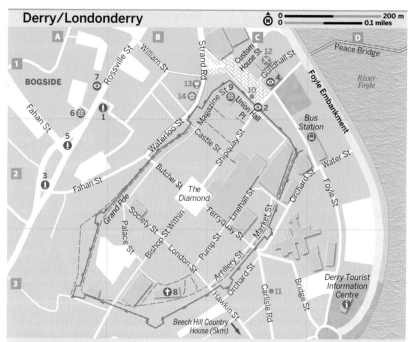

Derry/Londonderry

Derry/Londonderry

◎ Sights
1 Bloody Sunday Memorial	A1
2 Derry's City Walls	C1
3 Free Derry Corner	A2
4 Guildhall	C1
5 Hunger Strikers' Memorial	A2
6 Museum of Free Derry	A1
7 People's Gallery Murals	A1
8 St Columb's Cathedral	B3
9 Tower Museum	C1

◎ Activities, Courses & Tours
10 Bogside Artists Tours	C1
11 City Tours	C3

⊗ Eating
12 Custom House	C1

◎ Drinking & Nightlife
13 Peadar O'Donnell's	B1

⊕ Entertainment
14 Gweedore Bar	B1

of Bloody Sunday. 'Free Derry' ended with Operation Motorman on 31 July 1972, when thousands of British troops and armoured cars moved in to occupy the Bogside.

Since then the area has been extensively redeveloped, the old houses and flats demolished and replaced with modern housing, and the population is now down to 8000. All that remains of the old Bogside is **Free Derry Corner** (Map p178; cnr Fahan & Rossville Sts), where the gable end of a house painted with the famous slogan 'You are Now Entering Free Derry' still stands. Nearby is the H-shaped **Hunger Strikers' Memorial** (Map p178; Rossville St) and, a little further north along Rossville St, the **Bloody Sunday Memorial** (Map p178; Rossville St), a simple granite obelisk that commemorates the 14 civilians who were shot dead by the British Army on 30 January 1972.

Hands Across the Divide, Derry/Londonderry

Museum of Free Derry   Museum

Just off Rossville St, this museum chronicles the history of the Bogside, the civil rights movement and the events of Bloody Sunday through photographs, newspaper reports, film clips and the accounts of firsthand witnesses, including some of the original photographs that inspired the murals of the **People's Gallery** (Map p178; Rossville St). (www.museumoffreederry.org; 55-61 Glenfada Park; adult/child £3/2; ⏰9.30am-4.30pm Mon-Fri year-round, plus 1-4pm Sat Apr-Sep, 1-4pm Sun Jul-Sep)

⟳ TOURS

Bogside Artists Tours   Art

Guided one-hour walking tours of the famous People's Gallery murals led by the artists themselves. Book in advance by phone or on the website. (☎07514 052481; www.bogsideartists.com; per person £5)

City Tours   Walking Tour

One-hour Historic Derry walking tours start from Carlisle Stores at 10am, noon, 2pm and 4pm year-round. There are also tours of the Bogside and of Derry's murals. (☎028-7127 1996; www.derrycitytours.com; Carlisle Stores, 11 Carlisle Rd; adult/child £4/free)

✖ EATING

Pyke 'n' Pommes   Burgers £

Derry's single-best eatery is this quayside food truck. Chef Kevin Pyke's amazing, mostly organic burgers span his signature Notorious Pig (pulled pork, crispy slaw, beetroot and crème fraîche), Cheeky Monkey (monkfish, warm potato and smoked-apple purée) and Veganderry (chickpeas, lemon and coriander) to his Legenderry Burger (wagyu beef, pickled onions and honey-mustard mayo). Seasonal specials might include mackerel or oysters. (behind Foyle Marina, off Baronet St; dishes £5-15; ⏰noon-3pm Tue-Thu, to 5pm Fri & Sat, hours vary; ⚲⚇) ✿

Custom House   Modern Irish ££

You can just drop in for a drink in the bar fitted out with pewter, copper and walnut wood, but the 1876-built Custom House is a superb spot to dine on sea bass tajine;

OHN SONES SINGING BOWL MEDIA/GETTY IMAGES ©

Corner pub, Derry/Londonderry

sirloin with smoked bacon and turnip and celeriac dauphinoise; and rigatoni with roasted red onion, hazelnuts and Cashel blue cheese. Service goes above and beyond. (028-7137 3366; http://custom houserestaurant.com; Custom House St, Queen's Quay; mains lunch £8-10, dinner £13-19; noon-9.30pm Mon-Sat, to 9pm Sun)

Beech Hill
Country House　　Modern Irish ££

Secluded in a picturesque patch of woodland 4.3km southeast of Derry, this wonderfully atmospheric 18th-century manor house is surrounded by magnificent gardens and is steeped in history – it was a WWII base for US marines, and former US president Bill Clinton stayed several times. Its lake-view restaurant is sublime, offering imaginative, gourmet takes on traditional dishes. (028-7134 9279; www. beech-hill.com; 32 Ardmore Rd; 2-course meal from £25;)

🍸 DRINKING & NIGHTLIFE

Peadar O'Donnell's　　Pub

Done up as a typical Irish pub/grocery – with shelves of household items, shopkeepers scales on the counter and a museum's-worth of old bric-a-brac – Peadar's has traditional music sessions every night and often on weekend afternoons as well. Its adjacent **Gweedore Bar** (www.peadars.com; 59-61 Waterloo St; 11.30am-1.30am Mon-Sat, noon-12.30am Sun) hosts live rock bands every night, and a Saturday-night disco upstairs. (www.peadars.com; 59-63 Waterloo St; 11.30am-1.30am Mon-Sat, 12.30pm-12.30am Sun)

ℹ️ INFORMATION

Derry Tourist Information Centre (Map p178; 028-7126 7284; www.visitderry.com; 44 Foyle St; 9am-5.30pm Mon-Fri, 10am-5pm Sat & Sun;) Sells books and maps, has a bureau de change and can book accommodation.

ⓘ GETTING THERE & AWAY

AIR

City of Derry Airport (☎028-7181 0784; www.
cityofderryairport.com) About 13km east of Derry
along the A2 towards Limavady. Direct flights
daily to London Stansted, Liverpool and Glasgow
International, plus summer routes to Spain and
Portugal.

BUS

The bus station (Map p178; ☎028-7126 2261;
Foyle St) is just northeast of the walled city.

TRAIN

Derry's train station (always referred to as
Londonderry in Northern Ireland timetables) is
on the eastern side of the River Foyle; a free Rail
Link bus connects with the bus station.

Belfast £12, 2½ hours, nine daily Monday to
Saturday, six on Sunday

Coleraine £9.30, 45 minutes, 11 daily Monday to
Saturday, six on Sunday

Portrush £12, 1¼ hours, 10 daily Monday to
Saturday, six on Sunday

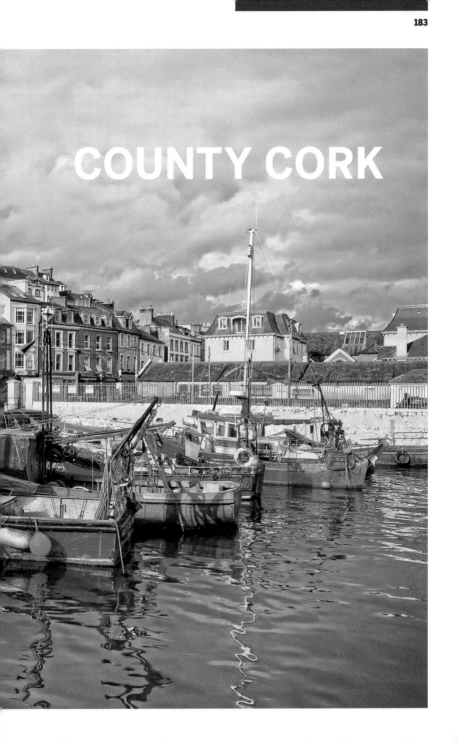

COUNTY CORK

County Cork

Everything good about Ireland can be found in County Cork. Surrounding the country's second city – a thriving metropolis made glorious by location and its almost Rabelaisian devotion to the finer things of life – is a lush landscape dotted with villages that offer days of languor and idyll.

Cork city's understated confidence is grounded in its plethora of food markets and ever-evolving cast of creative eateries, and in its selection of pubs, entertainment and cultural pursuits.

Further afield, you'll pass inlets along eroded coastlines and a multitude of perfectly charming old fishing towns and villages. The scenery is every bit as enchanting as the best bits of Ireland, particularly along the long Mizen Head, Sheep's Head and Beara Peninsulas, where you can tackle mountain passes and touch Ireland's ancient past.

☑ In This Section

❶ Arriving in County Cork

Cork Airport is 8km south of the city centre. Buses shuttle between the airport, the train station and bus station every half-hour between 6am and 10pm (€7.40, 30 minutes).

Kent Train Station is north of the River Lee, a 10- to 15-minute walk from the city centre.

Cork Bus Station is on Parnell Pl in the city centre.

Cork City Map (p191)

From left: grounds of Blarney Castle (p188); City Hall, Cork city (p190); water wheel, Bantry (p199)

© LISA KIMBERLY/GETTY IMAGES ©; GEOSTOCK/GETTY IMAGES ©; PETER UNGER/GETTY IMAGES ©

Gourmet goods for sale, English Market

GABRIELL12/SHUTTERSTOCK ©

Gourmet Cork

Ireland's largest county can fairly lay claim to being the foodie capital of Ireland. Farmers markets and fine dining are highlights of a visit.

Great For...

☑ Don't Miss
Cheeses and charcuterie at **On the Pig's Back** (Map p191; ☎021-427 0232; www.onthepigsback.ie; ☺9am-5.30pm Mon-Sat) 🖪 in the English Market.

English Market
Market

It could just as easily be called the Victorian Market for its ornate vaulted ceilings and columns, but the English Market is a true gem, no matter what you name it. Scores of vendors sell some of the regions's very best local produce, meats, cheeses and take-away food. On a sunny day, take your lunch to nearby Bishop Lucey Park, a popular al-fresco eating spot. (www.englishmarket.ie; Princes St (main entrance); ☺8am-6pm Mon-Sat)

Farmgate Cafe
Cafe, Bistro €€

An unmissable experience at the heart of the English Market, the Farmgate is perched on a balcony overlooking the food stalls below, the source of all that fresh local produce on your plate – everything from crab and oysters to the lamb for an Irish stew. Up the stairs and turn left for ta-ble service, right for counter service. (www.

ROBERT MCGRATH/GETTY IMAGES ©

❶ Need to Know

www.slowfoodireland.com lists local suppliers of farmhouse and artisan produce, mostly in County Cork.

✕ Take a Break

Buy picnic food in the English Market and take your lunch to nearby Bishop Lucey Park, a popular alfresco eating spot.

★ Top Tip

Cork city is also famous for its boutique coffee shops – try Cork Coffee Roasters or Filter.

farmgate.ie; Broderick St; mains lunch €12-20, dinner €18-30; ⊘noon-3.30pm Tue-Sat, 6.30-9.30pm Thu-Sat, cafe 9am-5pm Tue-Sat; 🚹)

Ballymaloe Cookery School   Cooking Course

TV personality Darina Allen (daughter-in-law of Myrtle Allen of Ballymaloe House (p196)) runs this famous cookery school. Darina's own daughter-in-law, Rachel Allen, is also a high-profile TV chef and author, and regularly teaches at the school. Demonstrations cost €75; lessons, from half-day sessions (€95 to €135) to 12-week certificate courses (€10,995), are often booked out well in advance. For overnight students, there are pretty cottages amid the 100 acres of grounds. It's 3km east of Ballymaloe House. (☎021-464 6785; www.cookingisfun.ie; Shanagarry)

farmgate.ie; Princes St, English Market; mains €6-15; ⊘8.30am-4.30pm Mon-Fri, to 5pm Sat) 📷

Midleton Farmers Market   Market €

Midleton's farmers market is one of Cork's best, with bushels of local produce on offer and producers who are happy to chat. It's behind the big roundabout at the north end of Main St. (www.midletonfarmersmarket.com; Main St; ⊘9.30am-1pm Sat) 📷

Farmgate Restaurant   Irish €€

The original, sister establishment to Cork city's Farmgate Café, the Midleton restaurant offers the same superb blend of traditional and modern Irish cuisine. Squeeze through the deli selling amazing baked goods and local produce, to the subtly lit, art-clad, 'farmhouse shed' cafe-restaurant, where you'll eat as well as you would anywhere in Ireland. (☎021-463 2771; www.

PATRYK KOSMIDER/SHUTTERSTOCK ©

Blarney Castle

If you need proof of the power of a good yarn, then join the queue to get into this 15th-century castle, one of Ireland's most popular tourist attractions.

The crowds are here, of course, to plant their lips on the Blarney Stone, which supposedly gives one the gift of gab – a cliché that has entered every lexicon and tour route. Blarney is 8km northwest of Cork and buses run every half-hour from Cork bus station (€7.30 return, 30 minutes).

The Blarney Stone is perched at the top of a steep climb up claustrophobic spiral staircases within the castle. On the battlements, you bend backwards over a long, long drop (with safety grill and attendant to prevent tragedy) to kiss the stone; as your shirt rides up, coachloads of onlookers stare up your nose. Once you're upright again, don't forget to admire the stunning views before descending. Try not to think of the local lore about all the fluids that drench the stone other than saliva. Better yet, just don't kiss it.

Great For...

☑ Don't Miss

While kissing the stone is the main focus for most visitors, the Poison Garden and Rock Close offer some stunning scenery and are must-sees.

Visitor kissing the Blarney Stone

❶ Need to Know

☎021-438 5252; www.blarneycastle.ie; adult/child €13/5; ☉9am-5.30pm daily year-round, to 6.30pm Mon-Sat May & Sep, to 7pm Mon-Sat Jun-Aug

✗ Take a Break

There's a cafe next to the castle's stable yard; also, the **Lemon Tree Restaurant** (www.blarneycastlehotel.com/dining; Blarney Castle Hotel, The Square, Blarney; ☉7.30am-11am, noon to 4.30pm & 6-9.30pm) is a 700m walk from the castle and offers hearty breakfasts, lunches and pub meals.

★ Top Tip

Book your tickets online via the castle's website and receive a discount. If you want to explore Blarney House, the nearby mansion, it's open from the beginning of June to the end of August (closed Sundays) each year.

💬 Full of Blarney?

The Irish reputation for being affable is largely well deserved, but it only hints at a more profound character, one that is more complex and contradictory than the image of the silver-tongued master of blarney might suggest. This dichotomy is best summarised by a quote usually ascribed to the poet William Butler Yeats: 'Being Irish, he had an abiding sense of tragedy, which sustained him through temporary periods of joy'.

The custom of kissing the stone is a relatively modern one, but Blarney's association with smooth talking goes back a long time. Queen Elizabeth I is said to have invented the term 'to talk blarney' out of exasperation with Lord Blarney's ability to talk endlessly without ever actually agreeing to her demands.

The famous stone aside, Blarney Castle itself is an impressive 16th-century tower set in gorgeous grounds. Escape the crowds on a walk around the Fern Garden and Arboretum, investigate toxic plants in the Harry-Potterish Poison Garden, or explore the landscaped nooks and crannies of the Rock Close.

Cork City

Ireland's second city is first in every important respect – at least according to the locals, who cheerfully refer to it as the 'real capital of Ireland'. It's a liberal, youthful and cosmopolitan place that was badly hit by economic recession but is now busily reinventing itself with spruced-up streets, revitalised stretches of waterfront, and – seemingly – an artisan coffee bar on every corner. There's a developing hipster scene, but the best of the city is still happily traditional – snug pubs with live-music sessions, restaurants dishing up top-quality local produce and a genuinely proud welcome from the locals.

◉ SIGHTS & ACTIVITIES

The best sight in Cork is the city itself – soak it up as you wander the streets. A new conference and events centre, complete

> *Locals cheerfully refer to Cork as the 'real capital of Ireland'.*

with 6000-seat concert venue, tourist centre, restaurants, shops, galleries and apartments, is planned for the former **Beamish & Crawford brewery site**, fronted by the landmark mock-Tudor 'counting house', a block west of the English Market.

Shandon, perched on a hillside overlooking the city centre to the north, is a great spot for the views alone, but you'll also find galleries, antique shops and cafes along its old lanes and squares. Those tiny old row houses, where generations of workers raised huge families in very basic conditions, are now sought-after urban pieds-à-terre. Pick up a copy of the *Cork Walks – Shandon* leaflet from the tourist office for a self-guided tour of the district.

Cork City Gaol   Museum

This imposing former prison is well worth a visit, if only to get a sense of how awful life was for prisoners a century ago. An audio tour guides you around the restored cells, which feature models of suffering prisoners and sadistic-looking guards. Take a bus to UCC – from there walk north along Mardyke Walk, cross the river and follow the signs uphill (10 minutes).

Cork City Gaol

ARSTY/GETTY IMAGES ©

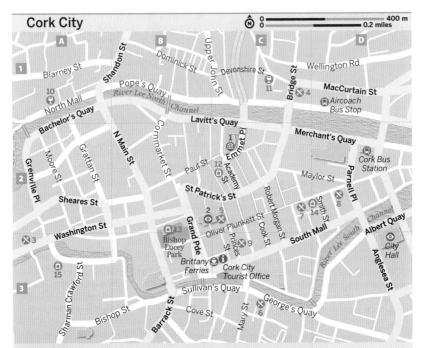

Cork City

Cork City

The tour is very moving, bringing home the harshness of the 19th-century penal system. The most common crime was that of poverty; many of the inmates were sentenced to hard labour for stealing loaves of bread. Atmospheric night tours take place on Thursday at 7pm (€10). The prison closed in 1923, reopening in 1927 as a radio station which continued in use until the 1950s. The Governor's House has been converted into a **Radio Museum** (www.corkcitygaol.com/radio-museum/; Cork City Gaol, Convent Ave; adult/child €8/5; ☺9.30am-5pm Mar-Oct, 10am-4pm Nov-Feb; ☐8 to the University College Cork) where, alongside collections of beautiful old radios, you can hear the story of Guglielmo Marconi's conquest of the airwaves. (☎021-430 5022; www.corkcitygaol.com; Convent Ave; adult/child €8/5; ☺9.30am-5pm Apr-Oct, 10am-4pm Nov-Mar)

Crawford Municipal Art Gallery · Gallery

Cork's public gallery houses a small but excellent permanent collection covering the 17th century to the modern day. Highlights include works by Sir John Lavery, Jack B Yeats, Nathaniel Hone and a room devoted to Irish women artists from 1886 to 1978 – don't miss the works by Mainie Jellet and Evie Hone. (☎ 021-480 5042; www.crawford artgallery.ie; Emmet Pl; ⏱ 10am-5pm Mon-Wed, Fri & Sat, to 8pm Thu) FREE

Lewis Glucksman Gallery · Gallery

This award-winning building – shortlisted for the 2005 Stirling Prize – is a startling construction of limestone, steel and timber. Two floors of galleries with suitably paint-spattered floors display the best in both national and international contemporary art and installation. Don't miss the free fortnightly curatorial tours. The on-site cafe is excellent. (☎ 021-490 1844; www.glucksman.org; University College Cork, Western Rd; suggested donation €5; ⏱ 10am-5pm Tue-Sat, 2-5pm Sun; ♿)

⊙ TOURS

Cork City Tour · Bus Tour
Hop-on-hop-off open-top bus linking the city's main points of interest. (☎ 021-430 9090; www.corkcitytour.com; adult/student/child €15/13/5; ⏱ Mar-Nov)

⊙ SHOPPING

O'Connaill · Food & Drink
O'Connaill creates exquisite chocolates; don't leave Cork without sampling its delicious Chocolatier's Hot Chocolate. (☎ 021-437 3407; 16b French Church St; ⏱ 10am-5.30pm Mon-Sat, noon-5pm Sun; ☏)

PLUGD Records · Music
Carries all kinds of music and is the place to keep up with the ever-changing club scene. (☎ 021-472 2022; www.plugdrecords.com; Triskel Arts Centre, Tobin St; ⏱ noon-7pm Mon-Sat; ☏)

Pro Musica · Music
A focal point and meeting place for Cork's musicians, with a full range of instruments from electric guitars to clarinets, recording equipment, sheet music, and a noticeboard. (☎ 021-427 1659; www.promusica.ie; 20 Oliver Plunkett St; ⏱ 9am-6pm Mon-Sat)

Time Traveller's Bookshop · Books
A fascinating antiquarian bookshop specialising in rare and unusual books, first editions and signed copies. (☎ 087 290 3613; www.timetraveller.ie; Wandesford Quay; ⏱ 11am-5pm)

⊗ EATING

Cork Coffee Roasters · Cafe €
In this foodiest of foodie towns it's not surprising to find a cafe run by artisan coffee roasters. The brew on offer in this cute and often crowded corner is some of the best in Ireland, guaranteed to jump-start your morning along with a buttery pastry, scone or tart. (☎ 021-731 9158; 2 Bridge St; mains €3-6; ⏱ 7.30am-6.30pm Mon-Fri, 8am-6.30pm Sat, 9am-5pm Sun)

Filter · Cafe €
The quintessential Cork espresso bar, Filter is a carefully curated shrine to coffee nerdery, from the rough-and-ready retro

Where to Stay

As the second most populous city in Ireland, Cork has accommodation options to fit every budget. Whether you stay on the main island, or to the north in Shandon or around MacCurtain St, you're right in the heart of the action. Western Rd, which runs southwest from the city centre to the large UCC campus, has the best selection of B&Bs; take a bus there from the central bus station – or walk (10 to 30 minutes). If less hustle-and-bustle is your scene, head to picturesque Cobh for a dose of maritime and transportation history.

decor to the highly knowledgeable baristas serving up expertly brewed shots made with single-origin, locally roasted beans. The sandwich menu is a class act too, offering a choice of fillings that includes pastrami, chorizo and ham hock on artisan breads. (021-455 0050; 19 George's Quay; mains €3-6; 8am-6pm Mon-Fri, 9am-6pm Sat, 10am-5pm Sun)

Market Lane   Irish, International €€

It's always hopping at this bright corner bistro. The menu is broad and hearty, changing to reflect what's fresh at the English Market: how about braised ox cheek in ale, or smoked haddock with bacon and cabbage? No reservations for fewer than six diners; sip a drink at the bar till a table is free. Lots of wines by the glass. (021-427 4710; www.marketlane.ie; 5 Oliver Plunkett St; mains €12-26; noon-10.30pm Mon-Sat, 1-9pm Sun;)

Cafe Paradiso   Vegetarian €€

A contender for best restaurant in town in any genre, Paradiso serves contemporary vegetarian dishes, including vegan fare: how about sweet chilli–glazed, pan-fried

Top Five Places to Eat

- Finn's Table (p198)
- Manning's Emporium (p201)
- Farmgate Restaurant (p187)
- Cafe Paradiso (p193)
- Market Lane (p193)

tofu with Asian greens in tamarind and coconut broth? Reservations are essential. Dinner, bed and breakfast rates staying in the funky upstairs rooms start from €100 per person. (021-427 7939; www.cafeparadiso.ie; 16 Lancaster Quay; 2-/3-course dinners €33/40; 5.30-10pm Mon-Sat;)

Nash 19   International €€

A sensational bistro and deli where locally sourced food is honoured at breakfast and lunch, either sit-in or take away. Fresh scones draw in the crowds early; daily lunch specials (soups, salads, desserts etc), free-range chicken pie and platters of smoked

Shops, Kinsale (p197)

GEORGE MUNDAY/DESIGN PICS/GETTY IMAGES ©

Smokin' Food

No trip to Cork is complete without a visit to an artisan food producer, and the effervescent Frank Hederman is more than happy to show you around **Belvelly** (021-481 1089; www.frankhederman.com; Belvelly; free for individuals, fee for groups; Mon-Fri) , the oldest traditional smokehouse in Ireland – indeed, the only surviving one. Call ahead to arrange a visit, or stop by his stall at the Cobh or Midleton farmers markets (you can also buy his produce at Cork's English Market). The smokehouse is 19km east of Cork on the R624 towards Cobh.

Seafood and cheese are smoked here – even butter – but the speciality is fish, particularly salmon. In a traditional process that takes 24 hours from start to finish, the fish is filleted and cured before being hung to smoke over beech woodchips. The result is subtle and delectable.

LONELY PLANET/GETTY IMAGES ©

fish from Frank Henderman keep them coming through the rest of the day. (021-427 0880; www.nash19.com; Princes St; mains €10-16; 7.30am-4pm Mon-Fri, 8.30am-4pm Sat)

Jacques Restaurant Modern Irish €€
Sisters Jacqueline and Eithne Barry draw on a terrific network of local suppliers they've built up over three decades to help them realise their culinary ambitions – the freshest Cork food cooked simply, without frills. The menu changes daily: smoked quail with celeriac remoulade, perhaps, or

Castletownbere crab with spaghetti and herbs. (021-427 7387; www.jacquesrestaurant. ie; 23 Oliver Plunkett St; mains lunch €7-14, dinner €22-26; 10am-4pm Mon, to 10pm Tue-Sat)

🍸 DRINKING & NIGHTLIFE

Sin É   Pub
You could easily while away an entire day at this great old place, which is everything a craic-filled pub should be – long on atmosphere and short on pretension (Sin É means 'That's it!'). There's music most nights (regular sessions Tuesday at 9.30pm, Friday and Sunday at 6.30pm), much of it traditional, but with the odd surprise. (www.corkheritagepubs.com; 8 Coburg St; 12.30-11.30pm Sun-Thu, to 12.30am Fri & Sat)

Franciscan Well Brewery   Pub
The copper vats gleaming behind the bar give the game away: the Franciscan Well brews its own beer. The best place to enjoy it is in the enormous beer garden at the back. The pub holds regular beer festivals with other small independent Irish breweries. (www.franciscanwellbrewery.com; 14 North Mall; 3-11.30pm Mon-Thu, to 12.30am Fri & Sat, to 11pm Sun;)

ℹ INFORMATION
Cork City Tourist Office (021-425 5100; www.discoverireland.ie/corkcity; Grand Pde; 9am-6pm Mon-Sat year-round, plus 10am-5pm Sun Jul & Aug) Souvenir shop and information desk. Sells Ordnance Survey maps.

ℹ GETTING THERE & AWAY
AIR
Cork Airport (021-431 3131; www.cork-airport.com) Airlines servicing the airport include Aer Lingus and Ryanair.

BOAT
Brittany Ferries (021-427 7801; www.brittanyferries.ie; 42 Grand Pde) Sails to Roscoff in France (foot passenger from €59, car with two people from €329, 14 hours, one a week) from the end of March to October. The ferry terminal

Houses, Cork city

is at Ringaskiddy, 15 minutes' drive southeast of Cork along the N28. Taxis cost €28 to €35. Bus 223E from South Mall in Cork city centre links up with departures (€10, 50 minutes); confirm times.

BUS

Bus Éireann operates from the bus station (cnr Merchant's Quay & Parnell Pl), but **AirCoach** (01-844 7118; www.aircoach.ie) and **Citylink** (091-564 164; www.citylink.ie;) services depart from St Patrick's Quay, across the river, while **GoBus** (091-564 600; www.gobus. ie;) uses a stop on Parnell Pl, around the corner.

Dublin (€15, 3¾ hours, six daily)

Dublin (AirCoach; €16, three hours, hourly)

Dublin (GoBus; €17, three hours, six to nine daily)

Dublin airport (AirCoach; €20, 3½ hours, hourly)

Galway (Citylink; €21, three hours, five daily)

Kilkenny (€21, three hours, two daily)

Killarney (€27, two hours, hourly)

Limerick (Citylink; €17, 1½ hours, five daily)

Waterford (€23.50, 2¼ hours, hourly)

TRAIN

Kent Train Station (021-450 4777) is north of the River Lee on Lower Glanmire Rd, a 10- to 15-minute walk from the city centre. Bus 205 runs into the city centre (€2, five minutes, every 15 minutes).

The train line goes through Mallow, where you can change for the Tralee line, and Limerick Junction, for the line to Ennis (and Galway), then on to Dublin.

Dublin (€64, 2¼ hours, eight daily)

Galway (€57, four to six hours, seven daily, two or three changes)

Killarney (€28, 1½ to two hours, nine daily)

Waterford (€31, three to five hours, five daily, one or two changes)

GETTING AROUND

TO/FROM THE AIRPORT

Bus Éireann service 226A shuttles between the train station, bus station and Cork Airport every half-hour between 6am and 10pm (€7.40, 30 minutes).

A taxi to/from town costs €20 to €25.

BUS
Most places are within easy walking distance of the centre. Single bus tickets cost €2 each; a day pass is €5. Buy all tickets on the bus.

CAR
Street parking requires scratch-card parking discs (€2 per hour, required 8.30am to 6.30pm Monday to Saturday), available from many city-centre shops. Be warned – traffic wardens are ferociously efficient. There are several sign-posted car parks around the central area, with charges around €2 per hour and €12 overnight.

You can avoid city-centre parking problems by using **Black Ash Park & Ride** on the South City Link Road, on the way to the airport. Parking costs €5 a day, with buses into the city centre at least every 15 minutes (10-minute journey time).

TAXI
For taxi hire, try **Cork Taxi Co-op** (☏021-427 22 22; www.corktaxi.ie) or **Shandon Cabs** (☏021-450 22 55).

Around Cork City

Midleton
Aficionados of a particularly fine Irish whiskey will recognise the name Midleton, and the main reason to linger in this bustling market town is to visit the old Jameson whiskey distillery. However, the surrounding region is full of pretty villages, craggy coastline and heavenly rural hotels like **Ballymaloe House** (☏021-465 2531; www.ballymaloe.ie; Shanagarry; s/d from €140/240; 📶🏊), which also has a much-celebrated restaurant attached.

◉ SIGHTS

Jameson Experience   Museum
Coachloads pour in to tour the restored 200-year-old distillery building housing the Jameson Experience. Exhibits and tours

St Coleman's Cathedral, Cobh

MICHELKSL/GETTY IMAGES ©

explain the process of taking barley and creating whiskey (Jameson is today made in a modern factory in Cork). There's a well-stocked gift shop, and the **Malt House Restaurant** (☺noon-3pm) has live music on Sundays. (☎021-461 3594; www.jamesonwhis-key.com; Old Distillery Walk, Midleton; tours adult/child €15/8; ☺shop 10am-6.30pm, tour times vary)

ⓘ GETTING THERE & AWAY

Midleton is 20km east of Cork. The train station (5 McSweeney Tce) is 1.5km (20 minutes' walk) north of the Jameson Experience. There are frequent trains from Cork (€5.70, 25 minutes, at least hourly).

There are also frequent buses from Cork bus station (€7.80, 30 minutes, every 15 to 45 minutes). You'll need a car to explore the surrounding area.

Cobh

Cobh (pronounced 'cove') is a charming waterfront town on a glittering estuary, dotted with brightly coloured houses and overlooked by a splendid cathedral. It's a far cry from the harrowing Famine years when 2.5 million people left Ireland through the port in order to escape the ravages of starvation. Cobh was also the final port of call for the *Titanic;* a poignant museum commemorates the fatal voyage's point of departure.

◎ SIGHTS

Cobh, The Queenstown Story   Museum
The howl of the storm almost knocks you off-balance, there's a bit of fake vomit on the deck, and the people in the pictures all look pretty miserable – that's just one room at Cobh Heritage Centre. Housed in the old train station (next to the current station), this interactive museum is way above average, chronicling Irish emigrations across the Atlantic in the wake of the Great Famine. (☎021-481 3591; www.cobhheritage.

com; Lower Rd; adult/child €9.50/5; ☺9.30am-6pm Apr-Sep, to 5pm Oct-Mar, last admission 1hr before closing)

Titanic Experience Cobh   Museum
The original White Star Line offices, from where 123 passengers embarked (and one lucky soul absconded) on the RMS *Titanic*, now house this powerful insight into the ill-fated liner's only voyage. Admission is by tour, which is partly guided and partly interactive, with holograms, audiovisual presentations and exhibits; allow at least an hour. The technical wizardry is impressive but what's most memorable is standing on the spot where passengers were ferried to the waiting ship offshore, most never to return. (☎021-481 4412; www.titanic experiencecobh.ie; 20 Casement Sq; adult/child €9.50/5.50; ☺9am-6pm)

Spike Island   Historic Site
This low-lying green island in Cork Harbour was once an important part of the port's defences, topped by an 18th-century artillery fort. In the second half of the 19th century, and again during the Irish War of Independence, it served as a prison and internment centre, gaining the nickname 'Ireland's Alcatraz'. Today you can enjoy a self-guided walking tour of the island and its fortifications, or pay more for a **guided tour** (adult/child €13.50/8.50); the ferry (www.spikeislandferry.com) from Kennedy Pier, Cobh, is included in price. (www.spikeislandcork.com; Cork Harbour; adult/child €8/5; ☺11am-5.30pm Jun-Aug, noon-4.30pm May, noon-4.30pm Sat & Sun only Apr & Sep, noon-4.30pm Sun only Oct)

ⓘ GETTING THERE & AWAY

Hourly trains connect Cobh with Cork (€5.50, 25 minutes). No buses serve the Cork to Cobh route.

Kinsale

The picturesque yachting harbour of Kinsale (Cionn tSáile) is one of many colourful gems strung along the coastline of County Cork. Narrow, winding streets

Top Three Cork Food Festivals

Whet your appetite at these culinary celebrations:

Kinsale Gourmet Festival Three days of tastings, cookery demonstrations and the All-Ireland seafood chowder cook-off competition add to the town's foodie reputation. (www.kinsale restaurants.com; ☺Oct)

Seafood & Wooden Boat Festival A showcase for local restaurants and seafood producers, and displays of seamanship as traditional wooden sailboats race around the harbour. (www.baltimore. ie; ☺May)

Taste of West Cork Food Festival If you're in town in mid-September, don't miss this foodie extravaganza, including a lively farmers market and events at local restaurants. (www.atasteofwestcork. com; ☺Sep)

Farmers market, Bantry
CARL BRUEMMER/DESIGN PICS/GETTY IMAGES ©

lined with galleries and gift shops, lively bars and superb restaurants, and a handsome natural harbour filled with yachts and guarded by a huge 17th-century fortress make it an engrossing place to spend a day or two.

Kinsale has been labelled the gourmet centre of southwest Ireland and, for such a small place, it certainly packs more than its fair share of international-standard restaurants. Most are situated near the harbour and within easy walking distance of the town centre.

⊙ SIGHTS

Charles Fort   Fort
One of Europe's best-preserved star-shaped artillery forts, this vast 17th-century fortification would be worth a visit for its spectacular views alone. But there's much more here: the 18th- and 19th-century ruins inside the walls make for some fascinating wandering. It's 3km southeast of Kinsale along the minor road through Scilly; if you have time, hike there along the lovely coastal **Scilly Walk**. (☏021-477 2263; www.heritageireland.ie; Summercove; adult/child €4/2; ☺10am-6pm mid-Mar–Oct, to 5pm Nov–mid-Mar)

Lusitania Museum   Museum
This 200-year-old signal tower has been restored and converted into a museum dedicated to the RMS *Lusitania,* which was torpedoed by a German U-boat in 1915 with the loss of 1200 lives. You can walk to the nearby clifftops for impressive views south towards the Old Head, the nearest point of land to the disaster; sadly, a privately-owned golf club prevents you from reaching the lighthouse at the tip of the headland. The tower is 13km south of town via the R604. (www.oldheadofkinsale.com; Signal Tower, Old Head of Kinsale; adult/child €5/free; ☺10am-6pm daily Jun-Aug, to 5pm Thu-Sun May & Sep, check hours Oct-Apr)

✖ EATING

Black Pig Wine Bar   Irish €€
This sophisticated hideaway offers no fewer than 80 wines by the bottle and 40 by the glass including many organic varieties. There's a charming cobbled courtyard out back, and a mouthwatering menu of snacks, charcuterie platters and cheese boards sourced from artisan local suppliers. Tables are coveted – book so you don't miss out. (☏021-477 4101; 66 Lower O'Connell St; mains €8-20; ☺5.30-11.30pm Wed-Mon) ⓟ

Finn's Table   Modern Irish €€€
Owning a gourmet restaurant in Kinsale means plenty of competition, but John

PETER UNGER/GETTY IMAGES ©

Market square, Bantry

and Julie Finn's venture is more than up to the challenge. Elegant but unstuffy, with a warm welcome, its menu of seasonal, locally sourced produce rarely fails to please. Seafood (including lobster in season) is from West Cork, while meat is from the Finn family's butchers. (☎021-470 9636; www. finnstable.com; 6 Main St; mains €20-30; ⏰from 5.30pm Thu-Mon)

Fishy Fishy Cafe   Seafood €€€

One of the most famous seafood restaurants in the country, Fishy Fishy has a wonderful setting with stark white walls splashed with bright artwork and steel fish sculptures, and a terrific decked terrace at the front. All the fish is caught locally, from the lobster thermidor to the chilled seafood platter served with homemade mayonnaise. (☎021-470 0415; www.fishyfishy. ie; Crowley's Quay; mains €17-30; ⏰noon-9pm Mar-Oct, to 4pm Sun-Wed, to 9pm Thu-Sat Nov-Feb)

ℹ INFORMATION

Tourist Office (☎021-477 2234; www.kinsale. ie; cnr Pier Rd & Emmet Pl; ⏰9.15am-5pm Tue-Sat year-round, 9.15am-5pm Mon Apr-Oct, 10am-5pm Sun Jul & Aug) Has a good map detailing walks in and around Kinsale.

ℹ GETTING THERE & AWAY

Bus Éireann (☎021-450 8188; www.buseireann. ie) service No 226 connects Kinsale with Cork bus station (€9.40, one hour, hourly) via Cork airport, and continuing to Cork train station. The bus stop is on Pier Rd, near the tourist office.

Bantry

Framed by the Sheep's Head hills and the craggy Caha Mountains, magnificent, sprawling Bantry Bay is one of the country's most attractive seascapes. Sheltered by islands at the head of the bay, Bantry town is neat and respectable, with narrow streets of old-fashioned, one-off shops and a picturesque harbourfront.

Pride of place goes to Bantry House, the former home of one Richard White, who earned his place in history when in 1798 he warned authorities of the imminent landing of patriot Wolfe Tone and his French fleet, in

PETER ZOELLER/DESIGN PICS/GETTY IMAGES ©

Bantry House & Garden

support of the United Irishmen's rebellion. In the end, storms prevented the fleet from landing and the course of Irish history was definitively altered – all Wolfe Tone got for his troubles was a square and a statue bearing his name.

Bantry struggled through the 19th century due to famine, poverty and mass emigration, but today its industry derives from the bay: you'll see Bantry oysters and mussels on menus throughout County Cork.

◉ SIGHTS

Bantry House & Garden
Historic Building

With its melancholic air of faded gentility, 18th-century Bantry House makes for an intriguing visit. From the Gobelin tapestries in the drawing room to the columned splendour of the library, it conjures up a lost world of aristocratic excess. But the gardens are its greatest glory, with lawns sweeping down towards the sea, and the magnificent Italian garden at the back with its staircase of 100 steps offering spectacular views. The entrance is 1km southwest of the town centre on the N71.

The house has belonged to the White family since 1729 and every room brims with treasures brought back from each generation's travels since then. The entrance hall is paved with mosaics from Pompeii, French and Flemish tapestries adorn the walls, and Japanese chests sit next to Russian shrines. Upstairs, worn bedrooms look out wanly over an astounding view of the bay – the 18th-century Whites had ringside seats to the French armada. Experienced pianists are invited to tinkle the ivories of the ancient grand piano in the library. If it looks like the sort of place you can imagine staying in, you can – the owners offer B&B accommodation in one of the wings. (☎027-50047; www.bantryhouse.com; adult/child €11/3; ☉10am-5pm daily Jun-Aug, Tue-Sun Apr, May, Sep & Oct)

✗ EATING

Organico
Cafe €

This bright and lively wholefood shop and cafe serves tinglingly fresh salads, sandwiches and soups, and lunch specials such as a falafel platter with hummus and tahini.

Ireland's Teardrop

So named because it was the last sight of the 'ould country' for emigrants sailing to America, the Fastnet Rock is the most southerly point of Ireland.

This isolated fang of rock, topped by a spectacular lighthouse, stands 6.5km southwest of Cape Clear Island, and in clear weather is visible from many places on the coastline from Baltimore to Mizen Head. Its image – usually with huge waves crashing around it – graces a thousand postcards, coffee-table books and framed art photographs.

The Fastnet lighthouse, widely considered the most perfectly engineered lighthouse in the world, was built in 1904 from ingeniously interlocked blocks of Cornish granite – there are exhibits about its construction at **Mizen Head Visitor Centre** (☎028-35115; www.mizenhead.ie; Mizen Head; adult/child €6/4.50; ☻10am-6pm Jun-Aug, 10.30am-5pm mid-Mar–May, Sep & Oct, Sat & Sun only Nov–mid-Mar; ♿) and **Cape Clear Museum** (☎028-39119; www.capeclearmuseum.ie; admission €3; ☻2.30-5pm Jun-Aug).

From June to August, **Fastnet Experience** (www.fastnettour.com; per person €32) operates boat trips to the rock, departing from Schull, Baltimore and Cape Clear Island. Tours are weather-dependent and last 2½ to three hours (one hour if departing from Cape Clear).

Fastnet lighthouse
MATTHIAS OESTERLE/GETTY IMAGES ©

Great coffee and cakes too. (☎027-55905; www.organico.ie; 2 Glengarriff Rd; mains €7-10; ☻9am-6pm Mon-Sat; 🛜♿) ♿

Manning's Emporium   Cafe, Deli €
This gourmet deli and cafe is an Aladdin's cave of West Cork's finest food. Tasting plates are the best way to sample the local artisan produce and farmhouse cheeses on offer. Foodie events take place regularly. It's on the N71 in Ballylickey (on the right as you're coming from Bantry). (www.manningsemporium.ie; Ballylickey; mains €8; ☻9am-6pm Mon-Sat, to 5pm Sun, 6-9pm Sat Jun-Aug) ♿

O'Connors Seafood Restaurant   Seafood €€
West Cork scallops with black pudding and smoked cauliflower puree, Castletownbere cod pan-roasted and topped with Irish-made feta cheese and truffle oil, and Bantry Bay mussels done four ways are among the innovative dishes here that make the most of the area's renowned seafood. The earlybird menu (5.30pm to 6.30pm) offers three courses for €27.50. (☎027-55664; www.oconnorseafood.com; Wolfe Tone Sq; mains €12-25; ☻12.30-3pm & 5.30-9pm; ♿) ♿

ⓘ INFORMATION

Tourist Office (☎027-50229; Wolfe Tone Sq; ☻9.15am-1pm & 2-5pm Mon-Sat Apr-Oct) In the old courthouse.

ⓘ GETTING THERE & AWAY

Bus Éireann (www.buseireann.ie) runs four to six buses daily between Bantry and Cork (€21, two hours).

COUNTY KERRY

County Kerry

County Kerry contains some of Ireland's most iconic scenery: surf-pounded sea cliffs and soft golden strands, emerald-green farmland criss-crossed by tumbledown stone walls, mist-shrouded bogs and cloud-torn mountain peaks.

With one of the country's finest national parks as its backyard, the lively tourism hub of Killarney spills over with colourful shops, restaurants and pubs loud with spirited trad music. The town is the jumping-off point for Kerry's two famed loop drives: the larger Ring of Kerry skirts the mountainous, island-fringed Iveragh Peninsula. The more compact Dingle Peninsula is like a condensed version of its southern neighbour, with ancient Christian sites, sandy beaches and glimpses of a hard, unforgiving land.

Kerry's exquisite beauty makes it one of Ireland's most popular tourist destinations. But if you need to escape from the crowds, there's always a mountain pass, an isolated cove or an untrodden trail to discover.

☑ In This Section

➊ Arriving in County Kerry

Kerry Airport (p217) is at Farranfore, about 17km north of Killarney on the N22.

Killarney's **train station** is behind the Malton Hotel, just east of the centre.

Bus Éireann runs one or two services a day to Killarney and Dingle Town from Dublin and Cork. **Citylink** also runs a service to Killarney from Galway.

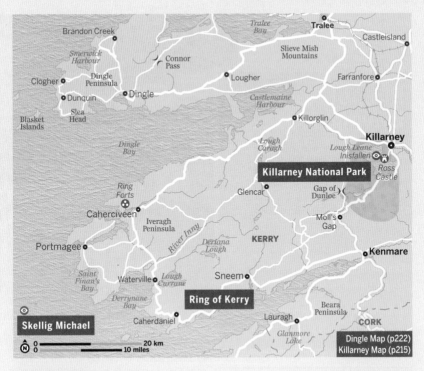

Tralee Bay
Tralee
Brandon Creek
Castleisland
Smerwick Harbour
Connor Pass
Slieve Mish Mountains
Dingle Peninsula
Lougher
Farranfore
Clogher
Dingle
Castlemaine Harbour
Dunquin
Killorglin
Killarney
Slea Head
Blasket Islands
Lough Caragh
Lough Leane
Inisfallen
Dingle Bay
Killarney National Park
Ross Castle
Ring Forts
Glencar
Gap of Dunloe
Caherciveen
Iveragh Peninsula
Moll's Gap
River Inny
KERRY
Portmagee
Deriana Lough
Kenmare
Saint Finan's Bay
Waterville
Lough Currane
Sneem
Derrynane Bay
Ring of Kerry
Beara Peninsula
Skellig Michael
Caherdaniel
Lauragh
CORK
Glanmore Lake

N 0 —— 20 km
   0 —— 10 miles

Dingle Map (p222)
Killarney Map (p215)

From left: Ross Castle (p212), Killarney National Park; Dingle Town (p221); Ring of Kerry (p206)
SASHA WELEBER/GETTY IMAGES © LITTLENY/SHUTTERSTOCK © AITORMMFOTO/GETTY IMAGES ©

Kerry Bog Village Museum

Ring of Kerry Driving Tour

Windswept beaches, Atlantic waves crashing against rugged cliffs, medieval ruins, soaring mountains and glinting loughs are some of the stunning distractions along the twisting 179km Ring of Kerry circle drive.

Distance: 179km
Duration: 1–2 days

Start Killorglin

❶ Killorglin

The first town on the Ring is Killorglin. For most of the year, the town is quieter than the waters of the River Laune that lap against its 1885-built eight-arched bridge. In August, however, there's an explosion of activity at the famous pagan festival, the Puck Fair. On the N70 between Killorglin and Glenbeigh, the **Kerry Bog Village Museum** (www. kerrybogvillage.ie; Ballincleave, Glenbeigh; adult/ child €6.50/4.50; ☉9am-6pm;) recreates a 19th-century bog village. The museum adjoins the sprawling Red Fox pub, which remains popular with locals for a sociable pint.

❷ Caherciveen

Caherciveen began life as a fishing harbour and market town. The former barracks has been beautifully restored as a **museum** (☏066-401 0430; www.oldbarrackscahersiveen. com; Bridge St; adult/child €4/2; ☉10am-5.30pm

Mon-Sat, 11am-5.30pm Sun), there are some excellent places to stay and eat, and the surrounding countryside is a delight to explore.

❸ Valentia Island

Take the ferry just west of Caherciveen to Knightstown on Valentia Island, a beautiful and under-visited corner of Kerry with a rich and fascinating history that is lovingly chronicled in the island's **heritage centre** (☏066-947 6411; School Rd, Knightstown; adult/ child €3.50/free; ☉10.30am-5.30pm May-Sep), a short distance from the ferry. A few miles west of Knightstown, Valentia is linked to the mainland by a bridge at Portmagee. Visit the **Skellig Experience** (☏066-947 6306; www.skelligexperience.com; adult/child €5/3, incl cruise €30/17.50; ☉10am-7pm Jul-Aug, to 6pm May, Jun & Sep, 10am-5pm Tue-Sat Mar-Apr & Oct-Nov;) before crossing to the village for lunch at the Bridge Bar (p219).

❹ Skellig Ring

The Skellig Ring, a scenic and little-travelled 18km detour from the Ring of Kerry (N70), links Portmagee and Water-

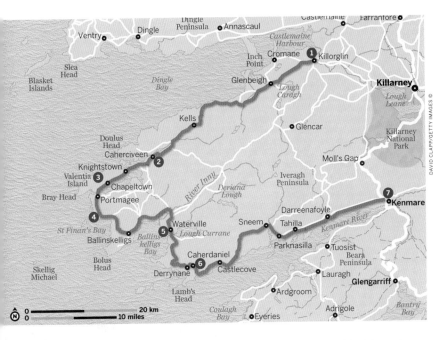

DAVID CLAPP/GETTY IMAGES ©

ville via a Gaeltacht (Irish-speaking) area centred on Ballinskelligs. The area is wild and beautiful, with the ragged outline of Skellig Michael never far from view.

❺ Waterville

Waterville is an old-fashioned seaside resort known for its golf and fishing. Silent-movie star Charlie Chaplin famously holidayed here in the 1960s with his extended family, returning every year for more than a decade. A bronze statue of Chaplin beams out from the seafront.

❻ Caherdaniel

The road between Waterville and Caherdaniel climbs high over the ridge of Beenarourke, providing grandstand views of some of the finest scenery on the Ring of Kerry. Caherdaniel, a tiny hamlet hidden among the trees at the head of Derrynane Bay, is the ancestral home of Daniel O'Connell, 'the Liberator', whose family made money smuggling from their base by the dunes. From Castlecove to Kenmare the main N70 Ring of Kerry road swings inland. Sneem (An tSnaidhm) is

a good place to pause and stretch your legs before the road dives into the woods for the final 27km stretch to Kenmare.

❼ Kenmare

Kenmare is a pretty little town with a neat triangle of streets lined with craft shops, galleries, cafes and good quality restaurants. The summit of the pass between Kenmare and Killarney at Moll's Gap is worth a stop for great views and good eating at the Avoca Cafe.

Finish Moll's Gap

❶ Need to Know

A number of Killarney tour companies run daily bus trips around the Ring.

❷ Take a Break

The Bridge Bar (p219) in Portmagee is a great place to stop for lunch.

☑ Top Tip

Drivers – start early or late, or travel anticlockwise, to avoid tour bus crowds.

Path to the monastery

RICK PRICE/GETTY IMAGES ©

Skellig Michael

A trip to the Skellig Islands, two wave-battered pinnacles of rock 12km off the coast, and the site of Ireland's most remote and spectacular ancient monastery, is an unforgettable experience.

Great For...

☑ Don't Miss

The 6th-century, stone-built beehive cells at the very summit of Skellig Michael.

The jagged, 217m-high rock of Skellig Michael (Archangel Michael's Rock; like St Michael's Mount in Cornwall and Mont St Michel in Normandy) is the larger of the two Skellig Islands and a Unesco World Heritage site. Early Christian monks established a community and survived here from the 6th until the 12th or 13th century. The monastic buildings perch on a saddle in the rock, some 150m above sea level, reached by 600 steep steps cut into the rock face.

The astounding 6th-century oratories and beehive cells vary in size; the largest cell has a floor space of 4.5m by 3.6m. You can see the monks' south-facing vegetable garden and their cistern for collecting rainwater. The most impressive structural achievements are the settlement's

Atlantic puffin, Skellig Michael

RICK PRICE/GETTY IMAGES ©

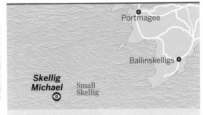

ℹ Need to Know

Boat trips usually run from Easter until September, depending on weather. See www.heritageireland.ie for more information.

✕ Take A Break

There are no facilities on Skellig Michael – take a packed lunch with you.

★ Top Tip

To see the islands up close without landing, consider a cruise with Skellig Experience from Valentia Island.

foundations – platforms built on the steep slope using nothing more than earth and drystone walls.

Influenced by the Coptic Church (founded by St Anthony in the deserts of Egypt and Libya), the monk's determined quest for ultimate solitude led them to this remote, wind-blown edge of Europe. Not much is known about the life of the monastery, but there are records of Viking raids in AD 812 and 823. Monks were kidnapped or killed, but the community recovered and carried on. In the 11th century a rectangular oratory was added to the site, but although it was expanded in the 12th century, the monks abandoned the rock around this time.

After the introduction of the Gregorian calendar in 1582, Skellig Michael became a popular spot for weddings. Marriages were forbidden during Lent, but since Skellig used the old Julian calendar, a trip to the islands allowed those unable to wait for Easter to tie the knot.

While Skellig Michael looks like two triangles linked by a spur, Small Skellig is longer, lower and much craggier. From a distance it looks as if someone battered it with a feather pillow that burst. Close up you realise you're looking at a colony of over 20,000 pairs of breeding gannets, the second-largest breeding colony in the world. Most boats circle the island so you can see the gannets and you may see basking seals as well. Small Skellig is a bird sanctuary; no landing is permitted.

TRISH PUNCH/GETTY IMAGES ©

Killarney National Park

Any cynicism engendered by Killarney's shamrock-filled souvenir stores evaporates when you begin to explore the lakes and woods of sublime Killarney National Park.

Great For...

☑ Don't Miss

Take a boat tour of the Killarney lakes and enjoy the serenity from a different perspective..

The core of the **national park** (www.killarney nationalpark.ie) [FREE] is the Muckross Estate, donated to the state by Arthur Bourn Vincent in 1932; the park was designated a Unesco Biosphere Reserve in 1982. The Killarney Lakes – Lough Leane (the Lower Lake, or 'Lake of Learning'), Muckross (or Middle) Lake and the Upper Lake – make up about a quarter of the park, surrounded by natural oak and yew woodland, and overlooked by the high crags and moors of Purple Mountain (832m) to the west and Knockrower (552m) to the south.

The park is rich in wildlife as well as scenic beauty: deer swim out to graze on the lake islands, red squirrels and pine martens scamper in the woods, and salmon and brown trout thrive in the clean waters. Fifteen white-tailed eagles were reintroduced

NICOLAS KIPOURAX PAQUET/GETTY IMAGES ©

ⓘ Need to Know

Killarney tourist office stocks walking guides and maps of the national park.

✕ Take A Break

There's a good cafe in the visitor centre near Muckross House.

> ### ★ Top Tip
> Take binoculars, and look out for rare white-tailed eagles circling above the Middle Lake.

1861. It's 5km south of Killarney, signposted from the N71. (🕿064-667 0144; www. muckross-house.ie; Muckross Estate; adult/child €9/6, incl Muckross Trad Farms €15/10.50; 🕘9am-7pm Jul & Aug, to 5.30pm Sep-Jun)

Muckross Traditional Farms Museum

These re-creations of 1930s farms evoke the sights, sounds and smells of real farming – cow dung, hay, wet earth and peat smoke, plus a cacophony of chickens, ducks, pigs and donkeys. Costumed guides bring the traditional farm buildings to life, and the petting area allows kids to get up close and personal with piglets, lambs, ducklings and chicks. The farms are immediately east of Muckross House; you'll need at least two hours to do justice to the self-guided tour. (🕿064-663 0804; www. muckross-house.ie; Muckross Estate; adult/child €9/6, incl Muckross House €15/10.50; 🕘10am-6pm Jun-Aug, 1-6pm May & Sep, 1-6pm Sat & Sun Apr & Oct)

here in 2007; by 2015 at least four nesting pairs were established in County Kerry, with one pair breeding successfully in the national park.

◎ Sights & Activities

Muckross House Historic Building

This impressive Victorian mansion is crammed with fascinating objects (70% of the contents are original). Portraits by John Singer Sargent adorn the walls alongside trophy stags heads and giant stuffed trout, while antique Killarney furniture, with its distinctive inlaid scenes of local beauty spots, graces the grand apartments along with tapestries, Persian rugs, silverware and china specially commissioned for Queen Victoria's visit in

Muckross Abbey   Ruins

This well-preserved ruin (actually a friary, though everyone calls it an abbey) was founded in 1448 and burned by Cromwell's troops in 1652. There's a square-towered church and a small, atmospheric cloister with a giant yew tree in the centre (legend has it that the tree is as old as the abbey). In the chancel is the tomb of the McCarthy Mòr chieftains, and an elaborate 19th-century memorial to local philanthropist Lucy Gallwey. The abbey is 1.5km north of Muckross House. (Muckross Estate; ⊗24hr) FREE

Ross Castle   Castle

Lakeside Ross Castle dates back to the 15th century, when it was a residence of the O'Donoghue family. It was the last place in Munster to succumb to Cromwell's forces, thanks partly to its cunning spiral staircase,

every step of which is a different height in order to break an attacker's stride. The castle is a lovely 3km walk or bike ride from the pedestrian park entrance; you may well spot deer along the way. (☎064-663 5851; www.heritageireland.ie; Ross Rd; adult/child €4/2; ⊗9am-5.45pm Mar-Oct)

Inisfallen   Island

The first monastery on Inisfallen (the largest of the lake's islands) was founded by St Finian the Leper in the 7th century. The extensive ruins of a 12th-century **Augustinian priory** and an oratory with a carved Romanesque doorway stand on the site of St Finian's original. You can hire a motor boat with boatman (around €10) from Ross Castle for the 10-minute trip to the island. In calm weather you can hire a rowing boat (€5 per hour; allow 30 minutes each way).

Muckross House

Knockreer House & Gardens   Park

Killarney House, built for the Earl of Kenmare in the 1870s, burned down in 1913; the present Knockreer House was built on the same site in 1958 and is now home to a national park education centre. It isn't open to the public, but its gardens, featuring a terraced lawn and a summerhouse, have magnificent views across the lakes to the mountains. From the park entrance opposite St Mary's Cathedral, follow the path to your right for about 500m. (⏰8am-7pm Jun-Aug, to 6pm Apr, May & Oct, to 5pm Nov-Mar) FREE

Killarney Lake Tours   Boat Tour

One-hour tours of Lough Leane in a comfortable, enclosed cruise boat depart four times daily from the pier beside Ross Castle, taking in the island of Inisfallen (no landing) and O'Sullivan's Cascade (a waterfall on the west shore). (☎064-663 2638; www.killarneylaketours.ie; Ross Castle Pier; adult/child €10/5; ⏰Apr-Oct)

ℹ Getting Around

Walking, cycling and boat trips are the best ways to explore the park. There are two pedestrian/bike entrances in Killarney town: opposite St Mary's Cathedral (24-hour access); and the so-called **Golden Gates** at the roundabout on Muckross Rd (open 8am to 7pm June to August, to 6pm April, May and October, to 5pm November to March).

Jaunting cars depart from Kenmare Pl in Killarney town centre, and from the Jaunting Car Entrance to Muckross Estate, at a car park 3km south of town on the N71. Expect to pay around €15 to €20 per person for a tour from Killarney to Ross Castle and back. There are no set prices; haggle for longer tours.

Killarney

Modern-day Killarney is a well-oiled tourism machine set in the midst of sublime scenery. Its manufactured tweeness is renowned – the shops selling soft-toy *shillelaghs* and shamrocks, the placards on street corners pointing to trad-music sessions.

However, it has attractions beyond its proximity to lakes, waterfalls and woodland spreading beneath a skyline of 1000m-plus peaks. In a town that's been practising the tourism game for more than 250 years, competition keeps standards high and visitors on all budgets can expect to find good restaurants, great pubs and comfortable accommodation.

Mobbed in summer, Killarney is perhaps at its best in the late spring and early autumn when the crowds are manageable, but the weather is still good enough to enjoy its outdoor activities.

> *County Kerry contains some of Ireland's most iconic scenery.*

Boat at Ross Castle

⊙ SIGHTS & ACTIVITIES

Killarney's biggest attraction, in every sense, is Killarney National Park (p210). The town itself can easily be explored on foot in an hour or two.

The traditional way to tour the national park is by horse-drawn **jaunting car**, which comes with a driver known as a jarvey. Jaunting cars depart from Kenmare Pl in Killarney town centre, and from the Jaunting Car Entrance to Muckross Estate, at a car park 3km south of town on the N71. Expect to pay around €15 to €20 per person for a tour from Killarney to Ross Castle and back. There are no set prices; haggle for longer tours.

Ross Castle
Traditional Boats   Boat Tour

The open boats at Ross Castle offer appealing trips with boatmen who define the word 'character'. Rates are around €10 per person for a trip to Inisfallen or the Middle Lake and back; €15 for a tour of all three lakes. (085 174 2997; Ross Castle Pier; ⊙9am-5.30pm)

PATRYK KOSMIDER/SHUTTERSTOCK ©

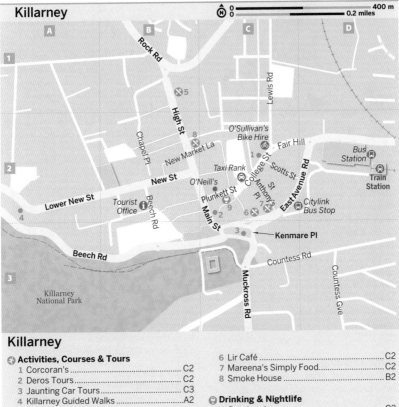

Killarney

Jaunting Car Tours   Tour

Killarney's traditional horse-drawn jaunting cars provide tours from the town to Ross Castle and Muckross Estate, complete with amusing commentary from the driver (known as a 'jarvey'). The cost varies depending on distance; cars can fit up to four people. The pick-up point, nicknamed 'the Ha Ha' or 'the Block', is on Kenmare Pl. (☎064-663 3358; www.killarneyjauntingcars.ie; per car €30-80)

Killarney Guided Walks Walking Tour

Guided two-hour walks through the national park woodlands leave at 11am daily from opposite St Mary's Cathedral at the western end of New St. Tours meander through Knockreer Gardens, then to spots where Charles de Gaulle holidayed, David Lean filmed *Ryan's Daughter* and Brother Cudda slept for 200 years. Tours available at other times on request. (☎087 639 4362; www.killarneyguidedwalks.com; adult/child €9/5)

Where to Stay

As the county's largest town, Killarney has the best accommodation offering. You'll find numerous B&Bs just outside the centre on Rock, Lewis and Muckross Rds. The town also has scores of generic hotels aimed at tour groups. Many places offer bike hire (around €12 to €15 per day) and discounted tours. Book ahead everywhere in summer. Dingle Town and Kenmare also have many charming midrange B&Bs and pubs that provide accommodation.

Village life
ANDHAL/GETTY IMAGES ©

Salmon Fishing   Fishing
The River Laune, which flows from Lough Leane to the sea, is one of Ireland's best salmon rivers. The season runs from 17 January to 30 September, with the best fishing from late July onwards. Both a permit (one day/seven days from €25/140) and a state rod licence (one day/three weeks €20/40) are required. You can also fish for salmon in the Killarney lakes (no permit needed, but state rod licence still required). Permits and licences available from **O'Neill's** (☑064-6631970; 6 Plunkett St; ⏰10am-9.30pm Mon-Fri, 10am-9pm Sat & Sun) in Killarney. (www.fishing inireland.info)

✪ EATING

Lir Café   Cafe €
Great coffee and hip atmosphere in Killarney's coolest cafe; food is limited to cakes, biscuits and the real treat, handmade chocolates, including Bailey's truffles.

(☑064-663 3859; www.lircafe.com; Kenmare Pl; mains €3-7; ⏰8am-9pm Mon-Thu, to 9.30pm Fri & Sat, to 7pm Sun; 📶)

Mareena's Simply Food   Irish €€
The clue is in the name – Mareena serves the finest of locally sourced produce, from scallops and sea bass to neck of lamb and pork fillet, cooked plainly and simply to let the quality of the food speak for itself. The decor matches the cuisine, unfussy and understated. (☑066-663 7787; www.mareenassimplyfood.com; East Avenue Rd; mains €17-23; ⏰noon-2.30pm & 6-9pm Tue-Sun) 🖉

Smoke House   Steak, Seafood €€
One of Killarney's busiest restaurants, this always-crowded bistro was the first establishment in Ireland to cook with a Josper (superhot Spanish charcoal oven). Stylish salads include Dingle prawn, and its Kerry surf'n'turf platter – a half-lobster and fillet steak – is decadence on a plate. Brunch served noon till 3pm includes eggs Florentine and Benedict. (☑087 233 9611; http://thesmokehouse.ie; 8 High St; mains lunch €7-16, dinner €15-29; ⏰9am-10pm)

Gaby's Seafood Restaurant   Seafood €€€
Gaby's is a refined dining experience serving superb seafood in a traditional manner. Peruse the menu by the fire before drifting past the wine racks to the low-lit dining room to savour exquisite Gallic dishes such as lobster in cognac and cream. The wine list is long and the advice unerring. (☑064-663 2519; 27 High St; mains €30-50; ⏰6-10pm Mon-Sat)

🍷 DRINKING & NIGHTLIFE

O'Connor's   Pub
This tiny traditional pub with leaded-glass doors is one of Killarney's most popular haunts. Live music plays every night; good bar food is served daily in summer. In warmer weather, the crowds spill out onto the adjacent lane. (7 High St; ⏰10.30am-11pm Mon-Thu, to 12.30am Fri & Sat, 12.30-11pm Sun)

Countryside near Caherdaniel

Courtney's   Pub

Inconspicuous on the outside, inside this timeless pub bursts at the seams with Irish music sessions many nights year-round. This is where locals come to see their old mates perform and to kick off a night on the town. (www.courtneysbar.com; Plunkett St; ⊙2-11.30pm Sun-Thu, to 12.30am Fri & Sat, from 5pm winter)

 INFORMATION

Tourist Office (☑064-663 1633; www.killarney. ie; Beech Rd; ⊙9am-5pm Mon-Sat; 🛜) Can handle most queries; especially good with transport intricacies.

🛈 GETTING THERE & AWAY

AIR

Kerry Airport (KIR; ☑066-976 4644; www. kerryairport.ie) Kerry Airport is at Farranfore, about 17km north of Killarney on the N22. There are daily flights to Dublin and London's Luton and Stansted airports, and less frequent services to Frankfurt-Hahn, Germany, Faro, Portugal and Alicante, Spain.

The small airport has a restaurant, bar, bureau de change and ATM. Virtually all the major car-hire firms have desks at the airport.

BUS

Bus Éireann (☑064-663 0011; www.buseireann.ie) operates from the bus station on Park Rd. For Dublin you need to change at Cork – the train is much faster. **Citylink** (☑091 564164; www. citylink.ie) buses to Galway leave from the coach stop outside the Malton Hotel on East Avenue Rd.

Cork (€27, two hours, hourly)

Dublin (€40, six hours, six daily)

Galway (Citylink; €30, three hours, two daily)

TRAIN

Killarney's train station is behind the Malton Hotel, just east of the centre. There are one or two direct services per day to Cork and Dublin; otherwise you'll have to change at Mallow.

Cork (€27.80, 1½ hours)

Dublin (€69, 3¼ hours, every two hours)

Cahergal ring fort, Caherciveen

ℹ️ GETTING AROUND

TO/FROM THE AIRPORT
Bus Éireann has hourly services between Killarney and Kerry Airport (€5.50, 20 minutes).

A taxi to Killarney costs about €35.

BICYCLE
Bicycles are ideal for exploring the scattered sights of the Killarney area, many of which are accessible only by bike or on foot.

O'Sullivan's Bike Hire (Map p215; 📞064-663 1282; www.killarneyrentabike.com; College St; per day/week €15/80) has branches on College St, on Beech Rd (opposite the tourist office) and on Muckross Rd (opposite Randles Court Hotel). Road, mountain and children's bikes are available.

Caherciveen

The main town of the Iveragh peninsula, Caherciveen (pronounced caar-suh-*veen;* from *cathair saidhbhín,* Little Sarah's Ring Fort) fell on hard times at the end of the

20th century – indeed, O'Connell St (north of Main St) still looks like a boulevard of broken dreams, lined with abandoned hotels and pubs.

But the last few years have seen a determined effort to reinvent the town as a tourism centre. The main street and waterfront areas have been spruced up, and the former barracks has been beautifully restored as a museum.

The town is indelibly linked with the fight for Irish independence – it was the birthplace of Daniel O'Connell, 'the Great Liberator', and was where the first shots of the 1867 Fenian Rising were fired.

◎ SIGHTS

Ring Forts   Ruin
Two impressive stone ring forts stand 3km northwest of Caherciveen, both reached from a shared parking area. **Cahergal**, the larger and more impressive, dates from the 10th century and has stairways on the inside walls, a *clochán* (beehive hut), and the remains of a roundhouse. The smaller,

9th-century **Leacanabuile** contains the outlines of four houses. Both have a commanding position overlooking Valentia Harbour, with superb views of the Kerry mountains. (Ballycarbery) FREE

EATING

Camo's
Cafe €

A friendly neighbourhood cafe that cooks familiar favourites really well – from fish and chips to steak sandwiches – Camo's also indulges in a bit of local foodie goodness with dishes such as oak-smoked salmon sandwiches on home-baked brown bread, and a delicious black-pudding salad. (066-948 1122; www.camos.ie; 24 Church St; mains €7-15; 10am-5pm Mon-Thu, to 9.30pm Fri & Sat, noon-6pm Sun May-Sep, shorter hours Oct-Apr;)

QCs Seafood Restaurant & Bar
Seafood €€

QCs is a modern take on a classic pub and as such is open pub hours for pints and craic. But when the kitchen's open, some of the finest food on the Ring pours forth (especially locally sourced seafood). Hours may vary – it's best to call ahead and book a table. Upstairs are six boutique B&B bedrooms (doubles from €109). (066-947 2244; www.qcsrestaurant.com; 3 Main St; mains €16-30; 12.30-2.30pm & 6-9.30pm Mon-Sat, 5-9pm Sun;)

Portmagee

Portmagee's much-photographed single street is a rainbow of colourful houses. On summer mornings, the small harbour comes to life with boats embarking on the choppy crossing to the Skellig Islands.

The focus of village life is the friendly **Bridge Bar** (mains €10-25; food served noon-9pm), a local gathering point that hosts traditional Irish music and set dancing sessions every Friday and Sunday night (plus Tuesdays in July and August). The bar's nautical-themed **Moorings Restaurant** (mains €20-25, 6-10pm Tue to Sun) specialises

Gap of Dunloe

The Gap of Dunloe is a wild and scenic mountain pass, studded with crags and bejewelled with lakes and waterfalls, that lies to the west of Killarney National Park, squeezed between Purple Mountain and the high summits of Macgillycuddy's Reeks (Ireland's highest mountain range).

Although it lies outside the national park, it has been a vital part of the Killarney tourist trail since the late 18th century when, inspired by the Romantic poets, wealthy tourists came in search of 'sublime' and 'savage' landscapes.

The traditional way to see the Gap is via a tour from Killarney – by bus to Kate Kearney's Cottage, then either on foot or by jaunting car through the Gap to Lord Brandon's Cottage on the Upper Lake, and finally by boat to Ross Castle and then bus back to town (per person €30, plus €20 for jaunting car). Most hostels, hotels and pubs in Killarney can set up these tours.

Corcoran's If you're pushed for time, this outfit offers half-day coach tours that take in Killarney, Ross Castle, Muckross House and the Gap of Dunloe. They also offer day-long tours of the Ring of Kerry (€18.50) and Dingle and Slea Head (€21.50. (064-663 6666; www.corcorantours.com; per person €20)

Deros Tours Gap of Dunloe (€27), Ring of Kerry (€19) and Dingle and Slea Head (€22) tours. (064-663 1251; www.derostours.com)

👓 Exploring Moll's Gap

Built in the 1820s to replace an older track to the east (the Old Kenmare Road, now followed by the Kerry Way hiking trail), the vista-crazy N71 Killarney to Kenmare road (32km) winds between rock and lake, with plenty of lay-bys to stop and admire the views (and recover from the switchback bends). Watch out for the buses squeezing along the road.

About 17km south of Killarney is Ladies' View, where the gorgeous panorama over the Upper Lake and Purple Mountain were enjoyed by Queen Victoria's ladies-in-waiting in 1861.

A further 5km south is the summit of the pass at **Moll's Gap**, worth a stop for great views and good eating – and not necessarily in that order. Avoca Cafe (064-663 4720; www.avoca.ie; Moll's Gap; mains €8-14; 9.30am-5pm Mon-Fri, 10am-5pm Sat & Sun;) has awesome panoramas and delicious fare like smoked salmon salad, pistachio-studded pork terrine and decadent cakes.

Horses at Moll's Gap
ANDY GOSS/GETTY IMAGES ©

in locally landed seafood, while the bar itself serves excellent fish and chips.

Sneem

The village's Irish name translates as 'the knot', which is thought to refer to the River Sneem that swirls, knot-like, into nearby

Kenmare Bay. The river splits the village in two, with separate village squares on either side and a picturesque waterfall tumbling below the old stone bridge.

From June to September the village hosts a weekly **farmers market** (Bridge St; 11am-4pm Tue). The **tourist office** (064-667 5807; South Sq; 11.30am-5.30pm May-Sep) is in the Joli Coeur craft shop.

🍴 EATING

Village Kitchen Irish €

For 25 years this family restaurant has been dishing up breakfast, lunch and dinner to locals and visitors alike. The menu runs from seafood chowder and fish specials to steak sandwiches, pizza and Irish stew. (064-664 5281; 3 Bridge St; mains €8-12; 10am-6pm, to 9pm Jun-Aug;)

Kenmare

Kenmare (ken-*mair*) is the thinking person's Killarney. Ideally positioned for exploring the Ring of Kerry (and the Beara Peninsula), but without the coach-tour crowds and calculated 'Oirishness' of its more famous neighbour, Kenmare is a pretty little town with a neat triangle of streets lined with craft shops, galleries, cafes and good quality restaurants.

🍴 EATING

Tom Crean Fish & Wine Irish €€

Named in honour of Kerry's pioneering Antarctic explorer, this venerable restaurant uses only the best of local organic produce, cheeses and fresh seafood, all served in modern, low-key surrounds. The oysters *au naturel* capture the scent of the sea; the homemade ravioli of prawn mousse, and sesame seed-crusted Atlantic salmon with lime and coriander are divine. (064-664 1589; www.tomcrean.ie; Main St; mains €16-30; 5-9.30pm Thu-Mon;)

ℹ GETTING THERE & AWAY

The twisting, 32km-long drive on the N71 from Kenmare to Killarney is surprisingly dramatic with tunnels and stark mountain vistas.

Buses run to Killarney (€12.10, 45 minutes, three daily) year-round.

Dingle Peninsula

The Dingle Peninsula (Corca Dhuibhne; www.dingle-peninsula.ie) is southwest Ireland's final flourish, a gnarled thumb of land cocked at the Atlantic and culminating in the Irish mainland's westernmost point. In the shadow of sacred Mt Brandon, a maze of fuchsia-fringed *boreens* (country lanes) weaves together an ancient landscape of prehistoric ring forts and beehive huts, early Christian chapels, crosses and holy wells, picturesque hamlets and abandoned villages.

But it's where the land meets the ocean – whether in a welter of wave-pounded rocks, or where the surf unrolls gently into secluded, sandy coves – that Dingle's beauty truly reveals itself.

Centred on charming Dingle town, the peninsula has long been a beacon for those of an alternative bent, attracting artists, craftspeople, musicians and a whole range of idiosyncratic characters who can be found in workshops, museums, trad sessions and folkloric festivals throughout Dingle's tiny settlements.

Dingle Town

Framed by its fishing port, the peninsula's charming little 'capital' manages to be quaint without even trying. Many pubs double as shops, so you can enjoy Guinness and a singalong among screws and nails, wellies and horseshoes. It has long drawn runaways from across the world, making it a cosmopolitan, creative place. In summer its hilly streets can be clogged with visitors; in other seasons its authentic charms are yours for the savouring.

Although Dingle is one of Ireland's largest Gaeltacht towns, the locals have voted to retain the name Dingle rather than go by the officially sanctioned – and signposted – Gaelige name of An Daingean.

Dingle town

LITTLENY/SHUTTERSTOCK ©

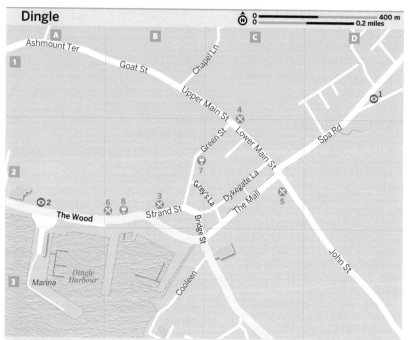

Dingle

◎ SIGHTS & ACTIVITIES

Dingle Oceanworld   Aquarium

Dingle's aquarium is a lot of fun, and includes a walk-through tunnel and a touch pool. Psychedelic fish glide through tanks that recreate such environments as Lake Malawi, the River Congo and the piranha-filled Amazon. Reef sharks and stingrays cruise the shark tank; water is pumped from the harbour for the spectacularly ugly wreck fish. (☏066-915 2111; www.dingle-oceanworld.ie; The Wood; adult/child €13/7.50; ◷10am-7pm Jul & Aug, to 5pm Sep-Jun; ⛵)

Dingle Brewing Company   Brewery

Housed in a 19th-century creamery building, this terrific craft brewery launched in 2011 on 20 July – not coincidentally Tom Crean's birthday (its single brew, a crisp, hoppy lager, is named after the local Antarctic explorer). Admission includes a self-guided or guided brewery tour as well as a pint. It's on the road towards the Connor Pass. (☏066-915 0743; www.dingle brewingcompany.com; Spa Rd; admission €6; ◷tours by reservation)

Dolphin Trips
Boat Tour

Boats run by the Dingle Boatmen's Association cooperative leave the pier daily for one-hour trips to see Dingle's most famous resident, Fungie the dolphin. It's free if Fungie doesn't show, but he usually does. The ticket office is next to the tourist office. (066-915 2626; www.dingledolphin.com; The Pier; adult/child €16/8)

Naomhòg Experience
Boating

Naomhòg is the Kerry name for a *currach*, a traditional Irish boat made from a wooden frame covered with tarred canvas (originally animal hides). They were used by the Blasket islanders for fishing, and are now maintained and raced by local enthusiasts. You can book a two-hour session in Dingle harbour learning how to row one. (087 699 2925; rowingdingle@gmail.com; Dingle Marina; per person €40)

✖ EATING

Chowder
Cafe €€

This unpretentious, always-busy cafe serves top-quality bistro food as well as breakfast pancakes and fry-ups – the signature seafood chowder is tasty, but lunch specials such as homemade crab tart, open sandwich of roast pork belly and stuffing, or mussels in garlic sauce are just superb. If it's sunny, try to bag one of the pavement tables. (Strand St; mains €9-15; 10am-5.30pm, to 9pm Jun-Aug)

Global Village Restaurant
International €€

With the sophisticated feel of a continental bistro, this restaurant offers a fusion of global recipes gathered by the well-travelled owner-chef, but utilises sustainable local produce, such as the Kerry mountain lamb. The wine list is excellent. (066-915 2325; www.globalvillagedingle.com; Upper Main St; mains €19-29; 5.30-9.30pm Mar-Oct)

Out of the Blue
Seafood €€€

'No chips', reads the menu of this funky blue-and-yellow, fishing-shack-style

🐦 Fungie the Dolphin

In 1983 a bottlenose dolphin swam into Dingle Bay and local tourism hasn't been quite the same since. Showing an unusual affinity for human company, he swam around with the local fishing fleet. Eventually somebody got the idea of charging tourists to go out on boats to see the friendly dolphin (nicknamed Fungie). Today up to 12 boats at a time and more than 1000 tourists a day ply the waters with Dingle's mascot, now a cornerstone of the local economy (there's even a bronze statue of him outside the tourist office).

In the wild, bottlenose dolphins live for an average of 25 years, though they have been know to live to over 40 in captivity. As Fungie has been around for more than 30 years (yes, it's still the same dolphin, recognisable by his distinctive markings), speculation is rife about how long it will be before he finally glides into the deep for the last time. And what will Dingle do without its dolphin?

Bottlenose dolphin, Dingle
CULTURA RM/GEORGE KARBUS PHOTOGRAPHY/GETTY IMAGES ©

restaurant on the waterfront. Despite its rustic surrounds, this is one of Dingle's best restaurants, with an intense devotion to fresh local seafood (and only seafood); if they don't like the catch, they don't open. With seafood this good, who needs chips? (066-915 0811; www.outoftheblue.ie; The Wood; mains €21-29; 5-9.30pm daily, plus 12.30-3pm Sun)

Idás   Irish €€€

Chef Kevin Murphy is dedicated to promoting the finest of Irish produce, much of it from Kerry, taking lamb and seafood and foraged herbs from the Dingle Peninsula and creating delicately flavoured concoctions such as braised John Dory fillet with fennel dashi cream, pickled cucumber, wild garlic and salad burnet. Early-bird menu offers two/three courses for €24.50/28.50. (066-915 0885; John St; mains €26-30; 5.30-9.30pm Tue-Sun)

🍷 DRINKING & NIGHTLIFE

John Benny's   Pub

A toasty cast-iron woodstove, stone slab floor, memorabilia on the walls, great staff and no intrusive TV make this one of Dingle's most enjoyable traditional pubs. Local musos pour in most nights for rockin' trad sessions. (www.johnbennyspub.com; Strand St; noon-11pm)

Dick Mack's   Pub

Stars in the pavement bear the names of Dick Mack's celebrity customers. Ancient wood and ancient snugs dominate the interior, which is lit like the inside of a whiskey bottle. Out the back there's a warren of tables, chairs and characters. (Green St; 3pm-late)

ℹ️ GETTING THERE & AWAY

Bus Éireann (www.buseireann.ie) buses stop outside the car park behind the supermarket. Up to six buses a day serve Killarney (€17.60, 1½ to two hours) via Tralee (€14.40, 1¼ hours).

Slea Head Drive

The signposted **Slea Head Drive** is a 50km loop that passes through the villages of Ventry, Dunquin, Ballyferriter and Ballydavid to the west of Dingle town, and takes in all the main sights. Including time for sightseeing, it's at least a half-day's drive or one or two days' bike ride. The road is very narrow in a few places, so it's recommended that all vehicles drive the route clockwise – ignore this rule and you risk holding up traffic as you try to squeeze past a tour bus going in the opposite direction.

John Benny's pub, Dingle Town

CHRIS HILL/GETTY IMAGES ©

Attractions include fine beaches, good walks and superbly preserved structures from Dingle's ancient past including bee-hive huts, ring forts, inscribed stones and early Christian sites.

◉ SIGHTS

Celtic & Prehistoric Museum   Museum

This museum squeezes in an astonishing collection of Celtic and prehistoric arte-facts, including the world's largest woolly mammoth skull and tusks, as well as a 40,000-year-old cave-bear skeleton, Viking horse-bone ice skates, stone battle-axes, flint daggers and jewellery. It started as the private collection of owner Harry Moore, a US expat musician (ask him to strike up a Celtic tune). It's 4km southwest of Ventry. (📞087 770 3280; Kilvicadownig, Ventry; admission €5; 🕙10am-5.30pm mid-Mar–Oct)

Blasket Centre   Cultural Centre

This wonderful interpretative centre cele-brates the rich cultural life of the now-abandoned Blasket Islands. It is housed in striking modern building with a long, white hall ending in a picture window looking directly at the islands. Great Blasket's rich community of storytellers and musicians is profiled along with its literary visitors like playwright JM Synge, author of *Playboy of the Western World*. The more prosaic practi-calities of island life are covered by exhibits on boatbuilding and fishing.

The centre has a good **cafe** with a view of the islands, and a useful **bookshop**. (Ionad an Bhlascaoid Mhóir; 📞066-915 6444; www.heritageireland.ie; adult/child €4/2; 🕙10am-6pm Apr-Oct)

Gallarus Oratory   Historic Site

Gallarus Oratory is one of Ireland's most beautiful ancient buildings, its smoothly constructed dry-stone walls in the shape of an upturned boat. It has stood in this lonely spot beneath the brown hills for some 1200

🔭 Views from Connor Pass

Topping out at 456m, the R560 across the Connor (or Conor) Pass from Dingle town to Cloghane and Stradbally is Ireland's highest public road. On a foggy day you'll see nothing but the tarmac just in front of you, but in fine weather it offers phenomenal views of Dingle Harbour to the south and Mt Brandon to the north. The road is in good shape, despite being narrow in places and steep and twisting on the north side (large signs portend doom for buses and trucks; caravans are a no-no).

The summit car park yields views down to glacial lakes in the rock-strewn valley below, where you can see the remains of walls and huts where people once lived impossibly hard lives. From the smaller, lower car park on the north side, beside a waterfall, you can make a 10-minute climb to hidden **Pedlar's Lake** and the kind of vistas that inspire mountain climbers.

JANMIKO/GETTY IMAGES ©

years and has withstood the elements perfectly. There is a narrow doorway on the western side and a single, round-headed window on the east. Gallarus is clearly signposted off the R559, 8km northwest of Dingle town. (📞066-915 6444; www.heritage ireland.ie) FREE

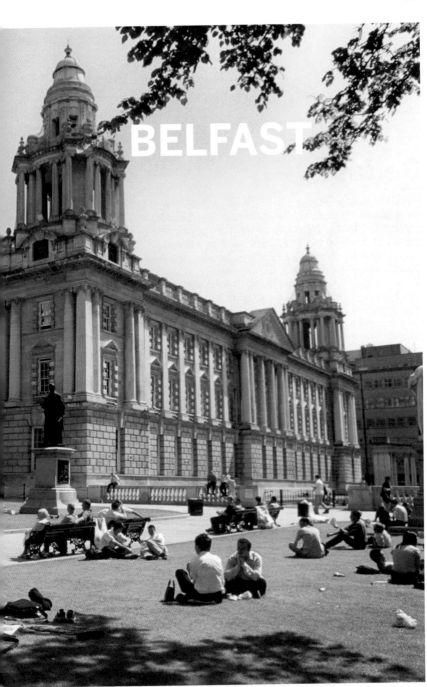

BELFAST

Belfast

Belfast is in many ways a brand-new city. Once lumped with Beirut, Baghdad and Bosnia as one of the four 'Bs' for travellers to avoid, in recent years it has pulled off a remarkable transformation from bombs-and-bullets pariah to a hip-hotels-and-hedonism party town.

The old shipyards on the Lagan continue to give way to the luxury apartments of the Titanic Quarter, whose centrepiece, the stunning, star-shaped edifice housing the Titanic Belfast centre, covering the ill-fated liner's construction here, has become the city's number-one tourist draw.

New venues keep popping up – already this decade historic Crumlin Road Gaol and SS Nomadic opened to the public, and WWI warship HMS Caroline is set to become a floating museum in 2016. They all add to a list of attractions that includes beautifully restored Victorian architecture, a waterfront lined with modern art, a fantastic foodie scene and music-filled pubs.

☑ In This Section

❶ Arriving in Belfast

Belfast International Airport Frequent buses to the city (return £10.50, 30 minutes) from 7am to 11pm, hourly through the night.

George Best Belfast City Airport Frequent buses to the city (return £3.80, 15 minutes) between 6am and 9.30pm.

Europa Bus Station Buses from Dublin arrive here; located right in the city centre.

Belfast Central Station Trains from Dublin arrive here; your rail ticket entitles you to a free bus ride into the city centre.

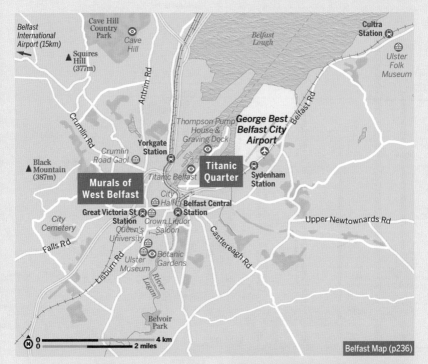

Belfast International Airport (15km)

Cave Hill Country Park

Cave Hill

▲ Squires Hill (377m)

Antrim Rd

Belfast Lough

Cultra Station

Ulster Folk Museum

Crumlin Rd

Black ▲ Mountain (387m)

Crumlin Road Gaol 🏛

Yorkgate Station

Thompson Pump House & Graving Dock

George Best Belfast City Airport

Belfast Rd

Titanic Belfast

Titanic Quarter

Sydenham Station

Murals of West Belfast

City Hall 🏛

Belfast Central Station

Great Victoria St Station

Crown Liquor Saloon

City Cemetery

Queen's University

Ulster Museum 🏛

Botanic Gardens

Falls Rd

Lisburn Rd

Castlereagh Rd

Upper Newtownards Rd

River Lagan

Belvoir Park

Ⓝ 0 —— 4 km
0 —— 2 miles

Belfast Map (p236)

➡ Belfast in One Day

Start with a free guided tour of **City Hall** (p234). Take a **black taxi tour** (p233) of the West Belfast murals, and ask the taxi driver to drop you off for lunch at **Holohan's** (p240). Afterwards, cruise the river on a **Lagan Boat Company** (p237) tour, then spend the rest of the afternoon exploring **Titanic Belfast** (p230), before dinner at the **Barking Dog** (p241).

➡ Belfast in Two Days

On your second day, explore the fascinating exhibits in the **Ulster Museum** (p234) and take a stroll through the **Botanic Gardens** (p235). In the afternoon either take a guided tour around historic **Crumlin Road Gaol** (p238), or go for a hike up Cave Hill. Spend the evening crawling traditional pubs such as **Kelly's Cellars** (p242), the **Duke of York** (p242), and **Crown Liquor Saloon** (p242).

From left: Belfast houses; Titanic Quarter (p230); River Lagan; Crown Liquor Saloon (p234 & p242)

Titanic Belfast

NAHLIK/SHUTTERSTOCK ©

Titanic Quarter

Belfast's former shipbuilding yards – the birthplace of RMS Titanic – stretch along the east side of the River Lagan, dominated by the towering yellow cranes known as Samson and Goliath.

Great For...

☑ **Don't Miss**

Taking a peek at the 1st-class toilets aboard the SS *Nomadic*.

Titanic Belfast

The head of the slipway where the Titanic was built is now occupied by the gleaming, angular edifice of **Titanic Belfast** (www. titanicbelfast.com; Queen's Rd; adult/child £15.50/7.25, combination ticket with Thompson Pumphouse & Graving Dock £19/9.25; ⊙9am-7pm Apr & Jun-Aug, 9am-6pm May & Sep, 10am-5pm Oct-Mar), an unmissable multimedia extravaganza that charts the history of Belfast and the creation of the world's most famous ocean liner. Cleverly designed exhibits enlivened by historic images, animated projections and soundtracks chart Belfast's rise to turn-of-the-20th-century industrial superpower, followed by a high-tech ride through a noisy, smells-and-all re-creation of the city's shipyards.

You can explore every detail of the Titanic's construction, from a computer

Titanic Memorial outside City Hall (p234)

HERITAGE IMAGES/GETTY IMAGES ©

❶ Need to Know

A series of information boards along Queen's Rd describe items and areas of interest.

✕ Take a Break

There are cafes in both Titanic Belfast and the Thompson Pump House.

★ Top Tip

Get a free self-guided tour of East Belfast (including Titanic Quarter) for your mobile device at http://belfast itours.com.

'fly-through' from keel to bridge, to replicas of the passenger accommodation. Perhaps most poignant are the few flickering images that constitute the only film footage of the ship in existence.

Behind the building you can see the massive slipways where the *Titanic* and her sister ship *Olympic* were built and launched.

SS Nomadic

Slightly to the southwest, you can take in the last remaining vessel of the White Star Line, the **SS Nomadic** (www.nomadicbelfast. com; Hamilton Dock, Queen's Rd; adult/child £7/5; ⏱10am-5pm daily Apr-Sep, Tue-Sun Oct-Mar). Built in Belfast in 1911, the little steam-ship ferried 1st- and 2nd-class passengers between Cherbourg Harbour and the ocean liners that were too big to dock at the French port. On 10 April 1912 it delivered

172 passengers to the ill-fated *Titanic*. First-come, first-served guided tours run every 30 minutes from 10am until an hour before closing. Alternatively, you're free to roam at will (don't miss the 1st-class toilets!).

Thompson Pump House & Graving Dock

At the far end of Queen's Rd is the most impressive monument to the days of the great liners – the vast **Thompson Graving Dock** (www.titanicsdock.com; Queen's Rd; graving dock free, pump house adult/child £6/4, combination ticket with Titanic Belfast £19/9.25; ⏱10am-5pm Sat-Thu, 9.30am-5pm Fri; 🛜) where the *Titanic* was fitted out.

Beside it is the Thompson Pump House, which has an exhibition on Belfast ship-building. Guided tours (2pm Saturday and Sunday) include a viewing of original film footage from the shipyards, a visit to the inner workings of the pump house and a walk along the floor of the dry dock.

Republican mural, Falls Rd, West Belfast

CARLOS SANCHEZ PEREYRA/GETTY IMAGES ©

Murals of West Belfast

The political murals of West Belfast are one of the city's most compelling sights, a colourful and visceral reminder of the tensions that once tore the city apart.

Great For...

☑ Don't Miss

A visit to the Peace Line, the corrugated steel wall that divides West Belfast's Protestant and Catholic communities.

Belfast's tradition of political murals is a century old, dating from 1908 when images of King Billy (William III, Protestant victor over the Catholic James II at the Battle of the Boyne in 1690) were painted by Unionists protesting against home rule for Ireland. The tradition was revived in the late 1970s as the Troubles wore on, with murals used to mark out sectarian territory, make political points, commemorate historical events and glorify terrorist groups.

Republican Murals

The first Republican murals appeared in 1981, when the hunger strike by Republican prisoners – demanding recognition as political prisoners – at the Maze Prison saw the emergence of dozens of murals of support. In later years, Republican muralists broadened their scope to cover wider political issues, Irish legends and historical events.

West Belfast mural featuring singer Tommy Sands

BRENDAN HOWARD/SHUTTERSTOCK ©

Loyalist Murals

Loyalist murals have traditionally been more militaristic and defiant in tone than the Republican murals. The Loyalist battle cry of 'No Surrender!' is everywhere, along with red, white and blue painted kerbstones, paramilitary insignia and images of King Billy, usually shown on a prancing white horse.

Murals Today

In recent years there has been a lot of debate about what to do with Belfast's murals. There's no doubt they have become an important tourist attraction, but there is now a move to replace the more aggressive and militaristic images with murals dedicated to local heroes and famous figures such as footballer George Best and *Narnia* novelist CS Lewis.

ⓘ Need to Know
The best way to see the murals is on a black taxi tour, but there's nothing to stop you exploring on foot.

✕ Take a Break
Bia (www.biabelfast.com; 216 Falls Rd; mains £8-22; ⊙9am-6pm Mon, 8am-8pm Tue-Sat, 10am-6pm Sun; 🛜🚼), in the Irish-language and arts centre Cultúrlann McAdam Ó Fiaich, makes a good lunch stop.

★ Top Tip
Photographing the murals is fine; people and police stations, not so much...

Taxi Tours

Black taxi tours of West Belfast's murals are offered by a large number of taxi companies and local cabbies. These can vary in quality and content, but in general they're an intimate and entertaining way to see the sights. Drivers will pick you up from anywhere in the city centre.

**Paddy Campbell's
Famous Black
Cab Tours**   Cultural Tour
Popular 1½-hour black cab tour. (📞07990 955227; www.belfastblackcabtours.co.uk; tour per 1-3 people £30)

Harpers Taxi Tours   Cultural Tour
Political and historical tours. (📞07711 757178; www.harperstaxitours.com; from £30)

**Official Black
Taxi Tours**   Cultural Tour
Customised tours lasting 1½ hours. (📞028-9064 2264; www.belfasttours.com; 1-2 passengers £25, 3+ per person £10)

◎ SIGHTS

◎ City Centre

City Hall   Historic Building

Belfast's classical Renaissance-style City Hall was built in fine, white Portland stone in 1906. Highlights of the free, 45-minute guided tour include the sumptuous, wedding-cake Italian marble and colourful stained glass of the entrance hall and rotunda; an opportunity to sit on the mayor's throne in the council chamber; and the idiosyncratic portraits of past lord mayors. Each is allowed to choose his or her own artist and the variations in personal style are intriguing. (www.belfastcity.gov.uk; Donegall Sq; ⏱guided tours 11am, 2pm & 3pm Mon-Fri, 2pm & 3pm Sat) FREE

Crown Liquor Saloon Historic Building

There are not too many historical monuments that you can enjoy while savouring a

Belfast is in many ways a brand-new city.

pint of beer, but the National Trust's Crown Liquor Saloon is one of them. Belfast's most famous bar was refurbished by Patrick Flanagan in the late 19th century and displays Victorian decorative flamboyance at its best (he was looking to pull in a posh clientele from the newfangled train station and Grand Opera House across the street). (www.nationaltrust.org.uk; 46 Great Victoria St; ⏱11.30am-11pm Mon-Wed, to midnight Thu-Sat, 12.30-10pm Sun) FREE

◎ South Belfast (Queen's Quarter)

Ulster Museum   Museum

You could spend hours browsing this state-of-the-art museum, but if you're pressed for time don't miss the Armada Room, with artefacts retrieved from the 1588 wreck of the Spanish galleon *Girona*; the Egyptian Room's Princess Takabuti, a 2500-year-old Egyptian mummy unwrapped in Belfast in 1835; and the Early Peoples Gallery's bronze Bann Disc, a superb example of Celtic design dating from the Iron Age. Free tours (10 people maximum; first-come, first served) run at 2.30pm Tuesday to Friday

Lanyon Building, Queen's University

and 1.30pm Sunday. (www.nmni.com; Stran-millis Rd; by donation; ⊙10am-5pm Tue-Sun)

Belfast Botanic Gardens   Gardens
The showpiece of Belfast's green oasis is
Charles Lanyon's beautiful **Palm House**
(⊙10am-5pm Apr-Sep, to 4pm Oct-Mar) [FREE],
built in 1839 and completed in 1852, with its
birdcage dome, a masterpiece in cast-iron
and curvilinear glass. Nearby is the **1889
Tropical Ravine** (⊙10am-5pm Apr-Sep, to
4pm Oct-Mar) [FREE], a huge red-brick greenhouse designed by the garden's curator
Charles McKimm. Inside, a raised walkway
overlooks a jungle of tropical ferns, orchids,
lilies and banana plants growing in a sunk-
en glen. It reopens in mid-2016 following
a £3.8 million restoration. (Stranmillis Rd;
⊙7.30am-sunset) [FREE]

Queen's University   Historic Building
Northern Ireland's most prestigious university was founded by Queen Victoria in 1845.
In 1908, the Queen's College became the
Queen's University of Belfast and today its
campus spreads across some 250 buildings. Queen's has around 25,000 students
and specialises in medicine, engineering
and law. Just inside the main entrance is
the **Queen's Welcome Centre** (www.queen-
seventus.com; University Rd; ⊙8am-6pm Mon-
Fri, 11am-4pm Sat & Sun) [FREE] with exhibitions
and a souvenir shop. Book ahead for guided
tours, or pick up or download a free leaflet
that outlines a self-guided tour. (University
Rd; guided tour per person £5)

◎ West Belfast (Gaeltacht Quarter)
Northwest of Donegall Sq, Divis St leads
across the Westlink Motorway to Falls
Rd and West Belfast. Though scarred by
decades of civil unrest during the Troubles,
this former battleground is one of the most
compelling places to visit in Northern Ireland. Recent history hangs heavy in the air,
but there is a noticeable spirit of optimism
and hope for the future.

The main attractions are the powerful
murals (p232) that chart the history of the
conflict, as well as the political passions of
the moment.

◫▯ Belfast's Titanic Connection

Perhaps the most famous vessel ever
launched, RMS *Titanic* was built in
Belfast's Harland & Wolff shipyard for
the White Star Line. When the keel was
laid in 1909, Belfast was at the height of
its fame as a shipbuilding powerhouse,
and the *Titanic* was promoted by White
Star as the world's biggest and most
luxurious ocean liner. Ironically, it was
also claimed to be 'unsinkable'.

Titanic was launched from H&W's
slipway No 3 on 31 May 1911, and spent
almost a year being fitted out in the
nearby Thompson Graving Dock before
leaving Belfast for the maiden voyage
on 2 April 1912. In one of the most notorious nautical disasters of all time, the
ship hit an iceberg in the North Atlantic
on 14 April 1912, and sank in the early
hours of the following day. Of the 2228
passengers and crew on-board, only
705 survived; there were only enough
lifeboats for 1178 people.

The Titanic Stories website (www.
the-titanic.com) contains a wealth
of information on the ship and its
passengers, and lists all *Titanic*-related
museums and memorials throughout
Ireland and the rest of the world.

Irish postage stamp commemorating the *Titanic*
CAT WAKER/SHUTTERSTOCK ©

West Belfast grew up around the
linen mills that propelled the city into
late-19th-century prosperity. It was an area
of low-cost, working-class housing, and
even in the Victorian era was divided along
religious lines. The advent of the Troubles

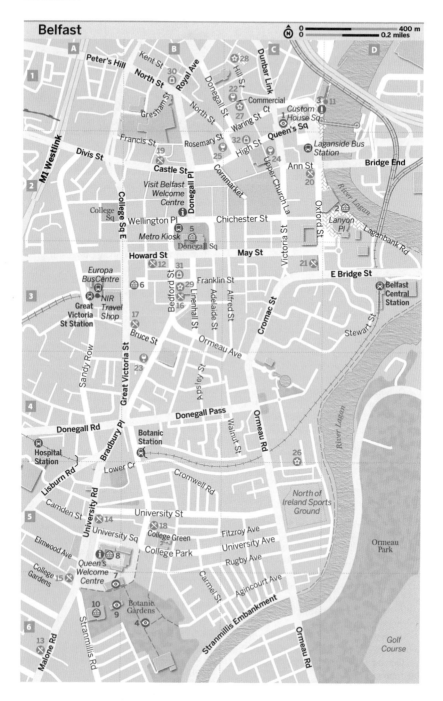

Belfast

0 — 400 m
0 — 0.2 miles

Peter's Hill
Kent St
North St
Royal Ave
Donegall Ave
Hill St
Dunbar Link
28
30
22
27
Commercial Ct
Custom House Sq
3
11
Gresham St
North St
Waring St
Queen's Sq
1
Francis St
Rosemary St
32
High St
Laganside Bus Station
Divis St
19
25
24
Ann St
Bridge End
Castle St
Cornmarket
20
Visit Belfast Welcome Centre
Donegall Pl
Upper Church La
College Sq
Chichester St
Oxford St
2
Lanyon Pl
Wellington Pl
Laganbank Rd
Metro Kiosk
5
Donegall Sq
May St
Victoria St
Howard St
31
21
E Bridge St
Europa BusCentre
12
Franklin St
6
29
Bedford St
Belfast Central Station
Great Victoria St Station
NIR Travel Shop
16
Adelaide St
Alfred St
Linenhall St
17
Bruce St
Stewart St
Sandy Row
23
Ormeau Ave
Cromac St
Great Victoria St
Apsley St
Donegall Pass
Bradbury Pl
Walnut St
Ormeau Rd
Donegall Rd
Botanic Station
River Lagan
Hospital Station
26
Lisburn Rd
Lower Cr
Cromwell Rd
North of Ireland Sports Ground
Camden St
University Rd
University St
14
Ormeau Park
Elmwood Ave
University Sq
18
College Green
Fitzroy Ave
University Ave
College Park
Rugby Ave
Queen's Welcome Centre
8
7
Carmel St
Agincourt Ave
College Gardens
15
10
9
Botanic Gardens
Stranmillis Embankment
Ormeau Rd
13
Malone Rd
Stranmillis Rd
4
Golf Course

Belfast

Sights

1 Albert Memorial Clock Tower C1
2 Belfast Barge D2
3 Bigfish Sculpture C1
4 Botanic Gardens B6
5 City Hall B2
6 Crown Liquor Saloon B3
7 Palm House A6
8 Queen's University A5
9 Tropical Ravine A6
10 Ulster Museum A6

Activities, Courses & Tours

11 Lagan Boat Company D1

Eating

12 Bar & Grill B3
13 Barking Dog A6
14 Beatrice Kennedy A5
15 Deanes at Queen's A6
16 Deanes Deli Bistro B3
Deanes Eipic .... (see 12)
17 Ginger B3
Holohan's .... (see 2)
James St South .... (see 12)
18 Molly's Yard B5
19 Mourne Seafood Bar B2
20 OX C2
21 St George's Market Bar & Grill C3

Drinking & Nightlife

Crown Liquor Saloon .... (see 6)
22 Duke of York C1
23 Filthy Quarter B4
Harlem Cafe .... (see 16)
Kelly's Cellars .... (see 19)
24 Muriel's Cafe-Bar C2
25 White's Tavern B2

Entertainment

26 An Droichead C4
27 Black Box C1
28 MAC C1
29 Ulster Hall B3

Shopping

30 Good Vibrations B1
St George's Market .... (see 21)
31 Steensons B3
32 Wicker Man C2

in 1968 solidified the sectarian divide, and since 1970 the ironically named Peace Line has separated the Loyalist and Protestant Shankill district (from the Irish *sean chill*, meaning 'old church') from the Republican and Catholic Falls district.

Despite its past reputation, the area is safe to visit. The best way to see West Belfast is on an informative and entertaining black taxi tour (p233), but there's nothing to stop you visiting under your own steam, either walking or using the shared black taxis that travel along the Falls and Shankill Rds. Alternatively, buses 10A to 10F from Queen St will take you along the Falls Rd; buses 11A to 11D from Wellington Pl go along Shankill Rd.

Free leaflets from the Visit Belfast Welcome Centre describe walking tours around the Falls and Shankill districts.

TOURS

You can find full details of organised tours at the Visit Belfast Welcome Centre (p244).

Lagan Boat Company Boat Tour

The Lagan Boat Company's excellent Titanic Tour explores the docklands downstream of Lagan Weir, taking in the slipways where the liners *Titanic* and *Olympic* were launched and the huge dry dock where they could fit with just nine inches (23cm) to spare. Tours depart from Donegall Quay near the Bigfish sculpture. (028-9024 0124; www.laganboat-company.com; adult/child £10/8; 12.30pm & 2pm daily Apr-Oct, Sat & Sun Nov-Mar, plus 3.30pm daily Apr-Sep)

Titanic Tours Guided Tour

A three-hour luxury tour led by the great-granddaughter of one of the *Titanic*'s crew, visiting various *Titanic*-related sites.

Planning Ahead

Book tickets for popular attractions such as Titanic Belfast and Crumlin Road Gaol. Reserve weekend dinner tables at top-end restaurants.

📖🍴 Crumlin Road Gaol

Guided tours of Belfast's notorious **Crumlin Road Gaol** (☎028-9074 1501; www.crumlinroadgaol.com; 53-55 Crumlin Rd; day tour adult/child £8.50/6.50, evening tour £7.50/5.50; ⏰10am-5.30pm, last tour 4.30pm, evening tour 6pm) take you from the tunnel beneath Crumlin Rd, built in 1850 to convey prisoners from the courthouse across the street (and allegedly the origin of the judge's phrase 'take him down'), through the echoing halls and cramped cells of C-Wing, to the truly chilling execution chamber.

Advance tour bookings are recommended. The gaol's pedestrian entrance is on Crumlin Rd; the car park entrance is reached via Cliftonpark Ave to the north.

Inner doors, Crumlin Road Gaol
TREVOR BUCHANAN/GETTY IMAGES ©

For groups of two to five people; includes pick-up and drop-off at your accommodation. (☎07852 716655; www.titanictours-belfast.co.uk; adult/child £30/15; ⏰on demand)

Belfast Pub Crawl   Guided Tour
A three-hour tour taking in four of the city's historic pubs (including a drink in each, plus live trad music), departing from the **Albert Memorial Clock Tower** at Queen's Sq. (☎07712 603764; www.belfastcrawl.com; per person £8; ⏰7.30pm Fri & Sat)

🔒 SHOPPING

St George's Market   Market
Ireland's oldest continually operating market was built in 1896. This Victorian beauty hosts a Friday variety market

(flowers, produce, meat, fish, homewares and secondhand goods), a Saturday City Food & Craft Market, with food stalls and live music, and a Sunday market (food, antiques and local arts and crafts). The **St George's Market Bar & Grill** (☎028-9024 0014; http://stgeorgesbargrill.com; Oxford St; breakfast £4.50-7, mains lunch £8-10, dinner £13-17; ⏰10am-2.30pm Tue, 10am-2.30pm & 5-9pm Wed & Thu, 9am-2.30pm & 5-10pm Fri & Sat, 10am-4pm Sun) 🖉 overlooks the action.

A free shuttle bus links the market with Donegall Sq and Adelaide St every 20 minutes from 11am to 3pm on Friday and Saturday. In early December, a two-day Christmas Fair and Market takes place here. (www.belfastcity.gov.uk; cnr Oxford & May Sts; ⏰6am-2pm Fri, 9am-3pm Sat, 10am-4pm Sun)

Wicker Man   Jewellery, Souvenirs
In addition to hosting exhibitions, arty Wicker Man sells a wide range of contemporary Irish crafts and gifts, including silver jewellery, glassware and knitwear. (www.thewickerman. co.uk; 44-46 High St; ⏰9.30am-6pm Mon-Wed, Fri & Sat, 9.30am-9pm Thu, 1.30-6pm Sun)

Good Vibrations   Music
Owned by music producer Terry Hooley (who released *Teenage Kicks* by the Undertones on his Good Vibrations label back in 1978), this is Belfast's best alternative record shop, and a source of info on the latest gigs, plus tickets. It's inside the Bigg Life Arts Centre, upstairs from Cafe Wah. (89-93 North St; ⏰8am-6pm)

Steensons   Jewellery
This city-centre showroom sells a range of stylish, contemporary, handmade jewellery in silver, gold and platinum, from a workshop (p176) in Glenarm, County Antrim. Steensons is the creator of *Game of Thrones* jewellery; look out for its similarly inspired designs. (www.thesteensons.com; Bedford House, Bedford St; ⏰10am-5.30pm Mon-Sat, to 8pm Thu)

⭐ ENTERTAINMENT

Ulster Hall   Concert Venue
Dating from 1862, Ulster Hall is a popular venue for a range of events including rock

concerts, lunchtime organ recitals, boxing bouts and performances by the Ulster Orchestra (http://ulsterorchestra.com). (www.belfastcity.gov.uk; 34 Bedford St)

MAC
Arts Centre

The Cathedral Quarter's beautiful new designer arts centre houses two theatres, and stages regular performances of drama, including shows for children. (Metropolitan Arts Centre; http://themaclive.com; St Anne's Sq)

Black Box
Arts Centre

Billing itself as a 'home for live music, theatre, literature, comedy, film, visual art, live art, circus, cabaret and all points in between', Black Box is an intimate venue in the heart of the Cathedral Quarter. (www.blackboxbelfast.com; 18-22 Hill St)

An Droichead
Music

Dedicated to Irish language, music and culture, this cultural centre offers Irish-language courses, stages traditional dance and *céilidh* workshops, hosts art exhibitions and serves as a live-music venue. It's a great place to hear live Irish folk music from big names from around the country, as well

Game of Thrones Tours

If you're driving around Northern Ireland, there are *Game of Thrones* filming locations aplenty – visit www.discovernorthernireland.com/gameofthrones. Alternatively, day-long bus tours depart from Belfast.

as up-and-coming local talent. (www.androichead.com; 20 Cooke St, The Bridge; tickets £5-15)

Lyric Theatre
Theatre

This stunning modern theatre opened to great dramatic and architectural acclaim in 2011. It's built on the site of the old Lyric Theatre, where Hollywood star Liam Neeson first trod the boards (he is now a patron). (www.lyrictheatre.co.uk; 55 Ridgeway St)

⊗ EATING

⊗ City Centre

Mourne Seafood Bar   Seafood ££

Hugely popular, this informal, pub-like place is all red brick and dark wood with

Christmas market, Belfast

PETER UNGER/GETTY IMAGES ©

Fresh seafood, Belfast

old oil lamps dangling from the ceiling. On the menu are oysters served *au naturel* or Rockefeller, meltingly sweet scallops, lobster and langoustines sourced from its own shellfish beds, along with luscious fish like gurnard and sea bass. Book ahead for dinner. (☏028-9024 8544; http://mourne seafood.com; 34-36 Bank St; mains £8-22; ⏱noon-9.30pm Mon-Thu, noon-4pm & 5-10.30pm Fri & Sat, 1-6pm Sun)

Holohan's   Modern Irish ££
Aboard the **Belfast Barge** (www.laganlegacy. com; Lanyon Quay; adult/child £4/3; ⏱10am-4pm), Holohan's is a sensational find for

inspired twists on seafood (deep-fried whitebait with garlic-and-herb aioli; roast cod with brown shrimp and boxty dumplings), as well as land-based dishes such as fillet steak with heirloom vegetables, desserts such as warm chocolate mousse with candied walnuts and Bailey's chocolate sauce, and by-the-glass wines from around the world. (☏028-9023 5973; Belfast Barge, Lanyon Quay; mains lunch £9.50-12.50, dinner £13-22; ⏱noon-4pm Mon & Tue, noon-3pm & 5-11pm Wed-Sat)

OX   Irish ££
A high-ceilinged space walled with cream-painted brick and furnished with warm golden wood creates a theatre-like ambience for the open kitchen at the back, where Michelin-trained chefs turn out some of Belfast's finest and best-value cuisine. The restaurant works with local suppliers and focuses on fine Irish beef, sustainable seafood, and seasonal vegetables and fruit. (☏028-9031 4121; http://oxbelfast.com; 1 Oxford St; mains lunch £10, dinner £19-25; ⏱noon-2.30pm & 6-9.30pm Tue-Fri, from 1pm Sat)

🍴 Top Five Places to Eat

- ● Barking Dog (p241)
- ● Holohan's (p240)
- ● Mourne Seafood Bar (p239)
- ● OX (p240)
- ● Deanes Eipic (p241)

Ginger
Bistro ££

Ginger is one of those places you could walk right past without noticing, but you'd be missing out. Cosy and informal, its food is anything but ordinary – the flame-haired owner/chef (hence the name) really knows what he's doing, sourcing top-quality Irish produce and creating exquisite dishes such as tea-smoked duck breast with ginger and sweet-potato puree. (📞028-9024 4421; www.gingerbistro.com; 7-8 Hope St; mains lunch £10-12.50, dinner £16-23; ⏰5-9pm Mon, noon-3pm & 5-9.30pm Tue-Thu, noon-3pm & 5-10pm Fri & Sat; 🖋) 🖋)

Deanes Eipic
French, Irish £££

Premium Irish and British produce – beef, game, lamb, seafood – is given the gourmet treatment at this flagship of chef Michael Deane's restaurant fleet. Within the same building are Deane's à la carte Love Fish and Meatlocker restaurants.Other venues from Belfast's best-known chef include and Deanes Deli Bistro (📞028-9024 8800; www.michaeldeane.co.uk; 44 Bedford St; mains £10-22; ⏰8am-10pm Mon-Fri, 9am-10pm Sat) and Deanes at Queen's (p242). (📞028-9033 1134; www.michaeldeane.co.uk; 34-40 Howard St; 4-/5-/6-course menu £40/50/60; ⏰noon-2.45pm Fri, 5.30-9.45pm Wed-Sat) 🖋

James St South
Modern Irish ££

Graced by a large, impressionistic landscape by Irish artist Clement McAleer, this starkly beautiful dining room with crisp white table linen creates a perfect stage for the presentation of starters such as grilled foie gras with pickled rhubarb, followed by mains such as venison with turnip and mushroom cottage pie. The service is relaxed yet highly professional.

Its **Bar & Grill** (📞028-9560 0700; www.belfastbargrill.co.uk; 21 James St S; mains £10.50-23; ⏰noon-10.30pm) is less formal but the quality of the food is just as high. (📞028-9043 4310; www.jamesstreetsouth.co.uk; 21 James St S; 1-/2-/3-course lunch menu £10/15.50/18.50, dinner mains £18.50-25; ⏰noon-2.30pm & 5.30-10.30pm Mon-Sat)

🎧 Van Morrison Trail

Fans of 'Van the Man' can take a self-guided, 3.5km walking tour of little-explored East Belfast, passing sights referenced in his lyrics, including the Hollow (immortalised in *Brown Eyed Girl*), Cypress Avenue and the modest house where he was born on Hyndford St (at number 125).

Morrison launched the trail in 2014 in collaboration with local council initiative Connswater Community Greenway (www.communitygreenway.co.uk/vanmorrisontrail). The free, downloadable map has audio snippets of songs relating to each of the trail's eight stops.

Van Morrison (r) with North Irish golfer Rory McIlroy
CHARLES MCQUILLAN/GETTY IMAGES ©

🥢 South Belfast

Barking Dog
Bistro ££

Chunky hardwood, bare brick, candlelight and quirky design create the atmosphere of a stylishly restored farmhouse. The menu completes the feeling of cosiness and comfort with simple but sensational dishes such as their signature burger of meltingly tender beef shin with caramelised onion and horseradish cream, and sweet potato ravioli with carrot and parmesan crisps. Superb service, too. (📞028-9066 1885; www.barkingdogbelfast.com; 33-35 Malone Rd; mains £14-24, tapas 1/5 dishes £3/12; ⏰noon-3pm & 5.30-10pm Mon-Thu, to 11pm Fri & Sat, noon-9pm Sun; 🖋🐾)

Molly's Yard
Irish ££

A restored Victorian stables courtyard is the setting for this quirky restaurant, with

Victorian Classics

Check out these other beautiful Belfast pubs.

Duke of York Down an inconspicuous alley in the heart of the city's former newspaper district, the snug, traditional Duke was a hangout for print workers and journalists, and Sinn Féin leader, Gerry Adams, worked behind the bar here during his student days back in 1971. The entire alley takes on a street-party atmosphere in warm weather. (www. dukeofyorkbelfast.com; 11 Commercial Ct; ⊙11.30am-11.30pm Mon-Wed, to 1am Thu & Fri, to 2am Sat, 2-8pm Sun)

Kelly's Cellars Kelly's is Belfast's oldest pub (1720) – as opposed to tavern – and was a meeting place for Henry Joy McCracken and the United Irishmen when they were planning the 1798 Rising. It pulls in a broad cross-section of Belfast society and is a great place to catch traditional music sessions at 8.30pm Tuesday to Thursday and 4.30pm Saturday. (www.kellyscellars.com; 30-32 Bank St; ⊙11.30am-1am Mon-Sat, 1pm-midnight Sun)

White's Tavern Established in 1630 but rebuilt in 1790, White's claims to be Belfast's oldest tavern (unlike a pub, a tavern provided food and lodging). Downstairs is a traditional Irish bar with an open peat fire and live music nightly; upstairs is like your granny's living room, stuffed with old armchairs and sofas, and hosting DJs and covers bands at the weekends. (1-4 Wine Cellar Entry; ⊙noon-11pm Mon & Tue, to 1am Wed-Sat, to midnight Sun)

a cosy bar-bistro on the ground floor, outdoor tables in the yard and a rustic dining room (open from 6pm) in the airy roof space upstairs. It has its own craft beers, brewed at **Lisburn's Hilden Brewery** (☎028-9266 0800; www.hildenbrewery.com;

Hilden House, Grand St, Lisburn; tour £6.50; ⊙tours by reservation 11.30am & 6.30pm Tue-Sat); the food menu is seasonal and sticks to half a dozen each of starters and mains. (☎028-9032 2600; www.mollysyard.co.uk; 1 College Green Mews; mains bistro £10, restaurant £14-23; ⊙bistro noon-5pm, restaurant 5-9pm Mon-Sat; ☑) ☑

Deanes at Queen's   Bistro ££
A chilled-out bar and grill from Belfast's top chef, Michael Deane, this place was once Queen's University's staff club. The menu focuses on what could be described as good-value, gourmet pub grub: salt and chilli squid, crisp pork belly with celeriac and horseradish, and whiskey-cured salmon with sea vegetables. (☎028-9038 2111; www.michaeldeane.co.uk; 1 College Gardens; mains lunch £7-12.50, dinner £14.50-22; ⊙noon-3pm & 5.30-11pm Mon-Sat, 1-6pm Sun)

Beatrice Kennedy   Irish ££
Organic veg and locally sourced meats are a staple at this perennial Queen's Quarter favourite (it's where students take their visiting parents for dinner). The dining room retains its Victorian elegance, while the menu adds a modern twist to traditional Irish seafood, lamb and beef. There's a separate vegetarian menu (though you may have to ask for it). (☎028-9020 2290; www. beatricekennedy.co.uk; 44 University Rd; mains £15-21.50; ⊙5-9.30pm Tue-Thu, to 10.30pm Fri & Sat, to 8.30pm Sun; ☑) ☑

🍷 DRINKING & NIGHTLIFE

Crown Liquor Saloon   Pub
Despite being a tourist attraction (p234), Belfast's most famous bar still fills up with crowds of locals at lunchtime and in the early evening. (www.nicholsonspubs.co.uk; 46 Great Victoria St; ⊙11.30am-11pm Mon-Wed, 11.30am-midnight Thu-Sat, 12.30-10pm Sun)

Filthy Quarter   Bar
Four individually and collectively fabulous bars make up the Filthy Quarter: retro-trad-style, bric-a-brac-filled Filthy McNastys, hosting local musicians from 10pm nightly;

the fairy-lit Secret Garden, a two-storey beer garden with watering cans for drinks coolers; Gypsy Lounge (Tuesday, Thursday, Friday, Saturday and Sundays nights), with a gypsy caravan DJ booth; and a chandelier- and candelabra-adorned cocktail bar, Filthy Chic. (www.thefilthyquarter.com; 45 Dublin Rd; ⏱1pm-1am Mon-Sat, to midnight Sun)

Harlem Cafe   Cafe, Bar
In a cornflower-blue building with eclectic art covering the walls, the Harlem is a great place for lounging over coffee, or enjoying a glass of wine after hitting the shops. A full food menu spans breakfast to brunch to pretheatre dinner; live music plays on Friday and Saturday. (http://harlembelfast. com; 34-36 Bedford St; ⏱8am-11pm Mon-Thu, 8am-1am Fri & Sat, 9am-7pm Sun; 🛜)

Muriel's Cafe-Bar   Bar
Hats meet harlotry (ask who Muriel was) in this delightfully snug and welcoming bar with retro-chic decor, old sofas and armchairs, heavy fabrics in shades of olive and dark red, gilt-framed mirrors and a cast-iron fireplace. Gin is Muriel's favourite tipple and there's a range of exotic brands

Where to Stay

From backpacker hostels to boutique havens, the range of places to stay gets wider every year. Most of Belfast's budget and midrange accommodation is south of the centre, in the leafy university district around Botanic Ave, University Rd and Malone Rd, around a 20-minute walk from City Hall.

Business hotels proliferate in the city centre; look out for new 40-room boutique hotel the Mutual, in the landmark turreted, red-sandstone 1904 Scottish Mutual building at 15–16 Donegall Sq S.

The Titanic Quarter, already home to a swish new branch of the Premier Inn chain, is set to welcome several new hotels in the coming years, including an 84-room *Titanic*-themed hotel with public spaces occupying the Harland & Wolff Drawing Offices (Queen's Rd), where the designs for the *Titanic* were first drawn up.

Book ahead on weekends, in summer, and during busy festival periods.

Enjoying a quiet Guinness at Crown Liquor Saloon

to mix with your tonic. The food menu is pretty good, too. (☎028-9033 2445; 12-14 Church Lane; ⏰11.30am-1am Mon-Fri, 11am-1am Sat, 11am-midnight Sun)

ℹ INFORMATION

DANGERS & ANNOYANCES
Even at the height of the Troubles, Belfast wasn't a particularly dangerous city for tourists. It's best, however, to avoid the so-called 'interface areas' – near the peace lines in West Belfast, Crumlin Rd and the Short Strand (just east of Queen's Bridge) – after dark; if in doubt about any area, ask at your hotel or hostel. You can follow the Police Service of Northern Ireland (PSNI) on Twitter (@policeserviceni) and receive immediate notification of any alerts.

If you want to take photos of fortified police stations, army posts or other military or quasi-military paraphernalia, get permission first, just to be on the safe side. In the Protestant and Catholic strongholds of West Belfast it's best not to photograph people without permission. Taking pictures of the murals is not a problem.

ℹ TOURIST INFORMATION
Visit Belfast Welcome Centre (☎028-9024 6609; http://visit-belfast.com; 9 Donegall Sq N; ⏰9am-7pm Mon-Sat, 11am-4pm Sun Jun-Sep, 9am-5.30pm Mon-Sat, 11am-4pm Sun Oct-May; 📶) Provides information about the whole of Northern Ireland and books accommodation. Services include left luggage (not overnight), currency exchange and free wi-fi.

ℹ GETTING THERE & AWAY

AIR
Belfast International Airport (BFS; ☎028-9448 4848; www.belfastairport.com) Located 30km northwest of the city; flights serve the UK and Europe, and in the USA, Las Vegas, Orlando and New York.

George Best Belfast City Airport (BHD; ☎028-9093 9093; www.belfastcityairport.com; Airport Rd) Located 6km northeast of the city centre; flights serve the UK and Europe.

BUS
There are **information desks** (⏰7.45am-6.30pm Mon-Fri, 8am-6pm Sat) at both of Belfast's bus stations, where you can pick up

Thompson Pump House (p231)

regional bus timetables. Contact Translink
(☎028-9066 6630; www.translink.co.uk) for
timetable and fares information.

National Express (☎08717 818 178; www.
nationalexpress.com) runs a daily coach service
between Belfast and London (£37 one way, 15½
hours) via the Cairnryan ferry, Dumfries, Milton
Keynes, Carlisle, Manchester and Birmingham.
The ticket office is in the Europa Bus Centre.

Scottish Citylink (☎0871 266 3333; www.
citylink.co.uk) operates three buses a day from
Glasgow to Belfast (£32, six hours), via the
Cairnryan ferry.

Europa BusCentre (☎028-9066 6630; Great
Victoria St, Great Northern Mall) Belfast's main
bus station is behind the Europa Hotel and
next door to Great Victoria St train station; it's
reached via the Great Northern Mall beside the
hotel. It's the main terminus for buses to Derry,
Dublin and destinations in the west and south of
Northern Ireland.

Laganside Bus Station (☎028-9066 6630;
Oxford St) The smaller of Belfast's two bus stations, Laganside is near the river and is mainly
for buses to eastern County Down and eastern
County Tyrone.

TRAIN

For information on train fares and timetables,
contact Translink (☎028-9066 6630; www.
translink.co.uk). The **NIR Travel Shop** (☎028-
9024 2420; Great Victoria St Station; ⊙9am-5pm
Mon-Fri, to 12.30pm Sat) books train tickets,
ferries and holiday packages.

Belfast Central Station (East Bridge St) East
of the city centre; trains run to Dublin and all
destinations in Northern Ireland. If you arrive by
train at Central Station, your rail ticket entitles
you to a free bus ride into the city centre.

Great Victoria St Station (Great Victoria St,
Great Northern Mall) Next to the Europa BusCen-
tre; has trains for Portadown, Lisburn, Bangor,
Larne Harbour and Derry.

ⓘ GETTING AROUND

TO/FROM THE AIRPORTS

Belfast International Airport Express 300 bus
runs to the Europa Bus Centre (one way/return

💬 12th of July in Belfast

In Northern Ireland the 12 July public
holiday marks the anniversary of the
Protestant victory at the 1690 Battle of
the Boyne. It is celebrated with bonfires,
marching bands and street parades
staged by the Orange Order, the biggest
of which takes place in Belfast.

Although the 12 July parades have
regularly been associated with sectarian
stand-offs and outbursts of violence,
there has been a concerted effort in
recent years to promote the Belfast
parade as a cultural celebration, even
rebranding it Orangefest.

However, many people still perceive
the parades as divisive and confronta-
tional, and with high levels of alcohol
consumption among the crowds there
is a potential for dangerous situations.
Visitors need to be alert for signs of trouble, follow local advice and expect extra
security if things escalate in any way.

Preparation for 12 July bonfires, Belfast
CHRISTOPHER FURLONG/GETTY IMAGES ©

£7.50/10.50, 30 minutes) every 10 or 15 minutes
between 7am and 8pm, every 30 minutes from
8pm to 11pm, and hourly through the night; a
return ticket is valid for one month. A taxi costs
about £30.

George Best Belfast City Airport Express 600
bus runs to the Europa BusCentre (one way/re-
turn £2.50/3.80, 15 minutes) every 20 minutes
between 6am and 9.30pm Monday to Saturday,
and every 40 minutes on Sunday. A return ticket
is valid for one month. The taxi fare to the city
centre is about £10.

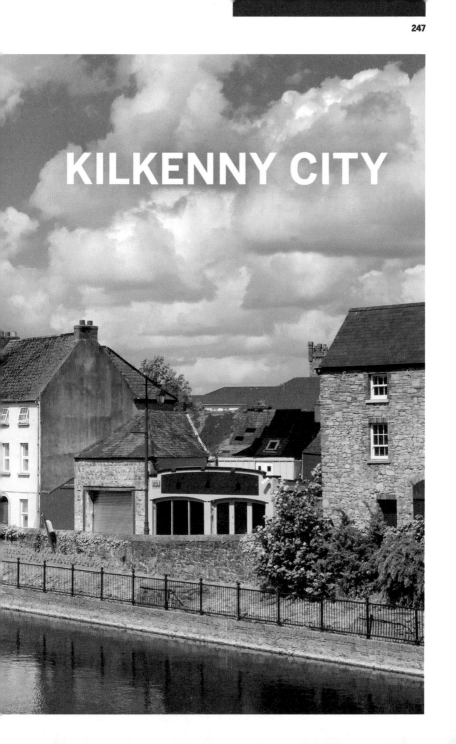

KILKENNY CITY

Kilkenny City

Kilkenny (from the Gaelic 'Cill Chainnigh', meaning the Church of St Canice) is the Ireland of many visitors' imaginations. Built from dark grey limestone flecked with fossil seashells, Kilkenny is also known as 'the marble city' – a centre for arts and crafts, and home to a host of fine restaurants, cafes, pubs and shops.

Whether it's strolling around Kilkenny's medieval quarters, lazing away the day on the banks of the River Nore or pub-hopping from one trad session to the next, you can't go out in this town and not find pleasure.

☑ In This Section

❶ Arriving in Kilkenny

Train Kilkenny MacDonagh train station is 10-minute walk northeast of the town centre.

Bus Bus Éireann services stop at the train station and on Ormonde Rd (nearer the town centre); JJ Kavanagh (www.jjkavanagh.ie) buses to Dublin airport stop on Ormonde Rd only.

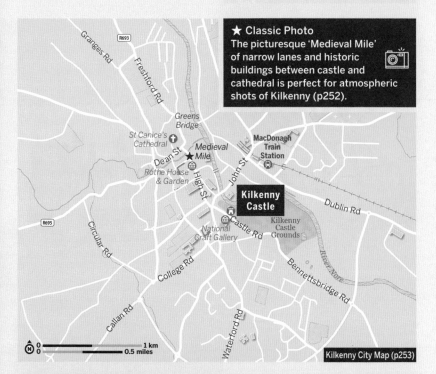

★ Classic Photo
The picturesque 'Medieval Mile' of narrow lanes and historic buildings between castle and cathedral is perfect for atmospheric shots of Kilkenny (p252).

Granges Rd

R693

Freshford Rd

Greens Bridge

St Canice's Cathedral

Dean St

Medieval Mile

Rothe House & Garden

High St

John St

MacDonagh Train Station

Kilkenny Castle

Dublin Rd

R695

Circular Rd

Castle Rd

National Craft Gallery

Kilkenny Castle Grounds

River Nore

College Rd

Bennettsbridge Rd

Callan Rd

Waterford Rd

N

0   1 km
0   0.5 miles

Kilkenny City Map (p253)

From left: Shops, Kilkenny city; riverside village, County Kilkenny; bridge over the River Nore (p258)

PATRYK KOSMIDER/SHUTTERSTOCK ©

Kilkenny Castle

Rising above the River Nore, Kilkenny Castle is one of Ireland's most visited heritage sites. Stronghold of the powerful Butler family, it has a history dating back to the 12th century, though much of its present look dates from Victorian times.

Great For...

☑ Don't Miss

The superbly sculpted Carrara marble fireplace in the Long Gallery.

History

Kilkenny Castle has a rich – and lengthy – past. The first structure on this strategic site was a wooden tower built in 1172 by Richard de Clare, the Anglo-Norman conqueror of Ireland better known as Strongbow. In 1192, Strongbow's son-in-law, William Marshall, erected a stone castle with four towers, three of which survive. The castle was bought by the powerful Butler family, (later earls and dukes of Ormonde) in 1391, and their descendants continued to live there until 1935. Maintaining the castle became such a financial strain that most of the furnishings were sold at auction. The property was handed over to the city in 1967 for the princely sum of £50.

Stone sculpture, Kilkenny Castle

Kilkenny Castle

Kilkenny Castle Grounds

❶ Need to Know

Map p253; www.kilkennycastle.ie; Castle Rd; adult/child €7/3; ⏱9.30am-5pm Mar-Sep, to 4.30pm Oct-Feb

✕ Take a Break

The Kilkenny Design Centre Restaurant (p257) is right across the street from the castle.

★ Top Tip

A path from the castle grounds leads down to the riverside, where you can walk back into town.

Visiting the Castle

During the winter months (November to January) there are 40-minute guided tours which shift to self-guided tours from February to October. For most visitors, the focal point of the visit is the Long Gallery which showcases portraits of Butler family members, the oldest dating from the 17th century. It is an impressive hall with a 19th-century timber roof vividly painted with Celtic, medieval and Pre-Raphaelite motifs by John Hungerford Pollen (1820–1902), who also created the magnificent Carrara marble fireplace, delicately carved with scenes from Butler family history.

The castle basement is home to the **Butler Gallery** (Map p253; www.butlergallery.

com) FREE, featuring contemporary artwork in temporary exhibitions. You can access the Butler Gallery and cafe without paying admission.

About 20 hectares of **public parkland** (Map p253; Castle Rd; ⏱8.30am-8.30pm May-Aug, to 7pm Apr & Sep, shorter hours Oct-Mar) extend to the southeast of Kilkenny Castle, framing a fine view of Mt Leinster, while a Celtic cross-shaped rose garden lies northwest of the castle.

Highlights of the guided tour include the Long Gallery with its painted roof and carved marble fireplace. There's an excellent tearoom in the former castle kitchens, all white marble and gleaming copper.

Kilkenny City

In the Middle Ages, Kilkenny was intermittently the unofficial capital of Ireland, with its own Anglo-Norman parliament. In 1366 the parliament passed the Statutes of Kilkenny aimed at preventing the adoption of Irish culture and language by the Anglo-Norman aristocracy – they were prohibited from marrying the native Irish, taking part in Irish sports, speaking or dressing like the Irish or playing any Irish music. Although the laws remained on the books for more than 200 years, they were never enforced with any great effect and did little to halt the absorption of the Anglo-Normans into Irish culture.

During the 1640s Kilkenny sided with the Catholic royalists in the English Civil War. The 1641 Confederation of Kilkenny, an uneasy alliance of native Irish and Anglo-Normans, aimed to bring about the return of land and power to Catholics. After

> *Kilkenny is the Ireland of many visitors' imaginations.*

St Canice's Cathedral

Charles I's execution, Cromwell besieged Kilkenny for five days, destroying much of the southern wall of the castle before the ruling Ormonde family surrendered. The defeat signalled a permanent end to Kilkenny's political influence over Irish affairs.

Today, tourism is the city's main economic focus, but Kilkenny is also the regional centre for more traditional pursuits such as agriculture – you'll see farmers on tractors stoically dodging tour buses.

◉ SIGHTS & ACTIVITIES

St Canice's Cathedral   Cathedral
Ireland's second-largest medieval cathedral (after St Patrick's in Dublin) has a long and fascinating history. The first monastery was built here in the 6th century by St Canice, Kilkenny's patron saint. The present structure dates from the 13th to 16th centuries, with extensive 19th-century reconstruction, its interior housing ancient grave slabs and the tombs of Kilkenny Castle's Butler dynasty. Outside stands a 30m-high round tower, one of only two in Ireland that you can climb.

IVICA DRUSANY/SHUTTERSTOCK ©

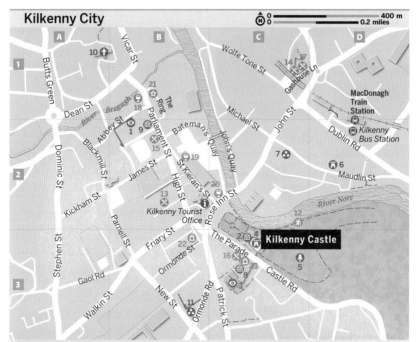

Kilkenny City

◉ Sights

◔ Activities, Courses & Tours

✸ Eating

◔ Drinking & Nightlife

✪ Entertainment

◔ Shopping

Records show that a wooden church on the site was burned down in 1087. The existing structure was raised between 1202 and 1285, but then endured a series of catastrophes and resurrections. The first disaster, the collapse of the church tower in 1332, was associated with Dame Alice Kyteler's conviction for witchcraft. Her maid Petronella was also convicted, and her nephew, William Outlawe, was implicated.

Kilkenny City Walls

Parts of Kilkenny's medieval city walls, mostly dating from the 14th and 15th centuries, can still be seen in several places, notably at **Talbot's Tower** (Map p253; cnr Ormonde Rd & New St), **Maudlin Tower** (Map p253; Maudlin St) and the Black Freren Gate (Map p253; Abbey St) – the only surviving city gate. **Maudlin Castle** (Map p253; Maudlin St) is a more substantial tower house that was built around 1500, and once protected the eastern approach to the city.

Kilkenny Castle (p250)
PETER ZOELLER/DESIGN PICS/GETTY IMAGES ©

The unfortunate maid was burned at the stake, but Dame Alice escaped to London and William saved himself by offering to reroof part of St Canice's Cathedral with lead tiles. His new roof proved too heavy, however, and brought the church tower down with it.

In 1650 Cromwell's forces defaced and damaged the church, using it to stable their horses. Repairs began in 1661; the beautiful roof in the nave was completed in 1863.

Inside, highly polished ancient grave slabs are set on the walls and the floor. On the northern wall, a slab inscribed in Norman French commemorates Jose de Keteller, who died in 1280; despite the difference in spelling he was probably the father of Alice Kyteler. The stone chair of St Kieran embedded in the wall dates from the 13th century. The fine 1596 monument to Honorina Grace at the western end of the southern aisle is made of beautiful local black limestone. In the southern transept is

the handsome black tomb of Piers Butler, who died in 1539, and his wife, Margaret Fitzgerald. Tombs and monuments (listed on a board in the southern aisle) to other notable Butlers crowd this corner of the church. Also worth a look is a model of Kilkenny as it was in 1642.

Apart from missing its crown, the 9th-century round tower is in excellent condition. Inside is a tight squeeze and you'll need both hands to climb the 100 steps up steep ladders (under 12s not admitted). Walking to the cathedral from Parliament St leads you over Irishtown Bridge and up St Canice's Steps, which date from 1614; the wall at the top contains fragments of medieval carvings. The leaning tombstones scattered about the grounds prompt you to look, at the very least, for a black cat. (www.stcanicescathedral.ie; St Canice's Pl; cathedral €4, round tower €3, combined €6; ⊙9am-6pm Mon-Sat, 1-6pm Sun, shorter hours Sep-May)

Rothe House & Garden   Museum

Dating from 1594 this is Ireland's finest example of a Tudor merchant's house, complete with restored medieval garden. Built around a series of courtyards, it now houses a museum with a rather sparse display of local artefacts including a rusted Viking sword and a grinning stone head sculpted by a Celtic artist. The highlight is the delightful walled garden, divided into fruit, vegetable and herb sections and a traditional orchard, as it would have been in the 17th century.

In the 1640s the wealthy Rothe family played a part in the Confederation of Kilkenny, and Peter Rothe, son of the original builder, had all his property confiscated. His sister was able to reclaim it, but just before the Battle of the Boyne (1690) the family supported James II and so lost the house permanently. In 1850 a Confederation banner was discovered in the house; it's now in the National Museum in Dublin. (www.rothehouse.com; Parliament St; adult/child €5.50/4.50; ⊙10.30am-5pm Mon-Sat, 3-5pm Sun Apr-Oct, 10.30am-4.30pm Mon-Sat Nov-Mar)

House doors, Kilkenny city

National Craft Gallery   Gallery

Contemporary Irish crafts are showcased at these imaginative galleries, set in former stables across the road from Kilkenny Castle, next to the shops of the Kilkenny Design Centre (p256). Ceramics dominate, but exhibits often feature furniture, jewellery and weaving from the members of the Crafts Council of Ireland. Family days are held the second Saturday of every month, with free hands-on workshops for children at 10am and 12.30pm. For additional workshops and events, check the website.

Behind the complex, look for the gate that leads into the beautiful **Butler House Gardens** (Map p253; ⏰10am-5pm Mon-Fri, to noon Sat & Sun) FREE with an unusual water feature constructed from remnants of the British-built Nelson Pillar, which once stood in Dublin's O'Connell St but was blown up by the IRA in 1966. (www.nationalcraftgallery. ie; Castle Yard; ⏰10am-5.30pm Tue-Sat, 11am-5.30pm Sun; 👪) FREE

Pat Tynan Walking Tours   Walking

Entertaining, informative 70-minute walking tours through Kilkenny's narrow lanes,

Top Festivals in Kilkenny

Kilkenny hosts several world-class events throughout the year that attract revellers in their thousands.

Kilkenny Rhythm & Roots (www. kilkennyroots.com; ⏰Apr/May) More than 30 pubs and other venues participate in hosting this major music festival in late April/early May, with an emphasis on country and 'old-time' American roots music.

Cat Laughs Comedy Festival (www. thecatlaughs.com; ⏰May/Jun) Acclaimed gathering of world-class comedians in Kilkenny's hotels and pubs over a long weekend in late May/early June.

Kilkenny Arts Festival (www.kilkenny arts.ie; ⏰Aug) The city comes alive with theatre, cinema, music, literature, visual arts, children's events and street spectacles for 10 action-packed days.

Where to Stay

There are many great accommodation options close to the centre of town. If you're arriving with no room booked (an unwise move at weekends, in summer and during festivals), the tourist office runs an efficient accommodation booking service (€4). Some of our favourite lodgings include:

Rosquil House (☏056-772 1419; www. rosquilhouse.com; Castlecomer Rd; r from €70, 2-person apt from €60; 🛜)

Butler House (☏056-772 2828; www.butler.ie; 16 Patrick St; s/d from €90/145; @🛜)

Celtic House (☏056-776 2249; www. celtic-house-bandb.com; 18 Michael St; r €80; @🛜)

Pembroke Hotel (☏056-778 3500; www. kilkennypembrokehotel.com; Patrick St; s/d from €104/144; @🛜).

steps and pedestrian passageways. There are two to three tours daily, mid-March to October. Meet at the tourist office. (☏087 265 1745; www.kilkennywalkingtours.ie; per person €6; ⊙2-3 tours daily mid-Mar–Oct)

🔒 SHOPPING

Kilkenny Design Centre   Arts, Crafts
Sells top-end Irish crafts and artworks, from artisans county-wide. Look for John Hanly wool blankets, Cushendale woollen goods, Foxford scarves and Bunbury cutting boards. (☏056-772 2118; www.kilkenny design.com; Castle Yard; ⊙10am-7pm)

Kilkenny Book Centre   Books
The largest bookshop in town, stocking plenty of Irish-interest fiction and non-fiction, periodicals and a good range of maps. There's a cafe upstairs. (10 High St; ⊙10am-5pm Mon-Sat)

⭐ ENTERTAINMENT

Watergate Theatre   Theatre
Kilkenny's top theatre venue hosts drama, comedy and musical performances. If you're wondering why intermission lasts 18 minutes, it's so patrons can nip into John Cleere's pub (p258) for a pint. (www. watergatetheatre.com; Parliament St)

🍴 EATING

Mocha's Vintage Tearooms   Cafe €
Cute retro tearoom with picture-cluttered walls and rose-patterned china. As well as tea and cakes, there's a breakfast menu (until 11.30am) with a choice of bagels or a full Irish fry-up, and hot lunch specials including fish and chips. (4 The Arches, Gashouse Lane; mains €6-13; ⊙8.30am-5.30pm Mon-Sat)

Foodworks   Bistro, Cafe €€
The owners of this cool and casual bistro keep their own pigs and grow their own salad leaves, so it would be churlish not to try their pulled pork brioche or confit pig's trotter – and you'll be glad you did. Delicious food, excellent coffee, and friendly service make this a justifiably popular venue; best to book a table. (☏056-777 7696; www. foodworks.ie; 7 Parliament St; lunch mains €7-14, 3-course dinners €28; ⊙noon-9.30pm Wed-Fri, to 10pm Sat, 12.30-4.30pm Sun; 🛜🚸) 🍃

Cafe Sol   Modern Irish €€
Leisurely lunches stretch until 5pm at this much-loved restaurant. Local organic produce is featured in dishes that emphasise what's fresh each season. The flavours are frequently bold and have global influences. Service, albeit casual, is excellent and the whole place exudes a modern Med-bistro look. (☏056-776 4987; www.restaurantskilkenny. com; William St; mains lunch €10-13, 2-/3-course dinners €25/29; ⊙11am-9.30pm Mon-Thu, to 10pm Fri & Sat, noon-9pm Sun; 🛜) 🍃

Kilkenny Design Centre Restaurant
Cafeteria €€

Upstairs from the craft shops, this arty, organic-oriented, self-service cafeteria offers home-baked breads and scones, tasty seafood chowder, salads in a vast variety, gourmet sandwiches, hot specials, and sumptuous desserts. (www.kilkenny design.com; Castle Yard; mains €7-15; ⊙10am-6pm Sun-Wed, to 9.30pm Thu-Sat; 🛜🛗)

Campagne
Modern Irish €€€

Chef Garrett Byrne, who gained fame and Michelin stars in Dublin, is the genius behind this bold, stylish restaurant in his native Kilkenny. He's passionate about supporting local and artisan producers and serves ever-changing, ever-memorable meals, with a French accent to every culinary creation. Two-/three-course lunch and early-bird menu €27/32. (📞056-777 2858; www.campagne.ie; 5 Gashouse Lane; mains €29-32; ⊙12.30-2.30pm Fri-Sun, 6-10pm Tue-Sat)

Kilkenny Pubs

You'll always find a pub with a song in its heart in Kilkenny. On boards battered by generations of drinkers, musicians perform impromptu trad sessions. Modern bands can be heard in one great setting after another on weekends.

🍷 DRINKING & NIGHTLIFE

Kyteler's Inn
Pub

Dame Alice Kyteler's old house was built back in 1224 and has seen its share of history: she was charged with witchcraft in 1323. Today the rambling bar includes the orignal building, complete with vaulted ceiling and arches. There is a beer garden, courtyard and a large upstairs room for the live bands, ranging from trad to blues. (www.kytelersinn.com; 27 St Kieran's St; ⊙11am-midnight Sun-Thu, to 2am Fri & Sat)

Butler House

SIMON GREENWOOD/GETTY IMAGES ©

Tynan's Bridge House

Tynan's Bridge House   Pub
This historic 1703 Georgian pub is the best traditional bar in town. There's barely a right angle left in the place, with its sagging, granite-topped horseshoe bar, original wood panelling, wonky shelves and loyal clientele of crusty locals – and no TV! Trad music on Wednesdays and weekends at 9pm. (St John's Bridge; ⏱10.30am-11.30pm Mon-Thu, to 12.30am Fri & Sat, 11.30am-11pm Sun)

John Cleere's   Pub
One of Kilkenny's finest venues for live music, theatre and comedy, this long bar has blues, jazz and rock, as well as trad music sessions on Monday and Wednesday. Food served throughout the day, including soup, sandwiches, pizza and Irish stew. (www.cleeres.com; 22 Parliament St; ⏱11.30am-11.30pm Mon-Thu, to 12.30am Fri & Sat, 1-11pm Sun)

O'Hara's Brewery Corner   Pub
Kilkenny's best venue for craft brews is a long, narrow beer hall of a place owned by Carlow Brewing Company. Service can be a bit hit or miss, especially at quiet times, but there's a wide selection of ale to choose from, including Carlow's own IPA. (www.carlowbrewing.com; 29 Parliament St; ⏱1-11.30pm Mon-Thu, to 12.30am Fri & Sat, to 11pm Sun)

🚶 The Peaceful River Nore

Flowing through the centre of Kilkenny, the inky waters of the River Nore reflect the city's stone-built beauty. A walk along its banks or a pause on a bench are the perfect breaks from touring the surrounding streets.

ℹ️ INFORMATION

Kilkenny Tourist Office (Map p253; www.visitkilkenny.ie; Rose Inn St; ⏱9.15am-5pm Mon-Sat) Stocks guides and walking maps. Located in Shee Alms House, dating from 1582 and built in local stone by benefactor Sir Richard Shee to help the poor.

 Top Places for Arts & Crafts

At least 130 full-time craftspeople and artists work commercially in County Kilkenny – one of the highest concentrations in Ireland – thanks to its fine raw materials and inspirational scenery.

Among the best places to see their work are:

Bennettsbridge Several craft studios are located in and around the village.

Graiguenamanagh Wool and crystal studios operate near the centre.

Kilkenny Design Centre (p256) has works by more than a dozen local craftspeople.

Stoneyford Home to a famous glass studio (www.jerpointglass.com; ☺10am-5.30pm Mon-Sat, noon-5pm Sun) and a cafe (www.knockdrinna.com; Main St; mains €5-10; ☺9.30am-6pm Mon-Sat, 11am-5pm Sun, shorter hours Oct-Mar; ⚐) ⚐ with locally produced foods.

Pick up a copy of the Made in Kilkenny craft trail (www.madeinkilkenny.ie) for a comprehensive list of studios and shops.

Irish crocheted blanket
CATHERINE MACBRIDE/GETTY IMAGES ©

ⓘ GETTING THERE & AWAY

BUS

Bus Éireann services stop at the train station and on Ormonde Rd (nearer the town centre); JJ Kavanagh (www.jjkavanagh.ie) buses to Dublin airport stop on Ormonde Rd only.

Cork €21.50, three hours, two daily

Dublin (€14, 2¼ hours, eight daily)

Dublin airport (€20, two to three hours, six daily)

Waterford €12.50, one hour, two daily

TRAIN

Kilkenny's MacDonagh train station is a 10-minute walk northeast of the town centre, with trains to Dublin Heuston (€26, 1½ hours, six daily) and Waterford (€13.85, 40 minutes, seven daily).

COUNTY TIPPERARY

County Tipperary

Landlocked Tipperary boasts the sort of fertile soil that farmers dream of. The central area of the county is low-lying, but rolling hills spill over from adjoining counties and an upper-crust gloss still clings to traditions here, with fox hunts in full legal cry during the winter season.

Walking and cycling opportunities abound, especially in the Glen of Aherlow near Tipperary town. But the real crowd-pleasers are the iconic Rock of Cashel and Cahir Castle. In between, you'll find bucolic charm along pretty much any country road you choose.

☑ In This Section

ⓘ Arriving in County Tipperary

Bus Éireann (p269) runs eight buses daily between Cashel and Cork (€15.50, 1½ hours). The bus stop for Cork is outside the Bake House on Main St. The Dublin stop (€15.50, three hours, six daily) is opposite.

Cahir is a hub for several **Bus Éireann** (p271) routes, including Dublin–Cork, Limerick–Waterford, Galway–Waterford, Kilkenny–Cork and Cork–Athlone. There are six buses per day to Cashel (€6, 20 minutes). Buses stop in the car park beside the tourist office.

From left: High street, Cashel (p268); religious mosaic, Cashel; Hore Abbey (p268)
ROBIN BUSH/GETTY IMAGES ©; MICHAEL INTERISANO/DESIGN PICS/GETTY IMAGES ©; JEREMY WALKER/ GETTY IMAGES ©

PATRICK SWAN/DESIGN PIC/GETTY IMAGES ©

Rock of Cashel

For more than 1000 years the Rock of Cashel was a symbol of power and the seat of kings and priests. Exploring this monumental complex offers a fascinating insight into Ireland's past.

Great For...

☑ **Don't Miss**

The carving of a centaur firing an arrow at a rampaging lion, on Cormac's Chapel.

The Rock of Cashel is one of Ireland's most spectacular archaeological sites. The 'Rock' is a prominent green hill, banded with limestone outcrops, rising from a grassy plain on the edge of town and bristling with ancient fortifications. Sturdy walls circle an enclosure that contains a complete round tower, a 13th-century Gothic cathedral and the finest 12th-century Romanesque chapel in Ireland, home to some of the land's oldest frescoes.

History

In the 4th century, the Rock of Cashel was chosen as a base by the Eóghanachta clan from Wales, who went on to conquer much of Munster and become kings of the region. For some 400 years it rivalled Tara as a centre of power in Ireland. The clan

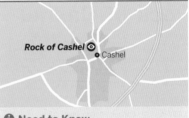

Rock of Cashel ⊙
• Cashel

❶ Need to Know

www.heritageireland.com; adult/child €7/3;
⊙ 9am-5.30pm mid-Mar–mid-Oct, to 7pm
mid-Jun–Aug, to 4.30pm mid-Oct–mid-Mar

✕ Take a Break

Head for Cafe Hans (p269) in the village
immediately below the rock.

★ Top Tip

Download a free audioguided tour
of the town from the tourist office
website (www.cashel.ie).

was associated with St Patrick, hence the
Rock's alternative name of St Patrick's
Rock. In the 10th century, the Eóghanachta
lost possession of the rock to the O'Brien
(or Dál gCais) tribe under Brian Ború's
leadership. In 1101, King Muircheartach
O'Brien presented the Rock to the Church
to curry favour with the powerful bishops
and to end secular rivalry over possession
of the Rock with the Eóghanachta, by now
known as the MacCarthys.

Buildings

Numerous buildings must have occupied
the cold and exposed Rock over the years,
but it is the ecclesiastical relics that have
survived even the depredations of the
Cromwellian army in 1647. The cathedral
was used for worship until the mid-1700s.

Among the graves are a 19th-century
high cross and mausoleum for local land-
owners, the Scully family; the top of the
Scully Cross was razed by lightning in 1976.

The word 'cashel' is an anglicised version
of the Irish word *caiseal,* meaning 'fortress'
(related to the English 'castle', from the
Latin *castellum*).

Getting There on Foot

It's a five-minute stroll from the town
centre up to the Rock, from where fantastic
views range over the Tipperary countryside.
You can take some pretty paths including
the Bishop's Walk from the gardens of the
Cashel Palace Hotel. Sheep grudgingly
allow you to pass. The scaffolding moves
from place to place each year as part of
the never-ending struggle to keep the Rock
caulked.

Call ahead for details of guided tours.

Rock of Cashel

For more than 1000 years the Rock of Cashel was a symbol of power and the seat of kings and churchmen who ruled over the region. Exploring this monumental complex offers a fascinating insight into Ireland's past.

Enter via the 15th-century **Hall of the Vicars Choral 1**, built to house the male choristers who sang in the cathedral. Exhibits in its undercroft include rare silverware, stone reliefs and the original St Patrick's Cross. In the courtyard you'll see the replica of **St Patrick's Cross 2**. A small porch leads into the 13th-century Gothic **Cathedral 3**. To the west of the nave are the remains of the **Archbishop's Residence 4**. From the cathedral's north transept on the northeastern corner is the Rock's earliest building, an 11th- or 12th-century **Round Tower 5**. The south transept leads to the compelling **Cormac's Chapel 6**, probably the first Romanesque church in Ireland. It dates from 1127 and the medieval integrity of its trans-European architecture survives. Inside the main door on the left is the sarcophagus said to house King Cormac, dating from between 1125 and 1150. Before leaving, take time for a close-up look at the Rock's **enclosing walls and corner tower 7**.

Hall of the Vicars Choral
Head upstairs from the ticket office to see the choristers' restored kitchen and dining hall, complete with period furniture, tapestries and paintings beneath a fine carved-oak roof and gallery.

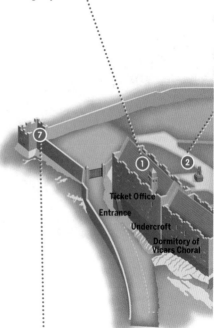

Ticket Office

Entrance

Undercroft

Dormitory of Vicars Choral

TOP TIPS

» Good photographic vantage points for framing the mighty Rock are on the road into Cashel from the Dublin Rd roundabout or from the little roads just west of the centre.

» The best photo opportunities, however, are from inside the atmospheric ruins of Hore Abbey, 1km to the north.

Enclosing Walls & Corner Tower
Constructed from lime mortar around the 15th century, and originally incorporating five gates, stone walls enclose the entire site. It's thought the surviving corner tower was used as a watchtower.

St Patrick's Cross
In the castle courtyard, this cross replicates the eroded Hall of the Vicars Choral original – an impressive 12th-century crutched cross depicting a crucifixion scene on one face and animals on the other.

GEORGE MUNDAY/GETTY IMAGES ©

Archbishop's Residence
The west side of the cathedral is taken up by the Archbishop's Residence, a 15th-century, four-storey castle, which had its great hall built over the nave, reducing its length. It was last inhabited in the mid-1700s.

Cathedral
A huge square tower with a turret on the southwestern corner soars above the cathedral. Scattered throughout are monuments, a 16th-century altar tomb, coats of arms panels, and stone heads on capitals and corbels.

JOE CORNISH/GETTY IMAGES ©

Turret

④

③

⑤

⑥

Choir

Scully Cross

Cormac's Chapel
Look closely at the exquisite doorway arches, the grand chancel arch and ribbed barrel vault, and carved vignettes, including a trefoil-tailed grotesque and a Norman-helmeted centaur firing an arrow at a rampaging lion.

STEPHEN SAKS/GETTY IMAGES ©

TRISH PUNCH/GETTY IMAGES ©

Round Tower
Standing 28m tall, the doorway to this ancient edifice is 3.5m above the ground – perhaps for structural rather than defensive reasons. Its exact age is unknown but may be as early as 1101.

Cashel

It's little wonder that Cashel (Caiseal Mumhan) is such a fabulous draw (the Queen included it on her historic visit in 2011). The iconic religious buildings that crown the blustery summit of the Rock of Cashel seem to emerge from the rocky landscape itself and the smallish market town of Cashel itself rewards rambles around its charming streets.

⊙ SIGHTS

Hore Abbey   Historic Site
Less than 1km north of the Rock, the formidable ruin of 13th-century Hore Abbey (also known as Hoare Abbey or St Mary's) stands in flat farmland. Originally Benedictine and settled by monks from Glastonbury in England at the end of the 12th century, it later became a Cistercian house. An enjoyably gloomy wreck, the abbey was gifted

Cashel is best known in Ireland and beyond for award-winning Cashel Blue cheese.

to the order by a 13th-century archbishop who expelled the Benedictine monks after dreaming that they planned to murder him.

Brú Ború   Heritage Centre
The privately run heritage and cultural centre is next to the car park below the Rock of Cashel, and offers absorbing insights into Irish traditional music, dance and song. The centre's main attraction, the Sounds of History exhibition, relates the story of Ireland and its music through imaginative audio displays; various other musical events take place in summer. (☏062-61122; www.comhaltas.ie/locations/detail/bru_boru; admission free, exhibitions from €5; ⊙9am-5pm Mon-Fri Sep–mid-Jun, 9am-5pm Mon, 9am-11pm Tue-Sat mid-Jun–Aug)

Cashel Folk Village   Museum
An engaging exhibition of old buildings, shopfronts and memorabilia from around the town. It's a bit slipshod in a heartwarming way. (☏062-63601; www.cashel-folkvillage.ie; Dominic St; adult/child €5/2; ⊙9am-7.30pm mid-Jun–mid-Sep, reduced hours rest of year)

Cashel Blue farmhouse cheese

OLIVER STREWE/GETTY IMAGES ©

Cashel Heritage
Town Centre Museum   Museum
Located in the town hall alongside the
tourist office, the displays include a scale
model of Cashel in the 1640s with an ac-
companying soundtrack. (Main St, Town Hall;
⊙9.30am-5.30pm mid-Mar–mid-Oct, 9.30am-
5.30pm Mon-Fri mid-Oct–mid-Mar) FREE

Bolton Library   Museum
This forbidding 1836 stone building houses
a splendid 18th-century collection of books,
maps and manuscripts from the dawn of
printing onwards, with works by writers
from Chaucer to Swift. (John St; admission
€2; ⊙10am-4pm by appointment, book at tourist
office)

⊗ EATING

Apart from the Rock, Cashel is best known
in Ireland and beyond for award-winning
Cashel Blue farmhouse cheese, Ireland's
first-ever blue cheese. Although it's still
handmade locally (and only locally), it's
surprisingly hard to find in shops and on
restaurant menus in town.

Cafe Hans   Cafe €€
Competition for the 32 seats is fierce at
this gourmet cafe run by the same family
as Chez Hans next door. There's a fantastic
selection of salads, open sandwiches
(including succulent prawns with tangy
Marie Rose sauce) and filling fish, shellfish,
lamb and vegetarian dishes, with a dis-
cerning wine selection and mouthwatering
desserts. No credit cards. (✆062-63660;
Dominic St; mains €13-18, 2-/3-course lunch
€16/20; ⊙noon-5.30pm Tue-Sat; 🚻)

Chez Hans   Irish €€€
Since 1968 this former church has been a
place of worship for foodies from all over
Ireland and beyond. Still as fresh and inventive as ever, the restaurant has a regularly
changing menu and gives its blessing to all
manner of Irish foods, including steamed
Galway mussels, goats-cheese tart and
pan-fried peppered skate wing. (✆062-

⤷ What's Nearby

Reached over a stile and across sometimes muddy fields, the atmospheric
and delightful ruins of Athassel Priory
sit in the shallow and verdant River Suir
Valley, 7km southwest of Cashel. The
original buildings date from 1205, and
Athassel was once one of the richest
and most important monasteries in
Ireland. What survives is substantial:
the gatehouse and portcullis gateway,
the cloister (ruined but recognisable)
and stretches of walled enclosure, as
well as some medieval tomb effigies.
To get here, take the N74 to the village
of Golden, then head 2km south along
the narrow L4304 road signed Athassel
Abbey. Roadside parking is limited and
quite tight. The welter of back lanes is
good for cycling.

61177; www.chezhans.net; Dominic St; mains €24-
38, 2-/3-course meal €28/33; ⊙6-10pm Tue-Sat)

ⓘ INFORMATION

Tourist Office (✆062-62511; www.cashel.ie;
Town Hall, Main St; ⊙9.30am-5.30pm Mon-Sat
mid-Mar–mid-Oct, 9.30am-5.30pm Mon-Fri mid-
Oct–mid-Mar) Helpful office with reams of info
on the area.

ⓘ GETTING THERE & AWAY

Bus Éireann (www.buseireann.ie) runs eight
buses daily between Cashel and Cork (€15.50,
1½ hours). The bus stop for Cork is outside the
Bake House on Main St. The Dublin stop (€15.50,
three hours, six daily) is opposite.

Cahir

At the eastern tip of the Galtee Mountains
15km south of Cashel, Cahir (An Cathair;
pronounced 'care') is a compact and
attractive town that encircles its sublime
castle. Walking paths follow the banks of

Where to Stay

While some visitors (mainly hikers) base themselves in Tipperary Town, there are lots of great B&B and hotel options nearby. Here are our favourites:

Cashel Town B&B (📞062-62330; www. cashelbandb.com; 5 John St; d €55-65, tr/q from €90/120; 🛜🍴) 🅿️

Tinsley House (📞052-744 1947; www. tinsleyhouse.com; The Square; d/f from €65/120; 🕐Apr-Sep; 🛜)

Baileys Hotel (📞062-61937; www. baileyshotelcashel.com; Main St; s/d from €55/70; 🛜🍴)

Cahir House Hotel (📞052-744 3000; www.cahirhousehotel.ie; The Square; s €95, d €160; 🕐bar food noon-9.30pm; @🛜🍴).

the River Suir – you can easily spend a couple of hours wandering about.

◎ SIGHTS

Cahir Castle   Historic Site
Cahir's awesome castle enjoys a river-island site with moat, massive walls, turrets and keep, stalwart defences, mullioned windows, vast fireplaces and dungeons. Founded by Conor O'Brien in 1142, it's one of Ireland's largest castles, passing to the Butler family in 1375. In 1599 the Earl of Essex shattered its walls with cannon fire, an event explained with a large model. With a huge set of antlers pinned to its white walls, the Banqueting Hall is an impressive sight; you can also climb the Keep.

The castle eventually surrendered to Cromwell in 1650 without a struggle; its future usefulness may have discouraged the usual Cromwellian 'deconstruction' – it is largely intact and still formidable. It was restored in the 1840s and again in the 1960s when it came under state ownership.A 15-minute audiovisual presentation puts Cahir in context with other Irish

castles. The buildings within the castle are sparsely furnished, although there are good displays, including an exhibition on 'Women in Medieval Ireland'. There are frequent guided tours. (📞052-744 1011; www. heritageireland.ie; Castle St; adult/child €4/2; 🕐9am-6.30pm mid-Jun–Aug, 9.30am-5.30pm mid-Mar–mid-Jun & Sep–mid-Oct, to 4.30pm mid-Oct–mid-Mar)

🔒 SHOPPING

The Craft Granary   Arts & Crafts
Hundreds of locals toiled away in a notorious linen mill during the 19th century. Almost 200 years later, the once ominous stone building has been reborn as the Cahir Craft Granary, with local artists creating and selling works including pottery, carvings, paintings and jewellery. It's just north of the Square, past the post office. (www.craftgranary.ie; Church St; 🕐10am-6pm Mon-Fri, 9am-5pm Sat year-round plus 1-5pm Sun Jul, Aug & Dec)

✖ EATING

Farmers Market   Market
Cahir's farmers market attracts the region's best food vendors. (Castle car park; 🕐9am-1pm Sat) 🅿️

Lazy Bean Cafe   Cafe €
Busy, breezy little cafe dishing out tasty sandwiches, salads, soups and wraps. Its adjacent tearoom, the Coffee Pod, is quieter. (www.thelazybeancafe.com; The Square; dishes €5-7; 🕐9am-6pm Mon-Sat, 10am-6pm Sun; 🛜)

River House   Cafe €
A change in ownership has turned this icon by the river into just another cafe, but the patio still has fine castle views. Enjoy them with your burger and chips. (📞052-744 1951; 1 Castle St; meals €6-12; 🕐9am-5pm)

Galileo   Italian €€
Serving fine pizzas and pasta to Cahir locals for over a decade, Galileo is a neat and smooth Italian restaurant, with a modern interior and efficient, friendly service.

Cahir Castle

The restaurant has no license, so BYO. (www.galileocafe.com; Church St; mains €9-22; ⊙noon-10pm)

❶ INFORMATION

Tourist Office (☎052-744 1453; www. discoverireland.ie/tipperary; Cahir Castle car park; ⊙9.30am-1pm & 1.45-5.30pm Tue-Sat Easter-Oct) Has information about the town and region.

❶ GETTING THERE & AWAY

BUS

Cahir is a hub for several Bus Éireann (www. buseireann.ie) routes, including Dublin–Cork, Limerick–Waterford, Galway–Waterford, Kilkenny–Cork and Cork–Athlone. There are six buses per day to Cashel (€6, 20 minutes). Buses stop in the car park beside the tourist office.

TRAIN

From Monday to Saturday, the Limerick Junction–Waterford train stops three times daily in each direction.

Galway street during the city's Food Festival (p122)

In Focus

Ha'penny Bridge (p59) over the Liffey, Dublin

Ireland Today

*Ireland has travelled a long way since the dawn of the
new millennium. It has yo-yoed out of recession and
back before once again emerging from the economic
gloom of the global financial crisis. It has grown
increasingly comfortable with its identity as a
multicultural melting pot, its gaze fixed firmly on being
a fully signed-up member of the global community.*

A Social Revolution

But the longest journey it has made is along the road of social change, moving from a
fiercely traditional and conservative nation to one that in May 2015 became the first country in the world to introduce marriage equality by universal plebiscite, by a margin of 62%.
The night of the result, Hillary Clinton tweeted 'Well done, Ireland!"

Back in the Black

The other bit of positive news was that Ireland has exited the restrictive austerity program
imposed on it in 2010 by its international creditors in exchange for a €78bn bailout that
saved the country from bankruptcy. Unemployment began to fall again – to below 10%

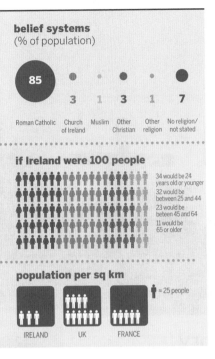

belief systems
(% of population)

85   3   1   3   1   7

Roman Catholic   Church of Ireland   Muslim   Other Christian   Other religion   No religion/ not stated

if Ireland were 100 people

34 would be 24 years old or younger

32 would be between 25 and 44

23 would be beteen 45 and 64

11 would be 65 or older

population per sq km

IRELAND   UK   FRANCE

= 25 people

for the first time in years. But the country could barely crack a smile in response: the cost of austerity was prohibitively high for many Irish, especially those on the vulnerable margins, who witnessed deep cuts to key social services, a fall in wages by an average of 15% and a slew of new indirect taxes that put additional burdens on households already put to the pin of their collars.

Even still, emigration numbers fell in 2015 and instead there was a rise in the number of returning Irish, eager it seems to take advantage of Europe's fastest-growing economy, with growth rates of over 3.5% (almost triple the European average).

A Vote of Confidence?

Needless to say, the government – a coalition of right-leaning Fine Gael and left-of-centre Labour who came to power in 2011 with the promise of repairing the damage of the financial crisis – are taking full credit for the recovery, which couldn't come at a better time. The pending election will determine whether the electorate buy the government's 'We did it for your own good' message or punish them for every cut and extra charge they've had to endure over the previous five years.

Waiting in the wings is Sinn Féin, the old political wing of the IRA. Still led by the old warhorse Gerry Adams, the party has reinvented itself dramatically. In Northern Ireland they're coalition partners in government with their bitterest rivals, the Democratic Unionist Party, while in the Republic they're now – according to some polls – the most popular party in the Republic due to a compelling (many say populist) rhetoric of anti-austerity that has a broad appeal.

Easter Rising Centenary

Whatever happens, the election will take place against the backdrop of the most significant anniversary for decades: the centenary of the Easter Rising of 1916, when republican nationalists declared a republic before being captured and executed by British forces. Every party wants to use the occasion to make political hay, but Fine Gael's own historical ideology as a conservative party staunchly opposed to violent rebellion makes it a tougher fit; not so for Sinn Féin, who see themselves as the natural heirs of the heroes of 1916...and won't miss an opportunity to remind the electorate in the run up to the elections.

Celtic cross in a cemetery, County Tipperary

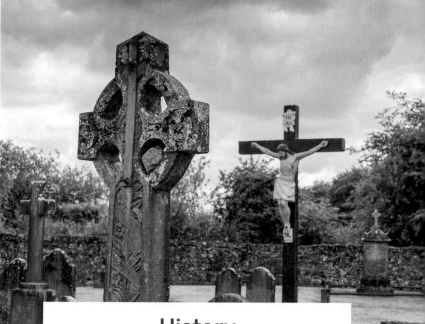

MORRBYTE/GETTY IMAGES ©

History

*From pre-Celts to Celtic cubs, Ireland's history is
a search for identity, which would be a little more
straightforward if this small island hadn't been of such
interest to so many invaders, especially the English.
Indeed, Ireland's fractious relationship with its nearest
neighbour has occupied much of the last 1000 years, and
it is through the prism of that relationship that a huge
part of the Irish identity is reflected.*

10,000–8000 BC	700–300 BC	AD 431–2
After the last ice age ends, the first humans arrive in Ireland.	The Celtic culture and language arrive, ushering in 1000 years of cultural and political dominance.	Arrival of the first Christian missionaries with Bishop Palladius and, a year later, St Patrick.

Replica Stone Age house, Ireland

Who the Hell are the Irish?

Hunters and gatherers may first have traversed the narrowing land bridge that once linked Ireland with Britain, but many more crossed the Irish Sea in small hide-covered boats. In the 8th century BC, Ireland came to the attention of the fearsome Celts, who, having fought their way across Central Europe, established permanent settlements on the island in the 3rd century BC.

Getting into the Habit

Arguably the most significant import into Ireland came between the 3rd and 5th centuries AD, when Christian missionaries first brought the new religion of Rome. Everyone has heard of St Patrick, but he was merely the most famous of many who converted the local pagan tribes by cleverly fusing traditional pagan rituals with the new Christian teaching, creating an exciting hybrid known as Celtic (Insular) Christianity. The artistic and

550–800	**795–841**	**1171**
The great monastic teachers begin exporting their knowledge across Europe, ushering in Ireland's 'Golden Age'.	Vikings plunder Irish monasteries before establishing settlements throughout the country.	King Henry II invades Ireland and forces Anglo-Norman warlords to accept him as their overlord.

St Patrick

Ireland's patron saint, St Patrick (AD 389–461), remembered all around the world on 17 March, wasn't even Irish. This symbol of Irish pride hailed from what is now Wales, which at the time of his birth was under Roman occupation. Kidnapped by Irish raiders when he was 16 and made a slave, he found religion, escaped from captivity and returned to Britain. He returned to Ireland vowing to make Christians out of the Irish, and within 30 years of his return his dream had come true.

So next St Paddy's Day, as you're swilling Guinness, think of who the man really was.

intellectual credentials of Ireland's Christians were the envy of Europe and led to the moniker 'the land of saints and scholars'.

More Invaders

The Celts' lack of political unity made the island easy pickings for the next wave of invaders, Danish Vikings. Over the course of the 9th and 10th centuries, they established settlements along the east coast, intermarried with the Celtic tribes and introduced red hair and freckles to the Irish gene pool.

The '800 years' of English rule in Ireland began in 1171, when the English king Henry II sent a huge invasion force, at the urging of the pope, to bring the increasingly independent Christian missionaries to heel. It was also intended to curb the growing power of the Anglo-Norman lords, who had arrived in Ireland two years before Henry's army, and who had settled quite nicely into Irish life, becoming – as the old saying went – *Hiberniores Hibernis ipsis* (more Irish than the Irish themselves). By the 16th century, they had divided the country into their own fiefdoms and the English Crown's direct control didn't extend any further than a cordon surrounding Dublin, known as 'the Pale'.

Divorce, Dissolution & Destruction

Henry VIII's failure to get the pope's blessing for his divorce augured badly for the Irish, who sided with the Vatican. Henry retaliated by ordering the dissolution of all monasteries in Britain and Ireland, and had himself declared King of Ireland. His daughter Elizabeth I went even further, establishing jurisdiction in Connaught and Munster before crushing the last of the rebels, the lords of Ulster, led by the crafty and courageous Hugh O'Neill, Earl of Tyrone.

With the native chiefs gone, Elizabeth and her successor, James I, could pursue their policy of Plantation with impunity. Though confiscations took place all over the country, Ulster was most affected both because of its wealthy farmlands and as punishment for being home to the primary fomenters of rebellion.

1366	**1534–41**	**1594**
Statutes of Kilkenny outlaw intermarriage and a host of Irish customs to stop Anglo-Norman assimilation.	Henry VIII declares war on the Irish Church and declares himself King of Ireland.	Hugh O'Neill, Earl of Tyrone, instigates open conflict with England and starts the Nine Years' War.

Bloody Religion

At the outset of the English Civil War in 1641, the Irish threw their support behind Charles I against the Protestant parliamentarians in the hope that victory for the king would lead to the restoration of Catholic power in Ireland. When Oliver Cromwell and his Roundheads defeated the Royalists and took Charles' head off in 1649, Cromwell then turned his attention to the disloyal Irish. His nine-month campaign was effective and brutal; yet more lands were confiscated – Cromwell's famous utterance that the Irish could 'go to hell or to Connaught' seems odd given the province's beauty, but there wasn't much arable land out there – and Catholic rights were restricted even more.

The Boyne & Penal Laws

Catholic Ireland's next major setback came in 1690. Yet again the Irish had backed the wrong horse, this time supporting James II after his deposition in the Glorious Revolution by the Dutch Protestant King William of Orange (who was married to James' own daughter Mary). After James had unsuccessfully laid siege to Derry for 105 days (the loyalist cry of 'No Surrender!', in use to this day, dates from the siege), in July he fought William's armies by the banks of the Boyne in County Louth and was roundly defeated.

The final ignominy for Catholic Ireland came in 1695 with the passing of the Penal Laws, known collectively as the 'popery code', which prohibited Catholics from owning land or entering any higher profession. Irish culture, music and education were banned in the hope that Catholicism would be eradicated. Most Catholics continued to worship at secret locations, but some prosperous Irish converted to Protestantism to preserve their careers and wealth. Land was steadily transferred to Protestant owners, and a significant majority of the Catholic population became tenants living in wretched conditions. By the late 18th century, Catholics owned barely 5% of the land.

If at First You Don't Succeed...

With Roman Catholics rendered utterly powerless, the seeds of rebellion against autocracy were planted by a handful of liberal Protestants, inspired by the ideologies of the Enlightenment and the unrest provoked by the American War of Independence and then the French Revolution.

The first of these came in 1798, when the United Irishmen, led by a young Dublin Protestant, Theobald Wolfe Tone (1763–98), took on the British at the Battle of Vinegar Hill in County Wexford – their defeat was hastened by the failure of the French to land an army of succour in 1796 in Bantry Bay.

The Liberator

The Act of Union, passed in 1801, was the British government's vain attempt to put an end to any aspirations towards Irish independence, but the nationalist genie was out of the bottle, not least in the body of a Kerry-born Catholic named Daniel O'Connell (1775–1847).

1601	1649–53	1690
O'Neill surrenders after the Battle of Kinsale and Irish rebellion against the Crown is broken.	Oliver Cromwell lays waste throughout Ireland after the Irish support Charles I.	Catholic King James II defeated by William of Orange in the Battle of the Boyne on 12 July.

Kilmainham Gaol (p40)

BENJAMIN KRALJ/SHUTTERSTOCK ©

In 1823 O'Connell founded the Catholic Association with the aim of achieving political equality for Catholics, which he did (in part) by forcing the passing of the 1829 Act of Catholic Emancipation, allowing some well-off Catholics voting rights and the right to be elected as MPs.

O'Connell's campaign now switched to the repeal of the Act of Union, but the 'Liberator' came to a sorry end in 1841 when he meekly stood down in face of a government order banning one of his rallies. His capitulation was deemed unforgivable given that Ireland was in the midst of the Potato Famine.

The Uncrowned King of Ireland

The baton of moderate opposition to British rule was then taken up by the extraordinary Charles Stewart Parnell (1846–91), who instigated the strategy of 'boycotting' (named after one particularly unpleasant agent named Charles Boycott) tenants, agents and landlords who didn't get on board with the demands of the Land League, an organisation set up to agitate for land reform, arguably the most important feature of the Irish struggle against British rule. The Land Act of 1881 improved life immeasurably for tenants, creating fair rents and the possibility of tenants owning their land.

Parnell's other assault on British rule was on agitating for Home Rule, a limited form of autonomy for Ireland. As leader of the Irish Parliamentary Party (IPP), he formed alliances with William Gladstone's Liberal Party in return for the introduction of a Home Rule Bill, which came (but was defeated) in 1886 and 1892 – although Parnell was not around for the second bill: in 1890 he was embroiled in a divorce scandal, was forced to resign and died a broken man in 1891.

Rebellion Once Again

Ireland's struggle for some kind of autonomy picked up pace in the second decade of the 20th century. The radicalism that had always been at the fringes of Irish nationalist aspirations was once again beginning to assert itself, partly in response to a hardening of attitudes in Ulster. Mass opposition to any kind of Irish independence had resulted in the

1801	1845–51	1879–82
The Act of Union unites Ireland politically with Britain, ending Irish 'independence'.	Between 500,000 and one million die during the Potato Famine; two million more emigrate.	The Land War sees tenant farmers defying their landlords en masse.

formation of the Ulster Volunteer Force (UVF), a loyalist vigilante group whose 100,000-plus members swore to resist any attempt to impose Home Rule on Ireland. Nationalists responded by creating the Irish Volunteer Force (IVF), and a showdown seemed inevitable.

Home Rule was finally passed in 1914, but the outbreak of WWI meant that its enactment was shelved for the duration. For most Irish, the suspension was disappointing but hardly unreasonable and the majority of the volunteers enlisted to help fight the Germans.

Beyond the Pale

The expression 'beyond the pale' came into use when the Pale – defined as a jurisdiction marked by a clear boundary – was the English-controlled part of Ireland, which stretched roughly from Dalkey, a southern suburb of Dublin, to Dundalk, north of Drogheda. Inland, the boundary extended west to Trim and Kells. To the British elite, the rest of Ireland was considered uncivilised.

The Easter Rising

A few, however, did not heed the call. Two small groups – a section of the Irish Volunteers under Pádraig Pearse and the Irish Citizens' Army led by James Connolly – conspired in a rebellion that took the country by surprise. A depleted Volunteer group marched into Dublin on Easter Monday 1916 and took over a number of key positions in the city, claiming the General Post Office on O'Connell St as its headquarters. From its steps, Pearse read out to passers-by a declaration that Ireland was now a republic and that his band was the provisional government. Less than a week of fighting ensued before the rebels surrendered to the superior British forces. The rebels weren't popular and had to be protected from angry Dubliners as they were marched to jail.

The Easter Rising would probably have had little impact on the Irish situation had the British not made martyrs of the rebel leaders. Of the 77 given death sentences, 15 were executed, including the injured Connolly, who was shot while strapped to a chair. This brought about a sea change in public attitudes and support for the Republicans rose dramatically.

War with Britain

By the end of WWI, Home Rule was far too little, far too late. In the 1918 general election, the Republicans stood under the banner of Sinn Féin and won a large majority of the Irish seats. Ignoring London's Parliament, where technically they were supposed to sit, the newly elected Sinn Féin deputies – many of them veterans of the 1916 Easter Rising – declared Ireland independent and formed the first Dáil Éireann (Irish assembly or lower house), which sat in Dublin's Mansion House under the leadership of Éamon de Valera (1882–1975). The Irish Volunteers became the Irish Republican Army (IRA) and the Dáil authorised it to wage war on British troops in Ireland.

1916	1919	1921
The Easter Rising rebels surrender to superior British forces in less than a week.	The Irish War of Independence begins in January.	War ends in a truce on 11 July; Anglo-Irish Treaty is signed on 6 December.

The Great Famine

As a result of the Great Famine of 1845–51, a staggering three million people died or were forced to emigrate from Ireland. This great tragedy is all the more inconceivable given that the scale of suffering was attributable to selfishness as much as to natural causes. Potatoes were the staple food of a rapidly growing, desperately poor population and, when a blight hit the crops, prices soared. The repressive Penal Laws ensured that farmers, already crippled with high rents, could ill afford to sell the limited harvest of potatoes not affected by blight or imported from abroad to the Irish.

Shamefully, during this time there were abundant harvests of wheat and dairy produce – the country was producing more than enough grain to feed the entire population and it's said that more cattle were sold abroad than there were people on the island.

Mass emigration continued to reduce the population during the next 100 years and huge numbers of Irish emigrants who found their way abroad, particularly to the US, carried with them a lasting bitterness.

As wars go, the War of Independence was pretty small fry. It lasted 2½ years and cost around 1200 casualties. But it was a pretty nasty affair, as the IRA fought a guerrilla-style, hit-and-run campaign against the British, their numbers swelled by returning veterans of WWI known as Black and Tans (on account of their uniforms, a mix of army khaki and police black), most of whom were so traumatised by their wartime experiences that they were prone to all kinds of brutality.

A Kind of Freedom

A truce in July 1921 led to intense negotiations between the two sides. The resulting Treaty, signed on 6 December 1921, created the Irish Free State, made up of 26 of 32 Irish counties. The remaining six – all in Ulster – remained part of the UK. The Treaty was an imperfect document: not only did it cement the geographic divisions on the island that 50 years later would explode into the Troubles, but it caused a split among nationalists – between those who believed the Treaty to be a necessary stepping stone towards full independence and those who saw it as capitulation to the British and a betrayal of Republican ideals. This division was to determine the course of Irish political affairs for virtually the remainder of the century.

Civil War

The Treaty was ratified after a bitter debate and the June 1922 elections resulted in a victory for the pro-Treaty side. But the anti-Treaty forces rallied behind de Valera, who, though president of the Dáil, had not been a member of the Treaty negotiating team (affording him, in the eyes of his critics and opponents, maximum deniability should the negotiations

1921–22	1922–23	1932
Treaty grants independence to 26 counties, allowing six Ulster counties to remain part of Great Britain.	Brief and bloody civil war between pro-Treaty and anti-Treaty forces results in victory for the former.	De Valera leads his Fianna Fáil party into government for the first time.

go pear-shaped) and objected to some of the Treaty's provisions, most notably the oath of allegiance to the English monarch.

Within two weeks of the elections, civil war broke out between comrades who, a year previously, had fought alongside each other. The most prominent casualty of this particularly bitter conflict was Michael Collins (1890–1922), mastermind of the IRA's campaign during the War of Independence and a chief negotiator of the Anglo-Irish Treaty – shot in an ambush in his native Cork. Collins himself had presaged the bitterness that would result from the Treaty: upon signing it he is said to have declared, 'I tell you, I have signed my own death warrant.'

The Making of a Republic

The Civil War ground to an exhausted halt in 1923 with the victory of the pro-Treaty side, who governed the new state until 1932. Defeated but unbowed, de Valera founded a new party in 1926 called Fianna Fáil (Soldiers of Ireland) and won a majority in the 1932 elections – they would remain in charge until 1948. In the meantime, de Valera created a new constitution in 1937 that did away with the hated oath of allegiance, reaffirmed the special position of the Catholic Church and once again laid claim to the six counties of Northern Ireland. In 1948 Ireland officially left the Commonwealth and became a Republic, but as historical irony would have it, it was Fine Gael, as the old pro-Treaty party were now known, that declared it – Fianna Fáil had surprisingly lost the election that year. After 800 years Ireland – or at least a substantial chunk of it – was independent.

Growing Pains & Roaring Tigers

Unquestionably the most significant figure since independence, Éamon de Valera's contribution to an independent Ireland was immense but, as the 1950s stretched into the 1960s, his vision for the country was mired in a conservative and traditional orthodoxy that was patently at odds with the reality of a country in desperate economic straits, where chronic unemployment and emigration were but the more visible effects of inadequate policy.

Partners in Europe

In 1972 the Republic (along with Northern Ireland) became a member of the European Economic Community (EEC), which brought an increased measure of prosperity thanks to the benefits of the Common Agricultural Policy, which set fixed prices and guaranteed quotas for Irish farming produce. Nevertheless, the broader global depression, provoked by the oil crisis of 1973, forced the country into yet another slump and emigration figures rose again, reaching a peak in the mid-1980s.

From Celtic Tiger...

In the early 1990s, European funds helped kick start economic growth. Huge sums of money were invested in education and physical infrastructure, while the policy of low corporate

1948	**1993**	**1994**
The new Fine Gael declares the Free State to be a republic.	Downing Street Declaration signed by British prime minister John Major and Irish Taoiseach Albert Reynolds.	Sinn Féin leader Gerry Adams announces a cessation of IRA violence on 31 August.

★ **Places Where History Happened**

General Post Office (Map p72)

Battle of Boyne Site (p92)

Tara (p92)

Kinsale (p197)

Battle of the Boyne reenactors

CHRIS MADDALONI/AFP/GETTY IMAGES ©

tax rates coupled with attractive incentives made Ireland very appealing to high-tech businesses looking for a door into EU markets. In less than a decade, Ireland went from being one of the poorest countries in Europe to one of the wealthiest: unemployment fell from 18% to 3.5%, the average industrial wage somersaulted to the top of the European league and the dramatic rise in GDP meant that the government had far more money than it knew what do with. Ireland became synonymous with the Celtic Tiger, an economic model of success that was the envy of the entire world.

...to Rescue Cat

From 2002, the Irish economy was kept buoyant by a gigantic construction boom that was completely out of step with any measure of responsible growth forecasting. The out-of-control international derivatives market flooded Irish banks with cheap money, and they were only too happy to lend it to anyone who wanted. And in Ireland, everyone wanted.

Then Lehman Brothers and the credit crunch happened. The Irish banks nearly went to the wall, were bailed out at the last minute and before Ireland could draw breath, the International Monetary Fund (IMF) and the European Union held the chits of the country's mid-term economic future. Ireland found itself yet again confronting the demons of its past: high unemployment, limited opportunity and massive emigration.

It's (Not So) Grim up North

Making sense of Northern Ireland isn't that easy. It's not because the politics are so entrenched (they are), or that the two sides are at such odds with each other (they are): it's because the fight is so old.

It began in the 16th century, with the first Plantations of Ireland ordered by the English Crown, whereby the confiscated lands of the Gaelic and Hiberno-Norman gentry were awarded to English and Scottish settlers of good Protestant stock. The policy was most effective in Ulster, where the newly arrived Protestants were given an extra leg-up by the Penal Laws, which successfully reduced the now landless Catholic population to second-class citizens with little or no rights.

mid-1990s	1998	2005
The 'Celtic Tiger' economy transforms Ireland into one of Europe's wealthiest countries.	After the Good Friday Agreement, the 'Real IRA' detonates a bomb in Omagh, killing 29 people and injuring 200.	The IRA orders all of its units to commit to exclusively democratic means.

Irish Apartheid

But fast-forward to 1921, when the notion of independent Ireland moved from aspiration to actuality. The new rump state of Northern Ireland was governed until 1972 by the Protestant-majority Ulster Unionist Party, backed up by the overwhelmingly Protestant Royal Ulster Constabulary (RUC) and the sectarian B-Specials militia. As a result of tilted economic subsidies, bias in housing allocation and wholesale gerrymandering, Northern Ireland was, in effect, an apartheid state, leaving the roughly 40% Catholic and Nationalist population grossly underrepresented.

Defiance of Unionist hegemony came with the Civil Rights Movement, founded in 1967 and heavily influenced by its US counterpart. In October 1968 a mainly Catholic march in Derry was violently broken up by the RUC amid rumours that the IRA had provided 'security' for the marchers. Nobody knew it at the time, but the Troubles had begun.

The Troubles

Conflict escalated quickly: clashes between the two communities increased and the police openly sided with the Loyalists against a Nationalist population made increasingly militant by the resurgence of the long-dormant IRA. In August 1969 British troops went to Derry and then Belfast to maintain law and order; they were initially welcomed in Catholic neighbourhoods but within a short time they too were seen as an army of occupation: the killing of 13 innocent civilians in Derry on Bloody Sunday (30 January 1972) set the grim tone for the next two decades, as violence, murder and reprisal became the order of the day in the province and, occasionally, on the British mainland.

Overtures of Peace

In the 1990s external circumstances started to alter the picture. Membership of the EU, economic progress in Ireland and the declining importance of the Catholic Church in the South started to reduce differences between the North and the Republic. Also, American interest added an international dimension to the situation.

A series of negotiated statements between the Unionists, Nationalists and the British and Irish governments eventually resulted in the historic Good Friday Agreement of 1998, which established the power-sharing Northern Ireland Assembly.

The agreement called for the devolution of legislative power from Westminster (where it had been since 1972) to a new Northern Ireland Assembly, but posturing, disagreement, sectarianism and downright pigheadedness made slow work of progress, and the assembly was suspended four times – the last from October 2002 until May 2007.

During this period, the politics of Northern Ireland polarised dramatically, resulting in the falling away of the more moderate UUP and the emergence of the hardline Democratic Unionist Party (DUP), led by Ian Paisley; and, on the Nationalist side, the emergence of the IRA's political wing, Sinn Féin, as the main torch-bearer of Nationalist aspirations, under the leadership of Gerry Adams and Martin McGuinness.

2008	2010	2015
The Irish banking system is declared virtually bankrupt following the collapse of Lehman Brothers.	Ireland surrenders financial sovereignty to IMF and EU in exchange for bailout package of €85bn.	Ireland becomes the first stricken eurozone country to successfully exit the terms of a bailout.

Lobster thermidor at Fishy Fishy (p199), Kinsale

Food & Drink

Ireland's recently acquired reputation as a gourmet destination is thoroughly deserved, as a host of chefs and producers are leading a foodie revolution that, at its heart, is about bringing to the table the kind of meals that have always been taken for granted on well-run Irish farms. Coupled with the growing sophistication of the Irish palate, it's now relatively easy to eat well in all budgets.

To Eat...

Potatoes

It's a wonder the Irish retain their good humour amid the perpetual potato-baiting they endure. But, despite the stereotyping, and however much we'd like to disprove it, potatoes are still paramount here and you'll see lots of them on your travels. The mashed potato dishes *colcannon* and *champ* (with cabbage and spring onion respectively) are two of the tastiest recipes in the country.

Meat & Seafood

Irish meals are usually meat based, with beef, lamb and pork common options. Seafood, long neglected, is finding a place on the table in Irish homes. It's widely available in restaurants

Dare to Try

Ironically, while the Irish palate has become more adventurous, it is the old-fashioned Irish menu that features some fairly interesting dishes:

Black pudding Made from congealed pork blood, suet and other fillings, it is a ubiquitous part of an Irish cooked breakfast.

Boxty A Northern Irish starchy potato cake made with a half-and-half mix of cooked mashed potatoes and grated, strained raw potato.

Carrageen The typical Irish seaweed that can be found in dishes as diverse as salad and ice cream.

Corned beef tongue Usually accompanied by cabbage, this dish is still found on a traditional Irish menu.

Lough Neagh eel A speciality of Northern Ireland typically eaten around Halloween; it's usually served in chunks and with a white onion sauce.

Poitín It's rare enough that you'll be offered a drop of the 'cratur', as illegally distilled whiskey (made from malted grain or potatoes) is called here. Still, there are pockets of the country with secret stills such as in Donegal, Connemara and West Cork.

and is often excellent, especially in the west. Oysters, trout and salmon are delicious, particularly if they're direct from the sea or a river rather than a fish farm. The famous Dublin Bay prawn isn't actually a prawn but a lobster. At its best, the Dublin Bay prawn is superlative, but it's priced accordingly. If you're going to splurge, do so here – but make sure you choose live Dublin Bay prawns because once these fellas die, they quickly lose their flavour.

Soda Bread

The most famous Irish bread, and one of the signature tastes of Ireland, is soda bread. Irish flour is soft and doesn't take well to yeast as a raising agent, so Irish bakers of the 19th century leavened their bread with bicarbonate of soda. Combined with buttermilk, it makes a superbly light-textured and tasty bread, and is often on the breakfast menus at B&Bs.

Cheese

Ireland has some wonderful cheeses, such as the flavoursome farmhouse Ardrahan with a rich nutty taste; the subtle Corleggy, a pasteurised goat's cheese from County Cavan; Durrus, a creamy, fruity cheese; creamy Cashel Blue from Tipperary; and the award-winning Camembert-style cheese, Cooleeney.

The Fry

Perhaps the most feared Irish speciality is the fry – the heart attack on a plate that is the second part of so many B&B deals. In spite of the hysterical health fears, the fry is still one of the most common traditional meals in the country. Who can say no to a plate of fried bacon, sausages, black pudding, white pudding, eggs and tomatoes? For the famous Ulster fry, common throughout the North, simply add *fadge* (potato bread).

To Drink...

Stout

While Guinness has become synonymous with stout the world over, few outside Ireland realise that there are two other major producers competing for the favour of the Irish drinker: Murphy's and Beamish & Crawford, both based in Cork city.

Freshly poured Guinness

RICHARD I'ANSON/GETTY IMAGES ©

★ **Memorable Meals**

Restaurant Patrick Guilbaud (p73)

Fishy Fishy Cafe (p199)

Farmgate Restaurant (p187)

Ginger (p241)

55 Degrees North (p169)

Tea

The Irish drink more tea, per capita, than any other nation in the world and you'll be offered a cup as soon as you cross the threshold of any Irish home. Taken with milk (and sugar, if you want) rather than lemon, preferred blends are very strong, and nothing like the namby-pamby versions that pass for Irish breakfast tea elsewhere.

Whiskey

At last count, there were almost 100 different types of Irish whiskey, brewed by only three distilleries – Jameson's in Midleton, County Cork, Bushmills on the Antrim Coast, and Cooley's on the Cooley Peninsula, County Louth. A visit to Ireland reveals a depth of excellence that will make the connoisseur's palate spin, while winning over many new friends to what the Irish call *uisce beatha* (water of life).

When to Eat

Irish eating habits have changed over the last couple of decades, and there are differences between urban and rural practices.

Breakfast

An important meal given the Irish tendency towards small lunches. Usually eaten before 9am as most people rush off to work; hotels and B&Bs will serve until 11am Monday to

---

Craft Beer Revolution

Although mainstream lagers like Heineken, Carlsberg and Coors Lite are most pubs' best-selling beers, the craft beer revolution has resulted in dozens of microbreweries spring up all over the island, making artisan beers that are served in more than 600 of Ireland's pubs and bars. Here's a small selection to whet the tastebuds.

Devil's Backbone (4.9% ABV) Rich amber ale from Donegal brewer Kinnegar.

The Full Irish (6% ABV) Pale ale by Eight Degrees Brewery outside Mitchelstown, County Cork; voted Irish beer of the year in 2015.

O'Hara's Leann Folláin (6% ABV) Dry stout with vaguely chocolate note produced by Carlow Brewing Company.

Metalman Pale Ale (4.3% ABV) American-style pale ale by the much-respected Metalman Brewing Company in Waterford; now available in cans.

Puck Pilsner (4.5% ABV) A light lager brewed by Jack Cody's Brewery in Drogheda.

Twisted Hop (4.7% ABV) Blond ale produced by Hilden just outside Lisburn, Ireland's oldest independent brewery.

Friday, to noon at weekends. Weekend brunch is popular in bigger towns and cities, although it pretty much copies traditional rural habits of eating a large, earthy breakfast late in the morning.

Lunch

Once the biggest meal of the day, lunch is now one of the more obvious rural/urban divides. Urban workers have succumbed to the eat-on-the-run restrictions of nine-to-five, with most eating a sandwich or a light meal between 12.30pm and 2pm (most restaurants don't begin to serve lunch until at least midday). At weekends, especially Sunday, the midday lunch is skipped in favour a substantial mid-afternoon meal (called dinner), usually between 2pm and 4pm.

Tea

No, not the drink, but the evening meal – also confusingly called dinner. For urbanites, this is the main meal of the day, usually eaten around 6.30pm. Rural communities eat at the same time but a more traditional tea of bread, cold cuts and, yes, tea. Restaurants follow more international habits, with most diners not eating until at least 7.30pm.

Supper

A before-bed snack of tea and toast or sandwiches, still enjoyed by many Irish although urbanites increasingly eschew it for health reasons. Not a practice in restaurants.

Dining Etiquette

The Irish aren't big on restrictive etiquette, preferring friendly informality to any kind of stuffy formality. Still, there are a few tips to dining with the Irish.

All restaurants welcome kids until 7pm, but pubs and some smarter restaurants don't allow them in the evening. Family restaurants have children's menus, others have reduced portions of regular menu items.

If the food is not to your satisfaction, it's best to politely explain what's wrong with it as soon as you can; any respectable restaurant will endeavour to replace the dish immediately.

If you insist on paying the bill, be prepared for a first, second and even third refusal to countenance such an *exorbitant* act of generosity. But don't be fooled: the Irish will refuse something several times even if they're delighted with it. Insist gently but firmly and you'll get your way!

Price Ranges

Our cafe and restaurant listings appear in budget order, with the cheapest budget range first.

BUDGET	REPUBLIC	NORTHERN IRELAND
€/£	<€12	£12
€€/££	€12-25	£12-20
€€€/£££	>€25	>£20

Vegetarians & Vegans

Vegetarians can take a deep breath. And then exhale. Calmly. For Ireland has come a long, long way since the days when vegetarians were looked upon as odd creatures; nowadays, even the most militant vegan will barely cause a ruffle in all but the most basic of rustic kitchens. Which isn't to say that travellers with plant-based diets are going to find the most imaginative range of options on menus outside the bigger towns and cities – or in the plethora of modern restaurants that have opened in the last few years – but you can rest assured that the overall quality of the home-grown vegetable is top-notch and most places will have at least one dish that you can tuck into comfortably.

Locals in a County Clare pub

The Pub

Simply put, the pub is the heart of Ireland's social existence, and we're guessing that experiencing it ranks pretty high on your list of things to do while you're here. But let's be clear: we're not just talking about a place to get a drink. Oh no. You can get a drink in a restaurant or a hotel, or wherever there's someone with a bottle of something strong. The pub is something far more than just that.

Role

The pub is the broadest window through which you can examine and experience the very essence of the nation's culture, in all its myriad forms. It's the great leveller, where status and rank hold no sway, where generation gaps are bridged, inhibitions lowered, tongues loosened, schemes hatched, songs sung, stories told and gossip embroidered. It's a unique institution: a theatre and a cosy room, a centre stage and a hideaway, a debating chamber and a place for silent contemplation. It's whatever you want it to be, and that's the secret of the great Irish pub.

Talk

Talk – whether it is frivolous, earnest or incoherent – is the essential ingredient. Once tongues are loosened and the cogs of thought oiled, the conversation can go anywhere and you should let it flow to its natural conclusion. An old Irish adage suggests you should never talk about sport, religion or politics in unfamiliar company. But as long as you're mindful, you needn't restrict yourself too much. While it's a myth to say you can walk into any pub and be befriended, you probably won't be drinking on your own for long – unless that's what you want of course. There are few more spiritual experiences than a solitary pint in an old country pub in the mid-afternoon.

★ **Traditional Music Pubs**

- Cobblestone (p76)
- Tig Cóilí (p116)
- O'Friel's Bar (p153)
- Peadar O'Donnell's (p180)

Tradition

Aesthetically, there is nothing better than the traditional haunt, populated by flat-capped pensioners bursting with delightful anecdotes and always ready to dispense a kind of wisdom distilled through generations' worth of experience. The best of them have stone floors and a peat fire; the chat barely rises above a respectful murmur save for appreciative laughter; and most of all, there's no music save the kind played by someone sitting next to you. Pubs like these are a disappearing breed, but there are still plenty of them around to ensure that you will find one, no matter where you are.

Etiquette

The rounds system – the simple custom where someone buys you a drink and you buy one back – is the bedrock of Irish pub culture. It's summed up in the Irish saying: 'It's impossible for two men to go to a pub for one drink.' Nothing will hasten your fall from social grace here like the failure to uphold this pub law.

Another golden rule about the system is that the next round starts when the first person has finished (preferably just about to finish) their drink. It doesn't matter if you're only halfway through your pint – if it's your round, get your order in.

Shamrocks

Irish Mythological Symbols

Ireland's collection of icons serves to exemplify the country – or a simplistic version of it – to an astonishing degree. It's referred to by the Irish as 'Oirishness', which is what happens when you take a spud, shove it in a pint of Guinness and garnish it with shamrock.

The Shamrock

Ireland's most enduring symbol is the shamrock, a three-leafed white clover known diminutively in Irish as *seamróg,* which was anglicised as 'shamrock'. According to legend, when St Patrick was trying to explain the mystery of the Holy Trinity to the recently converted Celtic chieftains, he plucked the modest little weed and used its three leaves to explain the metaphysically challenging concept of the Father, the Son and the Holy Spirit as being separate but part of the one being. This link is what makes the shamrock a ubiquitous part of the St Patrick's Day celebrations.

The Celtic Cross

Everywhere you go, you will see examples of the Celtic cross – basically, a cross surrounded by a ring. Its origins weren't simply a question of aesthetic design but more of practical necessity. The cross was a clever fusing of new Christian teaching (the cross itself) with established pagan beliefs, in this case, sun worship (marked by the circle).

The Luck of the Irish?

Nearly a millennium of occupation, a long history of oppression and exploitation, a devastating famine, mass emigration... how *exactly* are the Irish 'lucky'? Well, they're not – or at least not any more so than anybody else. The expression was born in the mid-19th century in the US during the gold and silver rush, when some of the most successful miners were Irish or of Irish extraction. It didn't really seem to matter that the Irish – recent escapees from famine and destitution in Ireland – were over-represented among the miners; the expression stuck. Still, the expression was always a little derisory, as though the Irish merely stumbled across good fortune.

Some of the most famous crosses in Ireland are in Monasterboice, County Louth, and Clonmacnoise, County Offaly.

The Leprechaun

The country's most enduring cliche is the myth of the mischievous leprechaun and his pot of gold, which he jealously guards from the attentions of greedy humans. Despite the twee aspect of the legend, its origin predates the Celts and belongs to the mythological Tuatha dé Danann (peoples of the Goddess Danu), who lived in Ireland 4000 years ago. When they were eventually defeated, their king Lugh (the demi-God father of Cúchulainn) was forced underground, where he became known as Lugh Chromain, or 'little stooping Lugh' – the origin of leprechaun.

The Irish can get visibly irritated if asked whether they believe in leprechauns (you might as well ask them if they're stupid), but many rural dwellers are a superstitious lot. They mightn't necessarily *believe* that malevolent sprites who dwell in faerie forts actually exist, but they're not especially keen to test the theory either, which is why there still exist trees, hills and other parts of the landscape that are deemed to have, well, supernatural qualities, and as such will never be touched.

The Harp

The Celtic harp, or *clársach,* is meant to represent the immortality of the soul, which is handy given that it's been a symbol of Ireland since the days of Henry VIII and the first organised opposition to English rule. The harp was the most popular instrument at the Celtic court, with the harpist (usually blind) ranked only behind the chief and bard in order of importance. In times of war, the harpist played a special, jewel-encrusted harp and served as the cheerleading section for soldiers heading into battle.

During the first rebellions against the English, the harp was once again an instrument of revolutionary fervour, prompting the crown to ban it altogether. This eventually led to its decline as the instrument of choice for Irish musicians but ensured its status as a symbol of Ireland.

The Claddagh Ring

The most famous of all Irish jewellery is the Claddagh ring (p126), made up of two hands (friendship) clasping a heart (love) and usually surmounted by a crown (loyalty). Made in the eponymous fishing village of County Galway since the 17th century, the symbolic origins are much older and belong to a broader family of rings popular since Roman times known as the *fede* rings (from *mani in fede,* or 'hands in trust'), which were used to symbolise marriage. Nevertheless, their popularity is relatively recent, and almost entirely down to their wearing by expat Americans who use them to demonstrate their ties to their Irish heritage.

Long Room (p39), Trinity College, Dublin

Literary Ireland

Of all their national traits, characteristics and cultural expressions, it's perhaps the way the Irish speak and write that best distinguishes them. Their love of language and their great oral tradition have contributed to Ireland's legacy of world-renowned writers and storytellers. All this in a language imposed on them by a foreign invader.

The Mythic Cycle

Before there was anything like modern literature, there was the Ulaid (Ulster) Cycle – Ireland's version of the Homeric epic – written down from oral tradition between the 8th and 12th centuries. The chief story is the Táin Bó Cúailnge (Cattle Raid of Cooley), about a battle between Queen Maeve of Connaught and Cúchulainn, the principal hero of Irish mythology. Cúchulainn appears in the work of Irish writers right up to the present day, from Samuel Beckett to Frank McCourt.

Modern Literature

From the mythic cycle, zip forward 1000 years, past the genius of Jonathan Swift (1667–1745) and his *Gulliver's Travels;* stopping to acknowledge acclaimed dramatist Oscar Wilde (1854–1900); *Dracula* creator Bram Stoker (1847–1912) – some have optimistically claimed that the name of the count may have come from the Irish *droch fhola* (bad blood); and the literary giant that was James Joyce (1882–1941), whose name and books elicit enormous pride in Ireland (although we've yet to meet five people who have read all of *Ulysses*!).

The majority of Joyce's literary output came when he had left Ireland for the artistic hotbed that was Paris, which was also true for another great experimenter of language and style, Samuel Beckett (1906–89). Influenced by the Italian poet Dante and French philosopher Descartes, Beckett's work centres on fundamental existential questions about the human condition and the nature of self. He is probably best known for his play *Waiting for Godot,* but his unassailable reputation is based on a series of stark novels and plays.

Of the dozens of 20th-century Irish authors to have achieved published renown, some names to look out for include playwright and novelist Brendan Behan (1923–64), who wove tragedy, wit and a turbulent life into his best works, including *Borstal Boy, The Quare Fellow* and *The Hostage*. Inevitably, as life imitated art, Behan died young of alcoholism.

Belfast-born CS Lewis (1898–1963) died a year earlier, leaving us *The Chronicles of Narnia,* a series of allegorical children's stories, three of which have been made into films. Other Northern writers have, not surprisingly, featured the Troubles in their work: Bernard McLaverty's *Cal* (also made into a film) and his more recent *The Anatomy School* are both wonderful.

The Gaelic Revival

While Home Rule was being debated and shunted, something of a revolution was taking place in Irish arts, literature and identity. The poet William Butler Yeats and his coterie of literary friends (including Lady Gregory, Douglas Hyde, John Millington Synge and George Russell) championed the Anglo-Irish literary revival, unearthing old Celtic tales and writing with fresh enthusiasm about a romantic Ireland of epic battles and warrior queens. For a country that had suffered centuries of invasion and deprivation, these images presented a much more attractive version of history.

Contemporary Scene

'I love James Joyce. Never read him, but he's a true genius.' Yes, the stalwarts are still great, but ask your average Irish person who their favourite home-grown writer is and they'll most likely mention someone who's still alive.

They might mention Roddy Doyle (1958–), whose mega-successful Barrytown trilogy – *The Commitments, The Snapper* and *The Van* – have all been made into films; his latest book, *The Guts* (2013), saw the return of *The Commitments* protagonist, Jimmy Rabbitte – older, wiser and battling illness. Doyle's novel *Paddy Clarke, Ha Ha Ha* won the Booker Prize in 1993.

Sebastian Barry (1955–) has been shortlisted twice for the Man Booker Prize, for his WWI drama *A Long Long Way* (2005) and the absolutely compelling *The Secret Scripture* (2008), about a 100-year-old inmate of a mental hospital called Roseanne who decides to write an autobiography. His latest novel, *The Temporary Gentleman* (2014), tells the story of Roseanne's brother-in-law, Jack McNulty, a former British Army officer posted to Africa during WWII but unable to return home to Ireland because of personal and professional guilt.

★ **Contemporary Fiction**

The Empty Family (Colm Tóibín)
Ghost Light (Joseph O'Connor)
The Forgotten Waltz (Anne Enright)
Room (Emma Donoghue)
John the Revelator (Peter Byrne)

Anne Enright (1962–) did nab the Booker for *The Gathering* (2007), a zeitgeist tale of alcoholism and abuse – she described it as 'the intellectual equivalent of a Hollywood weepie'. Her latest novel, *The Green Road* (2015), continues to mine the murky waters of the Irish family. Another Booker Prize winner is heavyweight John Banville (1945–), who won it for *The Sea* (2005); we also recommend either *The Book of Evidence* (1989) or the masterful roman-à-clef *The Untouchable* (1997), based loosely on the secret-agent life of art historian Anthony Blunt. Banville's literary alter-ego is Benjamin Black, author of a series of seven hard-boiled detective thrillers set in the 1950s starring a troubled pathologist called Quirke – the latest book is *Even the Dead* (2015).

Another big hitter is Wexford-born Colm Tóibín (1955–), author of nine novels including *Brooklyn* (2009; made into a film in 2015 starring Saoirse Ronan) and, most recently, *Nora Webster* (2014), a powerful study of widowhood.

Emma Donoghue (1969–) followed the award-winning *Room* (2010) with *Frog Music* (2014), about the real-life shooting of cross-dressing gamine Jenny Bonnet in late-19th-century San Francisco. John Boyne (1971–) made his name with Holocaust novel *The Boy in the Striped Pyjamas* (2006; the film version came out in 2008); his latest novel, *A History of Loneliness* (2014), explores the thorny issue of child abuse and the Catholic Church.

Colum McCann (1965–) left Ireland in 1986, eventually settling in New York, where his sixth novel, the post–September 11 *Let the Great World Spin* (2009), catapulted him to the top of the literary tree and won him the National Book Award for fiction as well as the International IMPAC Dublin Literary Award. His next novel, *TransAtlantic* (2013) weaves three separate stories together: the flight of Alcock and Brown, the visit of Frederick Douglass to Ireland in 1845 and the story of the Northern Irish peace process of the late 1990s.

The Troubles have been a rich and powerful subject for Northern Irish writers. Derry native Sean O'Reilly's (1969–) novels are populated by characters freed from sectarianism but irreparably damaged by it: his last novel was *Watermark* (2005), about a young woman on the edge of desire and reason in an unnamed Irish town. Eoin McNamee (1961–) has written a series that explores the conflict directly, teasing out the effects of religion and history on the lives of individuals. His latest novel, *Blue is the Night* (2014) is the final book of a trilogy that also includes *The Blue Tango* (2001) and *Orchid Blue* (2010).

Paul Murray's (1975–) second novel, *Skippy Dies* (2010), about a group of privileged students at an all-boys secondary school, won him lots of critical praise (and an upcoming movie version directed by Neil Jordan) but his follow-up, *The Mark and the Void* (2015), which is set against the backdrop of the financial crisis, met with far more lukewarm praise. Not so Shane Hegarty (1976–), who in 2015 published the first volume of *Darkmouth*, a YA novel set in a fictional Irish town where young Finn is learning about girls and fighting monsters.

Chick Lit

Authors hate the label and publishers profess to disregard it, but chick lit is big business, and few have mastered it as well as the Irish. Doyenne of them all is Maeve Binchy (1940–2012), whose mastery of the style saw her outsell most of the literary greats – her last novel before she died was *A Week in Winter* (2012). Marian Keyes (1963–) is another author with a long line of best-sellers, including her latest, *The Woman Who Stole My Life* (2014). She's a terrific storyteller with a rare ability to tackle sensitive issues such as alcoholism and depression, issues that she herself has suffered from and is admiringly honest about. Former agony aunt Cathy Kelly turns out novels at the rate of one a year: a recent book is *It Started with Paris* (2014), where a young man proposes beneath the Eiffel Tower before trouble begins...

Accordian player, County Kerry

Traditional Music

Irish music (known in Ireland as traditional music, or just trad) has retained a vibrancy not found in other traditional European forms, which have lost out to the overbearing influence of pop music. Although it has kept many of its traditional aspects, Irish music has itself influenced many forms of music, most notably US country and western.

Trad music's current success is also due to the willingness of its exponents to update the way it's played (in ensembles rather than the customary *céilidh* – communal dance – bands), the habit of pub sessions (introduced by returning migrants) and the economic good times that encouraged the Irish to celebrate their culture rather than trying to replicate international trends. And then, of course, there's Riverdance, which made Irish dancing sexy and became a worldwide phenomenon, despite the fact that most aficionados of traditional music are seriously underwhelmed by its musical worth.

Instruments

Despite popular perception, the harp isn't widely used in traditional music; the *bodhrán* (*bow*-rawn) goat-skin drum is much more prevalent. The uilleann pipes, played by squeezing bellows under the elbow, provide another distinctive sound, although you're not likely to see them in a pub. The fiddle isn't unique to Ireland but it is one of the main instruments in the country's indigenous music, along with the flute, tin whistle, accordion and bouzouki (a version of the mandolin). Music fits into five main categories (jigs, reels, hornpipes, polkas and slow airs), while the old style of singing unaccompanied versions of traditional ballads and airs is called *sean-nós*.

★ Traditional Albums

○ *The Quiet Glen* (Tommy Peoples)

○ *Paddy Keenan* (Paddy Keenan)

○ *Compendium: The Best of Patrick Street* (Various)

○ *The Chieftains 6: Bonaparte's Retreat* (The Chieftains)

○ *Old Hag You Have Killed Me* (The Bothy Band)

Tunes

The music was never written down, it was passed on from one player to another and so endured and evolved – regional 'styles' only developed because local musicians sought to play just like the one who seemed to play better than everybody else. The blind itinerant harpist Turlough O'Carolan (1670–1738) 'wrote' more than 200 tunes – it's difficult to know how many versions their repeated learning has spawned. This characteristic of fluidity is key to an appreciation of traditional music, and explains why it is such a resilient form today.

Popular Bands

Nevertheless, in the 1960s composer Seán Ó Riada (1931–71) tried to impose a kind of structure on the music. His ensemble group, Ceoltóirí Chualann, were the first to reach a wider audience, and from it were born the Chieftains, arguably the most important traditional group of them all. They started recording in 1963 – any one of their nearly 40 albums is worth a listen, but you won't go wrong with their 10-album eponymous series.

The other big success of the 1960s were the Dubliners. More folksy than traditional, they made a career out of bawdy drinking songs that got everybody singing along. Other popular bands include the Fureys, comprising four brothers with guitarist Davey Arthur. And if it's rousing renditions of Irish rebel songs you're after, you can't go past the Wolfe Tones.

Since the 1970s, various bands have tried to blend traditional with more progressive genres, with mixed success. The Bothy Band were formed in 1975 and were a kind of trad supergroup – bouzouki player Dónal Lunny, uillean piper Paddy Keenan, flute and whistle player Matt Molloy (later a member of the Chieftains), fiddler Paddy Glackin and accordion player Tony MacMahon – and their recordings are still as electrifying today.

Musicians tend to come together in collaborative projects. A contemporary group worth checking out is The Gloaming, who've taken traditional reels and given them a contemporary sound – their eponymous debut album (2011) is sensational. A key member of the group, fiddler Caoimhín Ó Raghallaigh, is also worth checking out in his own right; his latest album, *Laghdú,* displays both his beautiful fiddle playing and his superb understanding of loops and electronic texturing.

And if you want to check out a group that melds rock, folk and traditional music, you won't go far wrong with The Spook of the Thirteenth Lock, who've released a couple of albums since 2008 – their second album is *The Brutal Here and Now* (2012).

F.IEGUILUZ/GETTY IMAGES ©

Survival Guide

Directory A–Z

Accommodation

Accommodation options range from bare and basic to pricey and palatial. The spine of the Irish hospitality business is the ubiquitous B&B, in recent years challenged by a plethora of midrange hotels and guesthouses. Beyond Expedia, Booking. com, Trivago and other hotel price comparison sites, Ireland-specific online resources for accommodation include the following:

www.daft.ie Online classified paper for short- and long-term rentals.

www.elegant.ie Specialises in self-catering castles, period houses and unique properties.

www.familyhomes.ie Lists family-run guesthouses and self-catering properties.

www.irishlandmark.com Not-for-profit conservation group that rents self-catering properties of historical and cultural significance, such as castles, tower houses, gate lodges, schoolhouses and lighthouses.

www.imagineireland.com Modern cottage rentals throughout the whole island, including Northern Ireland.

www.stayinireland.com Lists guesthouses and self-catering options.

B&Bs & Guesthouses

Bed and breakfasts are small, family-run houses, farmhouses and period country houses with fewer than five bedrooms. Standards vary enormously, but most have some bedrooms with private bathroom at a cost of roughly €35 to €40 (£25 to £30) per person per night. In luxurious B&Bs, expect to pay €55 (£40) or more per person. Off-season rates – usually October through to March – are usually lower, as are midweek prices.

Guesthouses are like upmarket B&Bs, but bigger – the Irish equivalent of a boutique hotel. Facilities are usually better and sometimes include a restaurant.

Other tips:

❍ Facilities in B&Bs range from basic (bed, bathroom, kettle, TV) to beatific (whirlpool baths, rainforest showers) as you go up in price. Wi-fi is standard and most have parking (but check).

❍ Most B&Bs take credit cards, but the occasional rural one might not have facilities; check when you book.

❍ Advance reservations are strongly recommended, especially in peak season (June to September).

Book Your Stay Online

For more accommodation reviews by Lonely Planet authors, check out http://lonelyplanet.com/ireland/hotels. You'll find independent reviews, as well as recommendations on the best places to stay. Best of all, you can book online.

A 'Standard' Hotel Rate?

There is no such thing. Prices vary according to demand – or have different rates for online, phone or walk-in bookings. B&B rates are more consistent, but virtually every other accommodation will charge wildly different rates depending on the time of year, day, festival schedule and even your ability to do a little negotiating. The following price ranges have been used in our reviews of places to stay. Prices are all based on a double room with private bathroom in high season.

BUDGET	REPUBLIC	NORTHERN IRELAND
Budget (€/£)	<€80	<£50
Midrange (€€/££)	€80–180	£50–120
Top end (€€€/£££)	>€180	>£120

○ Some B&Bs and guest-houses in more remote regions only operate from Easter to September or other months.

○ If full, B&B owners may recommend another house in the area (possibly a private house taking occasional guests, not in tourist listings).

○ To make prices more competitive at some B&Bs, breakfast may be optional.

Hotels

Hotels range from the local pub to medieval castles. In most cases, you'll get a better rate than the one published if you book online or negotiate directly with the hotel, especially out of season. The explosion of bland midrange chain hotels (many Irish-owned) has proven to be a major challenge to the traditional B&Bs and guesthouses: they might not have the same personalised service, but their rooms are clean and their facilities generally quite good (although there may be a charge for wi-fi).

House Swapping

House swapping can be a popular and affordable way to visit a country and enjoy a real home away from home. There are several agencies in Ireland that, for an annual fee, facilitate international swaps. The fee pays for access to a website and a book giving house descriptions, photographs and the owner's details. After that, it's up to you to make arrangements. Use of the family car is sometimes included.

Homelink International House Exchange (www.homelink.ie) Home exchange service running for over 60 years.

Intervac International Holiday Service (www.intervac-home exchange.com) Long-established, with agents in 45 nations worldwide.

Rental Accommodation

Self-catering accommodation is often rented on a weekly basis and usually means an apartment, house or cottage where you look after yourself. The rates vary from one region and season to another. **Fáilte Ireland** (☑ Republic 1850 230 330, the UK 0800 039 7000; www.discoverireland.ie) publishes a guide for registered self-catering accommodation; you can check listings at their website.

Climate

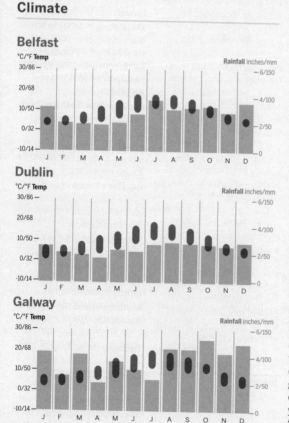

Belfast

°C/°F **Temp**
30/86 —
20/68 —
10/50 —
0/32 —
-10/14 —

Rainfall inches/mm
— 6/150
— 4/100
— 2/50
— 0

J F M A M J J A S O N D

Dublin

°C/°F **Temp**
30/86 —
20/68 —
10/50 —
0/32 —
-10/14 —

Rainfall inches/mm
— 6/150
— 4/100
— 2/50
— 0

J F M A M J J A S O N D

Galway

°C/°F **Temp**
30/86 —
20/68 —
10/50 —
0/32 —
-10/14 —

Rainfall inches/mm
— 6/150
— 4/100
— 2/50
— 0

J F M A M J J A S O N D

Customs Regulations

Both the Republic of Ireland and Northern Ireland have a two-tier customs system: one for goods bought duty-free outside the European Union (EU), the other for goods bought in another EU country where tax and duty is paid. There is technically no limit to the amount of goods transportable within the EU, but customs will use certain guidelines to distinguish personal use from commercial purpose. Allowances are as follows:

Duty free For duty-free goods from outside the EU, limits include 200 cigarettes, 1L of spirits or 2L of wine, 60ml of perfume and 250ml of eau de toilette.

Tax and duty paid Amounts that officially constitute personal use include 3200 cigarettes (or 400 cigarillos, 200 cigars or 3kg of tobacco) and either 10L of spirits, 20L of fortified wine, 60L of sparkling wine, 90L of still wine or 110L of beer.

Cats & Dogs

Cats and dogs from anywhere outside Ireland and the UK are subject to strict quarantine laws. The EU Pet Travel Scheme, whereby animals are fitted with a microchip, vaccinated against rabies and blood-tested six months *prior* to entry, is in force in the UK and the Republic of Ireland. No preparation or documentation is necessary for the movement of pets directly between the UK and the Republic. Contact the **Department of Agriculture, Food & Rural Development** (☎01-607 2000; www.agriculture.gov.ie) in Dublin for further details.

Electricity

230V/50Hz

Food

Our cafe and restaurant listings appear in budget order, with the cheapest budget range first. Within the ranges, listings are given in preference order.

For more information, see our Food & Drink chapter (p286).

Gay & Lesbian Travellers

Ireland is a pretty tolerant place for gays and lesbians. Bigger cities such as Dublin, Galway and Cork have well-established gay scenes, as do Belfast and Derry in Northern Ireland. In 2015, Ireland overwhelmingly backed same-sex marriage in a historic referendum. Nonetheless, you'll still find pockets of homophobia throughout the island, particularly in smaller towns and rural areas. Resources include the following:

Gaire (www.gaire.com) Message board and info for a host of gay-related issues.

Gay & Lesbian Youth Northern Ireland (www.cara-friend.org.uk/projects/glyni) Voluntary counselling, information, health and social space organisation for the gay community.

Gay Men's Health Project (☎01-660 2189; http://hse.ie/go/GMHS) Practical advice on men's health issues.

National Lesbian & Gay Federation (NLGF; ☎01-671 9076; http://nxf.ie) Publishes the monthly *Gay Community News* (http://theoutmost.com).

Northern Ireland Gay Rights Association (Nigra; ☎9066 5257; http://nigra.org.uk)

Outhouse (Map p72; ☎01-873 4932; www.outhouse.ie; 105 Capel St; ▣all city centre) Top gay, lesbian and bisexual resource centre in Dublin. Great stop-off point to see what's on, check noticeboards and meet

Practicalities

◉ **Currency** Republic of Ireland: Euro (€); Northern Ireland: Pound Sterling (£).

◉ **Newspapers** *Irish Independent* (www.independent.ie), *Irish Times* (www.irishtimes.com), *Irish Examiner* (www.examiner.ie), *Belfast Telegraph* (www.belfasttelegraph.co.uk).

◉ **Radio** RTE Radio 1 (88-90 MHz), Today FM (100-103 MHz), Newstalk 106-108 (106-108 MHz), BBC Ulster (92-95 MHz; Northern Ireland only).

◉ **Weights & Measures** Metric units; exception is for liquid measures of alcohol, where pints are used.

people. It publishes the free Ireland's *Pink Pages*, a directory of gay-centric services, which is also accessible on the website.

The Outmost (www.theoutmost.com) Excellent and resourceful for gay news, entertainment, lifestyle and opinion.

Health

No jabs are required to travel to Ireland. Excellent health care is readily available. For minor, self-limiting illnesses, pharmacists can give valuable advice and sell over-the-counter medication. They can also advise when more specialised help is required and point you in the right direction.

EU citizens equipped with a European Health Insurance Card (EHIC), available from health centres or, in the UK, post offices, will be covered for most medical care – but not nonemergencies or emergency repatriation. While other countries, such as Australia, also have reciprocal agreements with Ireland and Britain, many do not.

In Northern Ireland, everyone receives free emergency treatment at accident and emergency (A&E) departments of state-run NHS hospitals, irrespective of nationality.

Insurance

Insurance is important: it covers you for everything from medical expenses and luggage loss to cancellations or delays in your travel arrangements, depending on your policy.

While EU citizens have most medical care covered with an EHIC card, an additional insurance policy for all other issues is recommended.

Worldwide travel insurance is available at www.lonelyplanet.com/travel-insurance. You can buy, extend and claim online at any time – even if you're already on the road.

All cars on public roads must be insured. If you are bringing your own vehicle, check that your insurance will cover you in Ireland.

Internet Access

If using a laptop, tablet, phablet or smartphone to get online, the vast majority of hotels, B&Bs, hostels, bars and restaurants offer wi-fi access, usually for free (though there may be a charge in a minority of hotels).

Internet cafes are disappearing. The survivors generally charge up to €6/£5 per hour.

Legal Matters

Illegal drugs are widely available, especially in clubs. The possession of small quantities of marijuana attracts a fine or warning, but harder drugs are treated more seriously. Public drunkenness is illegal but commonplace – the police will usually ignore it unless you're causing trouble.

Contact the following for assistance:

Legal Aid Board (☎066-947 1000; www.legalaidboard.ie) Has a network of local law centres.

Legal Services Agency Northern Ireland (☎028-9076 3000; www.dojni.gov.uk/legalservices)

Administers the statutory legal aid scheme for Northern Ireland, but cannot offer legal advice.

Maps

Michelin's 1:400,000-scale Ireland map (No 923) is a decent single sheet map, with clear cartography and most of the island's scenic roads marked. The four maps – North, South, East and West – that make up the Ordnance Survey Holiday map series at 1:250,000 scale are useful for more detail.

The Ordnance Survey Discovery series covers the whole island in 89 maps at a scale of 1:50,000, also available as digital versions. These are all available through Ordnance Survey Ireland (www.osi.ie) and many bookshops around Ireland.

Collins also publishes a range of maps covering Ireland, also available at bookshops.

Money

The currency in the Republic of Ireland is the euro (€). The island's peculiar political history means that the six Ulster counties that make up Northern Ireland use the pound sterling (£). Although notes issued by Northern Irish banks are legal tender throughout

the UK, many businesses outside of Northern Ireland refuse to accept them and you'll have to swap them in British banks.

ATMs

Usually called 'cash machines', ATMs are easy to find in cities and all but the smallest of towns. Watch out for ATMs that have been tampered with; card-reader scams ('skimming') have become a real problem.

Credit & Debit Cards

Visa and MasterCard credit and debit cards are widely accepted in Ireland. American Express is only accepted by the major chains, and very few places accept Diners or JCB. Smaller businesses, such as pubs and some B&Bs, prefer debit cards (and will charge a fee for credit cards), and a small number of rural B&Bs only take cash.

Taxes & Refunds

Non-EU residents can claim Value Added Tax (VAT, a sales tax of 21% added to the purchase price of luxury goods – excluding books, children's clothing and educational items) back on their purchases, so long as the store operates either the Cashback or Taxback refund program (they should display a sticker). You'll get a voucher with your purchase that must be stamped at the *last point of exit* from the EU. If you're travelling on to Britain or mainland Europe

from Ireland, hold on to your voucher until you pass through your final customs stop in the EU; it can then be stamped and you can post it back for a refund of duty paid.

VAT in Northern Ireland is 20%; shops participating in the Tax-Free Shopping refund scheme will give you a form or invoice on request to be presented to customs when you leave. After customs have certified the form, it will be returned to the shop for a refund and the cheque sent to you at home.

Tipping

You're not obliged to tip if the service or food was unsatisfactory (even if it's been automatically added to your bill as a 'service charge').

Hotels Only for bellhops who carry luggage, then €1/£1 per bag.

Pubs Not expected unless table service is provided, then €1/£1 for a round of drinks.

Restaurants 10% for decent service, up to 15% in more expensive places.

Taxis 10% or rounded up to the nearest euro/pound.

Toilet attendants €0.50/50p.

Opening Hours

Hours in the Republic and Northern Ireland are roughly the same.

Banks 10am to 4pm Monday to Friday (to 5pm Thursday).

Offices 9am to 5pm Monday to Friday.

Post offices Northern Ireland 9am to 5.30pm Monday to Friday, 9am to 12.30pm Saturday; Republic 9am to 6pm Monday to Friday, 9am to 1pm Saturday. Smaller post offices may close at lunch and one day per week.

Pubs Northern Ireland 11.30am to 11pm Monday to Saturday, 12.30pm to 10pm Sunday, but pubs with late licences open until 1am Monday to Saturday and midnight Sunday; Republic 10.30am to 11.30pm Monday to Thursday, 10.30am to 12.30am Friday and Saturday, noon to 11pm Sunday (30 minutes of 'drinking up' time allowed). Pubs with bar extensions open to 2.30am Thursday to Saturday. All pubs close Christmas Day and Good Friday.

Restaurants Noon to 10.30pm in Dublin, till 9pm outside (aim to be seated by 8pm at the latest); many close one day of the week.

Shops 9am to 5.30pm or 6pm Monday to Saturday (until 8pm on Thursday & sometimes Friday), noon to 6pm Sunday (in bigger towns only). Shops in rural towns may close at lunch and one day per week.

Tourist offices 9am to 5pm Monday to Friday, 9am to 1pm Saturday. Many extend their hours in summer and open fewer hours/days or close from October to April.

Tourist sights Some sights only open from Easter through to September or October.

Photography

○ Natural light can be very dull, so use higher ISO speeds than usual, such as 400 for daylight shots.

○ In Northern Ireland, get permission before taking photos of fortified police stations, army posts or other military or quasi-military paraphernalia.

○ Don't take photos of people in Protestant or Catholic strongholds of West Belfast without permission; always ask and be prepared to accept a refusal.

Public Holidays

Public holidays can cause road chaos as everyone tries to get somewhere else for the break. It's wise to book accommodation in advance for these times.

The following are public holidays in both the Republic and Northern Ireland:

New Year's Day 1 January

St Patrick's Day 17 March

Easter (Good Friday to Easter Monday inclusive) March/April

May Holiday 1st Monday in May

Christmas Day 25 December

St Stephen's Day (Boxing Day) 26 December

St Patrick's Day and St Stephen's Day holidays are taken on the following Monday when they fall on a weekend. In the Republic, nearly everywhere closes on Good Friday even though it isn't an official public holiday. In the North, most shops open on Good Friday, but close the following Tuesday.

Northern Ireland

Spring Bank Holiday Last Monday in May

Orangemen's Day 12 July

August Holiday Last Monday in August

Republic

June Holiday 1st Monday in June

August Holiday 1st Monday in August

October Holiday Last Monday in October

Safe Travel

Ireland is safer than most countries in Europe, but normal precautions should be observed.

Northern Ireland is as safe as anywhere else, but there are areas where the sectarian divide is bitterly pronounced, most notably in parts of Belfast. It's probably best to ensure your visit to Northern Ireland doesn't coincide with the climax of the Orange marching season on 12 July; sectarian passions are usually inflamed and even many Northerners leave the province at this time.

Telephone

Area codes in the Republic have three digits and begin with a 0, eg ☏021 for Cork, ☏091 for Galway and ☏061 for Limerick. The only exception is Dublin, which has a two-digit code (☏01). Always use the area code if calling from a mobile phone, but you don't need it if calling from a fixed-line number within the area code.

In Northern Ireland, the area code for all fixed-line numbers is ☏028, but you only need to use it if calling from a mobile phone or from outside Northern Ireland. To call Northern Ireland from the Republic, use ☏048 instead of ☏028, without the international dialling code.

Other codes:

○ ☏1550 or ☏1580 – premium rate.

○ ☏1890 or ☏1850 – local or shared rate.

○ ☏0818 – calls at local rate, wherever you're dialling from within the Republic.

○ ☏1800 – free calls Free-call and low-call numbers are not accessible from outside the Republic.

Other tips:

○ Prices are lower during evenings after 6pm and weekends.

○ If you can find a public phone that works, local calls in the Republic cost €0.30 for around three minutes (around €0.60 to a mobile), regardless of when you call. From Northern Ireland local calls cost about 40p, or 60p to a mobile, although this varies somewhat.

○ Prepaid phonecards can be purchased at both news agencies and post offices, and work from all payphones for both domestic and international calls.

Directory Enquiries

For directory enquiries, a number of agencies compete for your business.

○ In the Republic, dial ☏11811 or ☏11850; for international enquiries it's ☏11818.

○ In the North, call ☏118 118, ☏118 192, ☏118 500 or ☏118 811.

○ Expect to pay at least €1/£1 from a land line and up to €2/£2 from a mobile phone.

International Calls

To call out from Ireland dial ☏00, then the country code (☏1 for USA, ☏61 Australia etc), the area code (you usually drop the initial zero) then the number. The Republic's international dialling code is ☏353, Northern Ireland's is ☏44.

Mobile Phone

○ Ensure your mobile phone is unlocked for use in Ireland.

○ Pay-as-you-go mobile phone packages with any of the main providers start at around €40 and usually include a basic handset and credit of around €10.

○ SIM-only packages are also available, but make sure your phone is compatible with the local provider.

Time

In winter, Ireland is on Greenwich Mean Time (GMT), also known as Universal Time Coordinated (UTC), the same as Britain. In summer, the clock shifts to GMT plus one hour, so when it's noon in Dublin and London, it's 4am in Los Angeles and Vancouver, 7am in New York and Toronto, 1pm in Paris, 7pm in Singapore, and 9pm in Sydney.

Tourist Information

In both the Republic and the North there's a tourist office or information point in almost every big town; most can offer a variety of services, including accommodation and attraction reservations, currency-changing services, map and guidebook sales, and free publications.

In the Republic, the tourism purview falls to **Fáilte Ireland** (☏Republic

1850 230 330, the UK 0800 039 7000; www.discoverireland. ie); in Northern Ireland, it's the **Northern Irish Tourist Board** (NITB; ☎head office 028-9023 1221; www.discover-northernireland.com). Outside Ireland, Fáilte Ireland and the NITB unite under the banner Tourism Ireland (www.tourismireland.com).

See the individual destinations for the location of major tourist offices in Dublin, Cork, Donegal, Galway and other cities/towns.

Travellers with Disabilities

All new buildings have wheelchair access, and many hotels have installed lifts, ramps and other facilities. Others, especially B&Bs, have not adapted as successfully so you'll have far less choice. Fáilte Ireland and NITB's accommodation guides indicate which places are wheelchair accessible.

In big cities, most buses have low-floor access and priority space onboard, but the number of kneeling buses on regional routes is still relatively small.

Trains are accessible with help. In theory, if you call ahead, an employee of Irish Rail (Iarnród Éireann) will arrange to accompany you to the train. Newer trains have audio and visual information systems for visually impaired and hearing-impaired passengers.

The **Citizens' Information Board** (☎0761 079 000; www.citizensinformationboard. ie) in the Republic and **Disability Action** (☎028-9066 1252; www.disabilityaction.org) in Northern Ireland can give some advice to travellers with disabilities.

Visas

If you're a European Economic Area (EEA) national, you don't need a visa to visit (or work in) either the Republic or Northern Ireland. Citizens of Australia, Canada, New Zealand, South Africa and the US can visit the Republic for up to three months, and Northern Ireland for up to six months. They are not allowed to work unless sponsored by an employer.

Full visa requirements for visiting the Republic are available online at www.dfa. ie; for Northern Ireland's visa requirements see www. gov.uk/government/ organisations/uk-visas-and-immigration.

To stay longer in the Republic, contact the local *garda* (police) station or the **Garda National Immigration Bureau** (☎01-666 9100; www.garda.ie; 13-14 Burgh Quay). To stay longer in Northern Ireland, contact the Home Office (www.gov.uk/ government/organisations/ uk-visas-and-immigration).

Women Travellers

Ireland should pose no problems for women travellers. Finding contraception is not the problem it once was, although anyone on the Pill should bring adequate supplies.

If you experience sexual assault, the following services are recommended:

Rape Crisis Network Ireland (☎091-563 676; www.rcni.ie) In the Republic. App available.

Nexus NI (☎028-9032 6803 (Belfast); www.nexusni.org; ⏰8.30am-5pm Mon & Thu, 8.30am-8pm Tue & Wed, 9am-4pm Fri) Offers counselling and support to survivors of sexual abuse and victims of sexual violence and sexual assault. Offices in Belfast, Londonderry, Portadown and Enniskillen.

Transport

Getting There & Away

Entering the Country

Dublin is the primary point of entry for most visitors to Ireland, although some do choose Shannon and Belfast.

○ The overwhelming majority of airlines fly into Dublin.

○ Dublin is home to two seaports that serve as the main points of sea transport with Britain; ferries from France arrive in the southern ports of Rosslare and Cork.

○ Dublin is the nation's rail hub.

Flights, tours and rail transfers can be booked online at www.lonelyplanet.com/bookings.

Air

Ireland's main airports:
Cork Airport (☏021-431 3131; www.cork-airport.com) Airlines servicing the airport include Aer Lingus and Ryanair.
Dublin Airport (☏01-814 1111; www.dublinairport.com) Ireland's major international gateway airport, with direct flights from the UK, Europe,

North America and the Middle East.
Shannon Airport (SNN; ☏061-712 000; www.shannonairport.com; ☏) Has a few direct flights from the UK, Europe and North America.

Northern Ireland's airport:
Belfast International Airport (BFS; ☏028-9448 4848; www.belfastairport.com) Has direct flights from the UK, Europe and North America.

Land

Eurolines (www.eurolines.com) has a daily coach and ferry service from London's Victoria Station to Dublin Busáras.

Sea

The main ferry routes between Ireland and the UK and mainland Europe:

○ Belfast to Liverpool (England; 8 hours)

○ Belfast to Cairnryan (Scotland; 1¾ hours)

○ Cork to Roscoff (France; 14 hours; April to October only)

○ Dublin to Liverpool (England; fast/slow four/8½ hours)

○ Dublin & Dun Laoghaire to Holyhead (Wales; fast/slow two hours/3½ hours)

○ Larne to Cairnryan (Scotland; two hours)

○ Larne to Troon (Scotland; two hours; March to October only)

○ Larne to Fleetwood (England; six hours)

○ Rosslare to Cherbourg/Roscoff (France; 18/20½ hours)

○ Rosslare to Fishguard & Pembroke (Wales; 3½ hours).

Competition from budget airlines has forced ferry operators to discount heavily and offer flexible fares.

A useful website is www.ferrybooker.com, which covers all sea-ferry routes and operators to Ireland.

Climate Change & Travel

Every form of transport that relies on carbon-based fuel generates CO_2, the main cause of human-induced climate change. Modern travel is dependent on aeroplanes, which might use less fuel per kilometre per person than most cars but travel much greater distances. The altitude at which aircraft emit gases (including CO_2) and particles also contributes to their climate change impact. Many websites offer 'carbon calculators' that allow people to estimate the carbon emissions generated by their journey and, for those who wish to do so, to offset the impact of the greenhouse gases emitted with contributions to portfolios of climate-friendly initiatives throughout the world. Lonely Planet offsets the carbon footprint of all staff and author travel.

Bus/Train & Ferry Combos

It's possible to combine bus, ferry and train tickets from major UK centres to most Irish towns. This might not be as quick as flying on a budget airline but leaves less of a carbon footprint. The journey between London and Dublin takes about 12 hours by bus, eight hours by train; the London to Belfast trip takes 13 to 16 hours by bus. Both can be had for as little as £30 one-way. **Eurolines** (www.eurolines.com) has bus-ferry combos while **Virgin Trains** (www.virgintrains.co.uk) has combos that include London to Dublin. For more options, look for SailRail fares.

Main operators include the following:

Brittany Ferries (www.brittanyferries.com) Cork to Roscoff; April to October.

Irish Ferries (www.irishferries.com) It has Dublin to Holyhead ferries (up to four per day year-round); and France to Rosslare (three times per week).

P&O Ferries (www.poferries.com) Daily sailings year-round from Dublin to Liverpool, and Larne to Cairnryan. Larne to Troon runs March to October only.

Stena Line (www.stenaline.com) Daily sailings from Holyhead to Dublin Port, from Belfast to Liverpool and Cairnryan, and from Rosslare to Fishguard.

Getting Around

The big decision in getting around Ireland is to go by car or use public transport. Your own car will make the best use of your time and help you reach even the most remote of places. It's usually easy to get very cheap rentals – €10 per day or less is common – and if two or more are travelling together, the fee for rental and petrol can be cheaper than bus fares.

The bus network, made up of a mix of public and private operators, is extensive and generally quite competitive – although journey times can be slow and lots of the points of interest outside towns are not served. The rail network is quicker but more limited, serving only some major towns and cities. Both buses and trains get busy during peak times; you'll need to book in advance to be guaranteed a seat.

Air

Ireland's size makes domestic flying unnecessary, but there are flights between Dublin and Belfast, Cork, Derry, Donegal, Galway, Kerry, Shannon and Sligo aimed at passengers connecting from international flights. Flights linking the mainland to the Aran Islands are popular.

Bicycle

Ireland's compact size and scenic landscapes make it a good cycling destination. However, dodgy weather, many very narrow roads and some very fast drivers are major concerns. Special tracks such as the 42km Great Western Greenway in County Mayo are a delight. A good tip for cyclists in the west is that the prevailing winds make it easier to cycle from south to north.

Buses will carry bikes, but only if there's room. For trains, bear in mind:

◉ Intercity trains charge up to €10 per bike.

◉ Book in advance (www.irishrail.ie), as there's only room for two bikes per service.

Companies that arrange cycling tours in Ireland:

Go Ireland (☎066-976 2094; www.govisitireland.com) Has guided and independent tours.

Irish Cycling Safaris (☎01-260 0749; www.cyclingsafaris.com) Organises numerous tours across Ireland.

Lismore Cycling Holidays (☎087-935 6610; www.cyclingholidays.ie) Runs tours around the southeast.

Boat

Ireland's offshore islands are all served by boat.

Ferries also operate across rivers, inlets and loughs, providing useful short cuts, particularly for cyclists.

Cruises are popular on the 258km-long Shannon–

Erne Waterway and on a variety of other lakes and loughs. Details of boat trips are given under the relevant sections throughout this book.

Border Crossings

Border crossings between Northern Ireland the Republic are unnoticeable; there are no formalities of any kind.

Bus

Private buses compete – often very favourably – with Bus Éireann in the Republic and also run where the national buses are irregular or absent. You'll find them listed throughout this book.

Distances are not especially long: few bus journeys will last longer than five hours. Bus Éireann bookings can be made online, but you can't reserve a seat for a particular service. Dynamic pricing is in effect on many routes: book early to get the lowest fares.

Note the following:

❍ Bus routes and frequencies are slowly contracting in the Republic.

❍ The National Journey Planner app by Transport for Ireland is very useful for planning bus and train journeys.

The main bus services in Ireland are:

Bus Éireann (☏01-836 6111; www.buseireann.ie) The Republic's main bus line.

Translink (☏028-9066 6630; www.translink.co.uk) Northern

Bus & Rail Passes

There are a few bus-, rail- and bus-and-rail passes worth considering:

Irish Explorer Offers customers five days unlimited Irish Rail travel out of 15 consecutive days (adult/child €160/80).

Open Road Pass Three days travel out of six consecutive days (€60) on Bus Éireann; extra days cost €16.50.

Sunday Day Tracker One day's unlimited travel (adult/child £9/4.50) on Translink buses and trains in Northern Ireland, Sunday only.

Trekker Four Day Four consecutive days of unlimited travel (€110) on Irish Rail.

Note that Eurail's one-country pass for Ireland is a bad deal in any of its permutations.

Ireland's main bus service; includes Ulsterbus and Goldline.

Car & Motorcycle

Travelling by car or motorcycle means greater flexibility and independence. The road system is extensive, and the network of motorways has cut driving times considerably. But also note that many secondary roads are very narrow and at times rather perilous.

Hire

Compared with many countries, hire rates are cheap in Ireland; you should find rates in advance for €10 to €20 per day for a small car (unlimited mileage). Shop around and use price comparison sites as well as company sites (which often have deals not available on booking sites).

Other tips:

❍ Most cars are manual; automatic cars are available,

but they're much more expensive to hire.

❍ If you're travelling from the Republic into Northern Ireland, it's important to be sure that your insurance covers journeys to the North.

❍ The majority of hire companies won't rent you a car if you're under 23 and haven't had a valid driving license for at least a year.

Parking

All big towns and cities have covered and open short-stay car parks that are conveniently signposted.

❍ On-street parking is usually by 'pay and display' tickets available from on-street machines or disc parking (discs, which rotate to display the time you park your car, are usually provided by rental agencies). Costs range from €1.50 to €5 per hour; all-day parking in a car park will cost around €24.

Motoring Organisations

The two main motoring organisations:

Automobile Association (AA; ☏ NI breakdown 00 800 8877 6655, Republic breakdown 1800 66 77 88; www.theaa.ie)

Royal Automobile Club (RAC; ☏ NI breakdown 0333 200 0999, Republic breakdown 0800 015 6000; www.rac.ie)

○ Yellow lines (single or double) along the edge of the road indicate restrictions. Double yellow lines mean no parking at any time. Always look for the nearby sign that spells out when you can and cannot park.

Roads & Rules

Ireland may be one of the few countries where the posted speed limits are often much faster than you'll find possible.

○ Motorways (marked by M+number on a blue background): modern, divided highways.

○ Primary roads (N+number on a green background in the Republic, A+number in NI): usually well-engineered two-lane roads.

○ Secondary and tertiary roads (marked as R+number in the Republic, B+number in NI): Can be very winding and exceedingly narrow.

○ Tolls are charged on many motorways, usually by machine at a plaza. On the M50, pay the automated tolls between junctions 6 and 7 at www.eflow.ie.

○ Directional signs often not in evidence.

○ GPS navigation via your smartphone or device is very helpful.

○ EU licences are treated like Irish licences.

○ Non-EU licences are valid in Ireland for up to 12 months.

○ If you plan to bring a car from Europe, it's illegal to drive without at least third-party insurance.

The basic rules of the road:

○ Drive on the left; overtake to the right.

○ Safety belts must be worn by the driver and all passengers.

○ Children aged under 12 aren't allowed to sit in the front passenger seat.

○ When entering a roundabout, give way to the right.

○ In the Republic, speed-limit and distance signs are in kilometres; in the North, speed-limit and distance signs are often in miles.

Speed limits:

Republic 120km/h on motorways, 100km/h on national roads, 80km/h on regional and local roads, and 50km/h or as signposted in towns.

Northern Ireland 70mph (112km/h) on motorways, 60mph (96km/h) on main roads, 30mph (48km/h) in built-up areas.

Drinking and driving is taken very seriously; you're allowed a maximum blood-alcohol level of 50mg/100mL (0.05%) in the Republic and 35mg/100mL (0.035%) in Northern Ireland.

Local Transport

Dublin and Belfast have comprehensive local bus networks, as do some other larger towns.

○ The Dublin Area Rapid Transport (DART) rail line runs roughly the length of Dublin's coastline, while the Luas tram system has two popular lines.

○ Taxis tend to be expensive: flagfall for daytime/nighttime is €3.60/4 plus €1.10/1.40 per km after the first 500m.

○ Uber is in Dublin and is expected to spread elsewhere.

Tours

Organised tours are a convenient way of exploring the country's main highlights if your time is limited. Tours can be booked through travel agencies, tourist offices, or through the tour companies. Some of the most reputable operators:

Bus Éireann (☏ 01-836 6111; www.buseireann.ie) Offers day trips from Dublin and Cork to popular destinations.

CIE Tours International (www.cietours.ie) Runs multi-day bus tours of the Republic and the North.

Paddywagon Tours (☏01-823 0822; www.paddywagontours. com) Activity-filled tours all over Ireland.

Railtours Ireland (☏01-856 0045; www.railtoursireland. com) For train enthusiasts.

Taxi Tours Ireland (☏085-276 5991; www.taxitoursireland.ie) One- to 14-day custom tours with your own vehicle and driver.

Train

Given Ireland's relatively small size, train travel can be quick and advance-purchase fares are competitive with buses.

❍ Many of the Republic's most beautiful areas, such as whole swaths of the Wild Atlantic Way are not served by rail.

❍ Most lines radiate out from Dublin, with limited ways of interconnecting between lines, which can complicate touring.

❍ There are four routes from Belfast in Northern Ireland; one links with the system in the Republic via Newry to Dublin.

❍ True 1st-class only exists on the Dublin–Cork and Dublin–Belfast lines. On all other trains, seats are the same size as in standard class, despite any marketing come-ons such as 'Premier' class.

Irish Rail (Iarnród Éireann; ☏1850 366 222; www.irishrail. ie) Operates trains in the Republic.

Translink NI Railways (☏028-9066 6630; www.translink. co.uk) Operates trains in Northern Ireland.

Language

Irish (Gaeilge) is Ireland's official language. In 2003 the government introduced the Official Languages Act, whereby all official documents, street signs and official titles must be either in Irish or in both Irish and English. Despite its official status, Irish is really only spoken in pockets of rural Ireland known as the Gaeltacht, the main ones being Cork (*Corcaigh*), Donegal (*Dún na nGall*), Galway (*Gaillimh*), Kerry (*Ciarraí*) and Mayo (*Maigh Eo*).

Ask people outside the Gaeltacht if they can speak Irish and nine out of 10 of them will probably reply *'ah, cupla focal'* (a couple of words) - and they generally mean it. Irish is a compulsory subject in schools for those aged six to 15, but Irish classes have traditionally been rather academic and unimaginative, leading many students to resent it as a waste of time. As a result, many adults regret not having a greater grasp of it. In recent times, at long last, a new Irish curriculum has been introduced cutting the hours devoted to the subject but making the lessons more fun, practical and celebratory.

For in-depth language information and a witty insight into the quirks of language in Ireland, check out Lonely Planet's *Irish Language & Culture*. To enhance your trip with this title or a phrasebook, visit **lonelyplanet.com**. Lonely Planet's Fast Talk app is available through the Apple App store.

Pronunciation

Irish divides vowels into long (those with an accent) and short (those without an accent), and distinguishes between broad (**a**, **á**, **o**, **ó**, **u**) and slender (**e**, **é**, **i** and **í**) vowels, which can affect the pronunciation of preceding consonants.

Other than a few odd-looking clusters, like **mh** and **bhf** (both pronounced as 'w'), consonants are generally pronounced as they are in English.

Irish has three main dialects: Connaught Irish (in Galway and northern Mayo), Munster Irish (in Cork, Kerry and Waterford) and Ulster Irish (in Donegal). The pronunciation guides given here are an anglicised version of modern standard Irish, which is essentially an amalgam of the three - if you read them as if they were English, you'll be able to get your point across in Gaeilge without even having to think about the specifics of Irish pronunciation or spelling.

Basics

Hello. (greeting)	
Dia duit.	deea gwit
Hello. (reply)	
Dia is Muire duit.	deeas moyra gwit
Good morning.	
Maidin mhaith.	mawjin wah
Good night.	
Oíche mhaith.	eekheh wah
Goodbye. (when leaving)	
Slán leat.	slawn lyat
Goodbye. (when staying)	
Slán agat.	slawn agut
Excuse me.	
Gabh mo leithscéal.	gamoh lesh scale
I'm sorry.	
Tá brón orm.	taw brohn oruhm
Thank you (very) much.	
Go raibh (míle) agat.	goh rev (meela) *maith* mah agut
Do you speak Irish?	
An bhfuil Gaeilge agat?	on wil gaylge oguht
I don't understand.	
Ní thuigim.	nee higgim
What is this?	
Cad é seo?	kod ay shoh
What is that?	
Cad é sin?	kod ay shin
I'd like to go to ...	
Ba mhaith liom dul go dtí ...	baw wah lohm dull go dee ...
I'd like to buy ...	
Ba mhaith liom ... a cheannach.	bah wah lohm ... a kyanukh

..., (if you) please....
más é do thoil é. ... maws ay do hall ay

Yes.
Tá. taw

No.
Níl. neel

It is.
Sea. sheh

It isn't.
Ní hea. nee heh

another/
ceann eile kyawn ella
one more

nice
go deas goh dyass

Making Conversation

Welcome.
Ceád míle fáilte. kade meela fawlcha
(lit: 100,000 welcomes)

How are you?
Conas a tá tú? kunas aw taw too

I'm fine.
Táim go maith. thawm go mah

What's your name?
Cad is ainm duit? kod is anim dwit

My name is (Sean Frayne).
(Sean Frayne) is (shawn frain) is
ainm dom. anim dohm

Impossible!
Ní féidir é! nee faydir ay

Nonsense!
Ráiméis! rawmaysh

That's terrible!
Go huafásach! guh hoofawsokh

Take it easy.
Tóg é gobogé. tohg ay gobogay

Cheers!
Slainte! slawncha

I'm never ever drinking again!
Ní ólfaidh mé go knee ohlhee mey
gubrách arís! brawkh ureeshch

Bon voyage!
Go n-éirí an go nairee on
bóthar leat! bohhar lat

Signs

Fir	*fear*	Men
Gardaí	*gardee*	Police
Leithreas	*lehrass*	Toilet
Mna	*mnaw*	Women
Oifig An	*iffig ohn*	Post Office
Phoist	*fwisht*	

Happy Christmas!
Nollaig shona! nuhlig hona

Happy Easter!
Cáisc shona! kawshk hona

Days of the Week

Monday	*Dé Luaín*	day loon
Tuesday	*Dé Máirt*	day maart
Wednesday	*Dé Ceádaoin*	day kaydeen
Thursday	*Déardaoin*	daredeen
Friday	*Dé hAoine*	day heeneh
Saturday	*Dé Sathairn*	day sahern
Sunday	*Dé Domhnaigh*	day downick

Numbers

1	*haon*	hayin
2	*dó*	doe
3	*trí*	tree
4	*ceathaír*	kahirr
5	*cúig*	kooig
6	*sé*	shay
7	*seacht*	shocked
8	*hocht*	hukt
9	*naoi*	nay
10	*deich*	jeh
20	*fiche*	feekhe

Behind the Scenes

Acknowledgements

Climate map data adapted from Peel MC, Finlayson BL & McMahon TA (2007) 'Updated World Map of the Koppen-Geiger Climate Classification', *Hydrology and Earth System Sciences*, 11, 163344.

Illustration pp104-5 by Javier Zarracina. Illustrations pp90-1 and pp266-7 by Michael Weldon.

This Book

This book was curated by Neil Wilson, who researched and wrote for it along with Fionn Davenport, Damian Harper, Catherine Le Nevez and Ryan Ver Berkmoes. This guidebook was commissioned in Lonely Planet's Melbourne office, and produced by the following:

Destination Editor James Smart
Series Designer Campbell McKenzie
Cartographic Series Designer Wayne Murphy
Product Editors Elizabeth Jones, Kate Mathews
Senior Cartographers Corey Hutchison, Anthony Phelan
Book Designer Katherine Marsh
Associate Product Directors Sasha Baskett, Liz Heynes
Assisting Editor Helen Koehne
Cartographers Julie Dodkins, Gabriel Lindquist
Cover Researcher Brendan Dempsey-Spencer
Thanks to Andrew Bigger, Katie Coffee, Daniel Corbett, Ruth Cosgrove, Mark Griffiths, James Hardy, Anna Harris, Kerrianne Jenkins, Indra Kilfoyle, Georgina Leslie, Dan Moore, Darren O'Connell, Katie O'Connell, Mazzy Prinsep, Kirsten Rawlings, Wibowo Rusli, Diana Saengkham, Dianne Schallmeiner, Ellie Simpson, Lyahna Spencer, John Taufa, Angela Tinson, Lauren Wellicome, Juan Winata

Send Us Your Feedback

We love to hear from travellers – your comments keep us on our toes and help make our books better. Our well-travelled team reads every word on what you loved or loathed about this book. Although we cannot reply individually to postal submissions, we always guarantee that your feedback goes straight to the appropriate authors, in time for the next edition. Each person who sends us information is thanked in the next edition, the most useful submissions are rewarded with a selection of digital PDF chapters.

Visit lonelyplanet.com/contact to submit your updates and suggestions or to ask for help. Our award-winning website also features inspirational travel stories, news and discussions.

Note: We may edit, reproduce and incorporate your comments in Lonely Planet products such as guidebooks, websites and digital products, so let us know if you don't want your comments reproduced or your name acknowledged. For a copy of our privacy policy visit lonelyplanet.com/privacy.

Map Legend & Symbols Key

Look for these symbols to quickly identify listings:

- ◎ Sights
- ✦ Activities
- ❸ Courses
- ◐ Tours
- ✹ Festivals & Events
- ✖ Eating
- ● Drinking
- ✪ Entertainment
- ⬤ Shopping
- ❶ Information & Transport

These symbols and abbreviations give vital information for each listing:

- ✎ Sustainable or green recommendation
- **FREE** No payment required

- ☎ Telephone number
- ☺ Opening hours
- Ⓟ Parking
- ◔ Nonsmoking
- ✳ Air-conditioning
- @ Internet access
- ☎ Wi-fi access
- ✈ Swimming pool

- ▣ Bus
- ⛴ Ferry
- ▣ Tram
- ℝ Train
- ◙ English-language menu
- ✐ Vegetarian selection
- ✦ Family-friendly

Find your best experiences with these Great For... icons.

- Budget
- Food & Drink
- Drinking
- Cycling
- Shopping
- Sport
- Art & Culture
- Events
- Photo Op
- Scenery
- Family Travel
- Short Trip
- Detour
- Walking
- Local Life
- History
- Entertainment
- Beaches
- Winter Travel
- Cafe/Coffee
- Nature & Wildlife

Sights

- ❀ Beach
- ◉ Bird Sanctuary
- ◉ Buddhist
- ◉ Castle/Palace
- ◉ Christian
- ◉ Confucian
- ◉ Hindu
- ◉ Islamic
- ◉ Jain
- ◉ Jewish
- ◉ Monument
- ⌂ Museum/Gallery/ Historic Building
- ◉ Ruin
- ◉ Shinto
- ◉ Sikh
- ◉ Taoist
- ◉ Winery/Vineyard
- ◉ Zoo/Wildlife Sanctuary
- ◉ Other Sight

Points of Interest

- ◉ Bodysurfing
- ◉ Camping
- ◉ Cafe
- ◉ Canoeing/Kayaking
- • Course/Tour
- ◉ Diving
- ◉ Drinking & Nightlife
- ◉ Eating
- ◉ Entertainment
- ◉ Sento Hot Baths/ Onsen
- ◉ Shopping
- ◉ Skiing
- ◉ Sleeping
- ◉ Snorkelling
- ◉ Surfing
- ◉ Swimming/Pool
- ◉ Walking
- ◉ Windsurfing
- ◉ Other Activity

Information

- ⑤ Bank
- ◉ Embassy/Consulate
- ◉ Hospital/Medical
- @ Internet
- ◉ Police
- ◉ Post Office
- ◉ Telephone
- ◉ Toilet
- ❶ Tourist Information
- • Other Information

Geographic

- ◉ Beach
- ⋈ Gate
- ◉ Hut/Shelter
- ◉ Lighthouse
- ◉ Lookout
- ▲ Mountain/Volcano
- ◉ Oasis
- ◉ Park
-)(Pass
- ◉ Picnic Area
- ◉ Waterfall

Transport

- ◉ Airport
- ⓑ BART station
- ⊗ Border crossing
- ◉ Boston T station
- ◉ Bus
- ⊶ Cable car/Funicular
- ◉ Cycling
- ◉ Ferry
- Ⓜ Metro/MRT station
- ◉ Monorail
- Ⓟ Parking
- ◉ Petrol station
- ⑤ Subway/S-Bahn/ Skytrain station
- ◉ Taxi
- ⊷ Train station/Railway
- ⋊⋉ Tram
- ◉ Tube Station
- ◉ Underground/ U-Bahn station
- • Other Transport